ZEN-EXISTENTIALISM:

The Spiritual Decline Of The West

— A POSITIVE ANSWER TO THE HIPPIES —

By

Lit-sen Chang

Former President of Kiang-nan University
Special Lecturer in Missions
Gordon Divinity School, Mass., U. S. A.

WIPF & STOCK · Eugene, Oregon

Wipf and Stock Publishers
199 W 8th Ave, Suite 3
Eugene, OR 97401

Zen-Existentialism
The Spiritual Decline of the West
By Chang, Lit-sen
Copyright©1969 by Chang, Lit-sen
ISBN 13: 978-1-60899-918-7
Publication date 8/20/2010
Previously published by Presbyterian and Reformed Publishing, Co., 1969

ACKNOWLEDGEMENTS

The author wishes to express his gratitude to the members of the Chinese Evangelical Literature Committee and to all those who have supported my ministry and helped to make this book possible. Sincere appreciation is hereby extended to Drs. Burton L. Goddard and Roger Nicole for their encouragement and suggestions; to Dr. Carl F. H. Henry, former editor of *Christianity Today*, for his initiative in urging the author to write on this subject (which has been published in part under the title, "The Challenge of the Cults," by Zondervan Publishing House to whom the author also gives thanks) and especially for his persuasion, for otherwise, this book would never have been written at all.

Special appreciation must be extended to Dr. Gordon H. Clark, not only for writing the Preface but also for his unusual patience and devotion in reviewing my manuscript and for making many valuable suggestions.

During the course of preparation for this book, the author has gathered ideas and quotations from various sources. Though it is not possible to list each one by name, the author wishes to express his hearty gratitude to them.

The author is also grateful to Dr. Christopher Kaiser, Rev. David Kleis and Rev. Alan Ruscito for help in proofreading the manuscript and to Mrs. Quentin Small for typing a part of the inital draft. A word of appreciation should also be given to my twin daughters June and Jean for typing the manuscript and reading the proof, and especially to my wife Ling-Nie who "looks well to the ways of her household" (Prov. 31:27) so as to enable the author to devote all his time to writing.

And finally the author wishes to thank Director Charles H. Craig of Presbyterian and Reformed Publishing Company and The Craig Press, for his Christian devotion and dedication which made possible the publication of this book.

Gordon Divinity School Lit-sen Chang
Wenham, Massachusetts, U.S.A.
March, 1969

TABLE OF CONTENTS

Acknowledgments --- III

Preface --- V

Foreword --- IX

INTRODUCTION --- 1

    I. The Crisis of Our Age
       — Religious Trends of the West —

   II. The Truth of God Changes for a lie
       — The Avenues of Pseudo-escape —

  III. The "Opiate" of the people becomes a Religion
       — The 'Drug" induced mysticism —
         ("Mystical cult of the Feelings")

  IV. The Root of Human Problem
       — "History passes over into theology" —

PART ONE
FANTASY OF THE EAST
— The Spirit of Zen —

CHAPTER ONE   HISTORY AND NATURE OF ZEN --- 26

    I. THE HISTORY OF ZEN
       1. Its Origin in India
       2. Its Development in China and Japan
       3. Its Impact on the West

   II. THE MEANING OF ZEN
       1. Its Etymological Rendering
       2. Its Different Interpretations

  III. THE ELUSIVE NATURE OF ZEN
       1. Is Zen Philosophy?
       2. Is Zen Religion?
       3. Is Zen Buddhism?
       4. Is Zen Taoism?
       5. Is Zen Atheism, etc?

  IV. THE ICONOCLASTIC STANCE OF ZEN
       1. A Revolt Against Language
       2. A Revolt Against Reason
       3. A Revolt Against Authority

CHAPTER II   TEACHINGS AND PRACTICE OF ZEN _____ 36

   I. THE TEACHINGS OF ZEN
1. The Method of Teaching
2. Schools of Teaching
3. Teachings on Original Nature
4. Teachings on Non-duality
5. Teachings on Egolessness
6. Teachings on Voidness
7. Teachings of Nothing

   II. THE PRACTICE OF ZEN
1. Object of Zen Practice
2. Ways of Zen Practice
3. Means of Zen Practice
4. Experience of Zen Practice
5. Result of Zen Practice

PART TWO

CRISIS IN THE WEST

— The Impact of Zen —

CHAPTER ONE   CRISIS IN CULTURE _____ 54
— CULTURAL BACKGROUND OF ZEN'S IMPACT —

   I. Failure of humanism
   II. Age of Tension

CHAPTER TWO   CRISIS IN PHILOSOPHY _____ 64
— PHILOSOPHICAL BACKGROUND OF ZEN'S IMPACT —

   I. Skeptical Futility of Human Wisdom
   II. Morbid Reaction Against Easy Rationalism

CHAPTER THREE   CRISIS IN RELIGION _____ 79
— RELIGIOUS BACKGROUND OF ZEN'S IMPACT —

   I. Scheme of self-negation
   II. Wave of Syncretism
   III. Mood of Secularism

CHAPTER FOUR   CRISIS IN THEOLOGY _____ 97
— THEOLOGICAL BACKGROUND OF ZEN'S IMPACT —

   I. Pantheistic Theology
     — The Oneness of God and Man —
     ("Art of Godmanship")

   II. Theology of Immanence
     — Sons of Schleiermacher —

   III. "Death-of-God" Movement
     — Cult of Iconoclasm —

   IV. "Christian Atheism"
     — Strategy of the Old Serpent —

PART THREE

THE TWINS OF ZEN—EXISTENTIALISM
(East and West Meet)
— DOOM OF AUTO-SOTERISM —

CHAPTER ONE   A TREND IN MODERN THOUGHT _____ 114
   I. Points of Correspondence
  II. Witness of Heidegger
 III. Shift of Mentality

CHAPTER TWO   THE FUTILITY OF PSEUDO RELIGION __ 125
   I. Appealing Features of Zen
     1. It Opposes Rationalism and Humanism
     2. It Teaches Self-denial and "Great Death"
     3. It Casts Some Dim Light on Way of Life

  II. Serious Inadequacy of Zen
     1. It Supersedes the Doctrine of Real Creator
     2. It Engenders a Spirit of Mysticism
     3. It Disregards the Holiness of God
     4. It Denies the Need of a Saviour

 III. Utter Failure of Zen
     1. In "Seeing into One's Own Nature"
     2. In the Attainment of Enlightenment
     3. In the Way of Salvation

 IV. Conclusion

CHAPTER THREE   A MOVEMENT TO ETERNAL
                             DESTRUCTION _____ 151
   I. Disastrous Surrender to Nihilism
  II. Man's Autonomy Over Against God
 III. Sweeping Apostasy of Modern Man
 IV. Urgent Message for this Generation

CONCLUSION _____ 173
   I. The Highest Goal of Man
  II. The Vanity of the Mind
 III. The Perversion of the Truth
 IV. The Divine Plan of Salvation
  V. The Power of the Gospel
 VI. The Hope of the World

EPILOGUE
      A POSITIVE ANSWER TO THE HIPPIES _____ 195

APPENDIX   I. THE WAY TO THE TRUE ENLIGHTEN-
                MENT _____ 202
                — From Zen to Christ —
                — Brief Testimony of the Author —

APPENDIX II. LSD, A NEW RELIGION? _____ 210
                Is There an Alternative to Hallucinogens?

APPENDIX III. THE ANTI-MIND MOOD OF OUR ERA ____ 218

APPENDIX IV. WHEHE IS MODERN THEOLOGY GOING? _ 222

GLOSSARY _____ 236

BIBLIOGRAPHY _____ 241

PREFACE

Americans by and large, and perhaps Europeans as well, have been, to the present at least, ignorant of the complex of ideas that dominate oriental minds. Vague and usually inaccurate notions of Buddhism circulate among us; Shintoism played some forgotten part in World War II; Zen and Yoga are names we have heard without learning their meanings.

After World War II and the Korean war had brought us into closer contact with Asia, we now find ourselves deeply engaged in Viet Nam. India and Indonesia are also on our minds. Obviously we shall have to learn more about the Far East.

In contrast with the general ignorance some knowledge has penetrated restricted circles. On a high academic level the University of Hawaii sponsors East-West studies. Even so, it can hardly be said that this program exerts massive force on the American Philosophical Association. On a more popular level a few curious souls, spiritual descendants of Madame Blavatsky, continue to affect eastern airs. But this Theosophy now faces rivals in the beatniks' attraction to Zen and Yoga. Not only this, but—quite apart from the Black Muslims—orthodox Islam, not originally far eastern, yet predominant in Indonesia, has gathered a following in the United States. Buddhism exerts more of a philosophic than a religious influence, though there is no sharp line separating philosophy from religion. Bahai has a gorgeous temple north of Chicago. As for Shintoism, whatever revival it may experience in Japan, I doubt that it will ever count for much here in America. But Zen, the subject of this book, appears to hold considerable attraction. With these eastern religions gaining adherents in our midst, it is time for exotic ignorance to give way to more accurate knowledge.

If Zen in its distinctive eastern dress never becomes widespread, yet, to the surprise of thoroughly western minds, some of the ideas of Zen appeal in the form of contemporary existentialism. To be sure, neither of these movements is historically dependent on the other. Their actual ancestries are totally different. Nevertheless, the despair, the pessimism, the frustration that have taken possession of European thinkers and have driven them to a mystic affirmation of freedom and a striving toward authentic being, have produced attitudes and ideas parallel to those of Zen in the passive, long-suffering east. For all the differences in the two ancestries, in the oriental and occidental dress, the deep and somewhat hidden similarities deserve analysis.

The present volume recommends itself by having as its author a gentleman who was once an adherent of Zen in its true eastern form. He knows Zen from the inside. He lived it, as an oriental, not as an American beatnik. For a time he was an ardent advocate of this resurgent movement in Buddhism. But he is not ignorant of the west, either. After his college education in China, he took postgraduate work in Law and Politics at the Université de Paris, at Louvain, Belgium, and did some research in Cambridge and London. This gave him first hand knowledge of Europe. Returning to China he became Professor of Law and Political Science. In addition to university work, including the presidency of Kiang-nan University, he served the government as Deputy Cabinet Member, as delegate to the Constituent National Assembly, plus some other official appointments. The combination of such important eastern experience with his studies in western Europe and now with almost fourteen years of experience in America constitute an advantage most authors do not have.

Modern existentialist theory, with its insistence on the existential situation and responsible choice, cannot possibly object to testing a theory by living it. Professor Lit-sen Chang has weighed Zen in the balances of experience and has found it wanting. Authentic being turned out to be nothingness. Freedom became nausea. In this volume Professor Chang recounts his early life; here he analyzes the Zen mentality; and here he shows the superiority of Christianity—"the Way of True Enlightenment." The contrast between these two religions is immense. Overweening pride gives way to humility; instead of Sartre's "all things are permitted," there are the *Thou shalt nots* of the Ten Commandments; and the defeat of death, which not only frustrates Sartre but plunges Bertrand Russell into unyielding despair, is vanquished by the Resurrection. Truly these are contrasts worth pondering.

Gordon H. Clark

FOREWORD

Here is a book in which we of the West may see ourselves as others see us. In a world of shrinking size, the boundaries of eastern and western cultures inter-penetrate one another. It is the judgment of Professor Chang that the West is "soulless." He makes this judgment by cultural and scriptural criteria, tempered by a background in the Orient and a vast experience in the West. His philosophical and theological insights perceptively trace the parallels between Zen Buddhism and the existentialist mood of liberal thought in the West.

There are many advocates of Zen among intellectuals in the United States. It is seen by some as a bridge between eastern and western thought. It is "this-worldly" and dissolves the dichotomous tension between the nominal and phenomenal worlds. It is essentially subjectivistic. It professes to liberate the individual from the necessity of differentiating between good and evil, sacred and profane, nirvana and sansara; and declares the advent of the "new humanity" without theistic reference.

Zen Buddhism begins its emergence in the West at a time when Western theology has "come of age" and does without God. It challenges Christianity at a time when the liberal church has lost its sense of mission and has become indistinguishable from the secular processes. The vast masses of the disillusioned who turn to "every new thing" to escape the revelational, the rational, and the responsible may turn to Zen. There is an undoubted affinity between the cultural propensity in the West to embrace the absurd and Professor Chang's view of Zen as "a disastrous surrender to nihilism."

The author puts the principles and implications of Zen alongside the plumbline of God's Word. The root of the human problem is in the soul. Zen is as soulless as Western culture. Both Zen and Western culture are godless. They are essentially pessimistic and say nothing to the ultimate implacabilities of human experience.

Professor Chang speaks of his own experience of Zen and this gives his words the authoritative power of witness. The positive dimension of the book is the clarity of the Biblical statement of both judgment and hope. This is a relevant word for a "sensate" culture and deserves the widest circulation among thinking people. One who has found "The Way" in Jesus Christ can speak meaningfully to those who are seeking God's truth for the pilgrimage.

     JAMES FORRESTER, Former President
     Gordon College and Gordon Divinity School

INTRODUCTION

I. THE CRISIS OF OUR AGE

— Religious Trends of the West —

After the first World War, Oswald Spengler, in his noted book *The Decline of the West*, warned mankind that the world-city is now soulless and that exact science must presently fall upon its own keen sword.[1] This book, though widely read by the thinking people of the world both in the West and the East, only gives a diagnosis of the disease of modern man, but provides no positive answer, for it fails to explore the deep roots of human problems, and consequently its philosophy of history indicates no exit from the human endeaver. It is indeed ironic that while Spengler diagnosed the world-city as "soulless," his remedy was also somewhat "soulless." Dr. Abraham Kuyper, the former Prime Minister and founder of the Free University of the Netherlands, in his Stone Foundation Lectures on Calvinism, pointed out that the crisis of the modern man "starts from the unbelief of the French Revolution." He said, "Voltaire's mad cry: 'Down with the scoundrel,' was aimed at Christ Himself; but this cry was merely the expression of the most hidden thought from which the French Revolution sprang. The fantastic outcry 'We no more need a God,' and the odious shibboleth 'No God, no master' of the Convention . . . were the sacrilegious watchwords which at that time heralded the liberation of man as an emancipation from all Divine Authority. The leaders of the French Revolution declared war against every religious confession and henceforth God was to be considered as a hostile power, yea, even as dead.'' (Here we discover the historic origin of "the death-of-God" movement!) "The principle of that revolution remains thoroughly anti-Christian and has since spread like a cancer, dissolving and undermining all that stood firm and constant before our Christian faith." Since that time Christianity has been imperiled by the greatest and most serious of dangers: "among the Protestant nations, Pantheism, born from the new German Philosophy and owing its concrete evolution-form to Darwin, claims for itself supremacy in every sphere of human life, even in that of theology, and under all sorts of names tries to overthrow our Christian traditions and is bent upon exchanging the heritage of our fathers for hopeless modern Buddhism."[2]

On the other hand, Abraham Kuyper further pointed out that there flows in modern life a side current. A host of high-minded men arose, who, shrinking from the uneasy chill of the moral atmosphere and taking alarm at the brutality of the prevailing egotism, endeavored to put new warmth in life partly by means of altruism, partly by means of a mystical cult of the feelings, and partly even by means of the name Christianity. Some of them claimed the right to emancipate the inner life of the soul from all the restraints of intellectual criticism. Losing one's self in the Infinite and feeling the stream of the Infinite pulsate through the deepest recesses of inner life temporarily satisfied the desire for the practice of piety. Others again, especially theologians, set themselves to the task of so metamorphosing the Christ that He might continue to glitter from the throne of humanism as the highest ideal of the modernized human heart. These endeavors may be traced from Schleiermacher to Ritschl. They extolled the normal character of their cosmology over against the abnormalism of historic Christian teaching; and the Christian religion being abnormalistic in principle and mode of manifestation, inevitaby lost ground to such an extent that some of its best men did not shrink from professing that they preferred not only Spiritism, but Mohammedanism and Schopenhauer, or even Buddhism, to the old evangelical faith. The name of the Christian religion is still being retained, but in essence, it has become a quite different religion in principle, indeed one of a diametrically opposite character.[3]

The modern sensate culture, as a result of its alienation from the historic Christian faith, is thus going through a process of disintegration. Modern man has lost all metaphysical certainties and has substituted in their place the ideals of material security. But a superficial glance at our contemporary world shows us that the so-called material progress adds only greater force to the threat of more stupendous catastrophe. Science has destroyed even the refuge of inner life. Since the beginning of the 19th century, man has given a more prominent place to the role of his psyche. He has turned his attention from contemplating the Word of God to his own subjective processes. Thus Freudian psychology has become dearer than the Gospel.[4] Now there are two evident trends in the Western mentality toward religion: (1) the denial of God and the renunciation of the Christian faith in terms of the free development of men as the "world come of age"; (2) the process of turning toward "inwardness" and an emphasis on the autonomy and transcendence of man, even to the point of resorting to "drugs" and making "the opiate" a "religion" of the people, so as to secure hallucinogenic experiences and magic power and thus plunge the nations into pagan darkness.[5]

II. "THE TRUTH OF GOD EXCHANGED FOR A LIE"

— The Avenues of Pseudo-escape —

In this age of tension and anxiety, while science has destroyed the refuge of the inner life and the false prophets provide no remedy for this soulless world-city, Zen, (known as Hsing Tsung, meaning 'mind doctrine' which teaches the way of full realization of the mind) steps in and appeals to the western mind weary of conventional religion and philosophy. It is the claim of Zen that it can reduce the tension of all opposites by leaping above them.[6] For Zen claims to bring about the "unity of man and the universe," to effect the "rhythm of the mind with the changing forms," and to produce the state of "oneness."[7] It teaches such doctrines as non-duality, non-discrimination and non-differentiation. Completely ignoring the deadly problem of sin, it even blames God by misinterpreting the Bible in alleging that the real human tragedy began when nature was to be dominated by man (Gen. 1:28), we are told. It teaches that when the idea of power (domination) comes in, all kinds of struggles arise.[8]

Alan Watts, a former Episcopal priest, now an interpreter of Zen in the West even says that "if there is a man of such spiritual courage as to call the Lord's bluff, what he is actually refusing to believe, what he will not take seriously, is not the Lord but his '*maya*,' he will not admit that agony and tragedy, death and hell, fear and nothingness, are ultimate realities. Above all, he is not admitting the final reality of separateness, of the seeming distinction between man and cosmos, creature and Creator." He further asserts that the fundamental dynamics of the universe is the game of hide and seek, the play of yes-and-no. Hence, explicitly, the light and dark are enemies, but implicitly they are really friends, and not only twins, not only co-conspirators, but they constitute a unity which cannot be described. Therefore, when the Lord and the Devil came out officially . . . they are implacable foes, but may we not suppose that before the show of creation began, there was an "original agreement"? Without an antithesis between the light and the dark, Alan Watts can explain away "original sin" in terms of "original illusion" in which the Creator seems to become the creature. It is the flaming sword that turns in all directions and guards the way of return to Paradise, preventing us from daring to recognize, upon pain of the utmost blasphemy, that we are each the Lord in hiding.[9] However, such a view is nothing new, but simply reflects the iconoclastic stance of Zen, i.e., every man is a potential Buddha. Thus it is only natural for Alan Watts to conclude that "we are each the Lord in hiding."

It is sad to say that a man who was so near to the truth could allow himself to drift away from it and neglect so great salvation (cf. Heb. 2:1-3). Being induced by those specious falsehoods of men, (cf. I Tim. 4:1,2), he is even unable to discern the distinction between the light and the darkness, the Lord and the Devil and the Creator and the creature, but rather presumes such distinctions are from his *Maya,* and concludes that the idea of Original Sin is in reality the production of the "original illusion."

In order to eradicate such distinction, there is now a movement in the West "to remove the concept of a Personal God and all that implies a salvation by grace alone. Salvation has no use for God"; thus we are told, "look to no Person or God for help."[10] Liberal theologians disregard the "God" of the Bible and proceed to characterize Christianity as "non-theistic religion," "religion without God" or "Atheistic religion."

John A. T. Robinson even could twist the story of the prodigal son in Luke to prove that a man's reconciliation is to himself and not to God. Robinson gives no solid treatment of man or of sin or of the Redeemer. He changes the vocabulary of theology — using "ultimate reality" or "ground of Being" for God, and leads only to greater confusion. For he argues that there is no God "up there" or "out there," that the mental picture of such a God may be more of a stumbling block than an aid to belief in the Gospel. He further charges that "our basic commitment to Christ" may have been "buttressed by many lesser commitments—to a particular projection of God, a particular myth of the Incarnation, a particular code of words, a particular pattern of religion." He further alleges that "we must beware of clinging to the buttresses instead of to Christ," for "they are barriers rather than supports."[11]

Paul Tillich who reduced all divine attributes to symbolic representation, likewise rejected a Deity who deprives him of his subjectivity because He is all powerful and all knowing. He asserted that "this is the God Nietzche said had to be killed, because nobody can tolerate being made into a mere object of absolute knowledge and absolute control ." [12] He further asserted that "God will remain somehow remote and 'out there' unless there is a complete turn about in which all references to the high and the beyond are translated into terms of depth. This infinite and inexhaustible depth and ground of all beings is God. That depth is what the word God means. He who knows about depth knows about God."[13] His speculative philosophy postulated the "unconditioned" over against the God of the Bible and paved the way for the "death of God" movement. He was so credited by Thomas J. J. Altizer, one of the most articulate "death-of-God" theologians, who blasphemously asserts that "only the death of God can make possible the advent of a new humanity. Just as apocalyptic imagery centers upon the defeat of Satan or Anti-Christ whose death alone ushers in the victory of the Kingdom of God, so the contemporary thought and sensibility is rooted in an absolute negation of God. ". . . . Just as the Jew was born out of a passage through the death of his own sacred history, we may hope that a new Christianity be born out of the death of Christendom."[14]

The radical proponents of the "death-of-God" theology have taken upon themselves the "iconoclastic role" of Zen which was represented by one of the outstanding Zen masters, Linchi (or Rinzai), who advocated with all vehemence: "O! Brethren, If you want to grasp the correct view of Dharma . . . . Smash whatever you come across . . . . Smash the Buddha, Patriarchs and Arhats, smash your parents and all your relations if you come across them; . . . you will be in real emancipation."[15] In other words, the emancipation of man demands the death of Buddha and the abolition of all authority. In this respect, we could say that the "death-of-God" theology has nothing new to offer; it is simply the revival of the Spirit of Zen. Thus Altizer said; "Today, Buddhism is the religion that is most profoundly challenging Christianity (particularly in its Zen form). Contemplation is the highest of man's activity. For therein he can become God and therein can he become immortal." "Genuine Christianity is the ultimate form of rebellion."[16]

Alan Watts stresses the spirit of Zen when he advocates that: "Every Easter Sunday should be celebrated with a solemn and reverent burning of the Holy Scriptures, for the whole meaning of the resurrection and ascension of Christ into heaven (which is within you) is that Godmanhood is to be discovered here and now inwardly, not in the letter of the Bible." "The eternal home will never be found so long as you are seeking it for the simple reason that it is yourself—not the self that you are aware of or that you can love or hate, but the one that always vanishes when you look for it. As soon as you realize that you are the center you have no further need to see it."[17] He completely disregards our Lord's own promises and thus distorts Biblical truth by alleging that: "In its early ages, the church was in constant expectation of the Parousia, the second coming of the Lord. Obviously, the church has been looking for the Parousia in the wrong direction—in the outward skies not in the realm of heaven which is 'within.' The true Parousia comes at the moment of crisis in consciousness."[18] Like other non-Christian scholars, this former Episcopal priest ignores the deadly problem of the sin of mankind, that we were dead through the trespasses and sins, following the evil ways of this present age. Only Christ has broken down the dividing wall of hostility and reconciles us to God in one body through the Cross thereby bringing the hostility to an end.[19] Man cut himself off from God by sin. It is only when sin is removed that we can have fellowship again. Thus it is not merely a psychological problem, as Alan Watts imagines, that "Centuries before Western psychology invented the idea of the unconscious aspect of one's 'own' mind, Indian and Chinese philosophers devised experiments whereby consciousness could be expanded or deepened so as to include vast areas of experience entirely ignored (or 'screened out') by conscious attention as we are normally taught to use it. It was from such experience that the Indian and the Chinese derived their sense of unity and continuity between the depths of man (Atman) the depths of the universe (Brahman)."[20]

Such a view is not only useless speculation, but also the work of "the mystery of iniquity." It is essentially a rebellion of human nature against the idea of objective order in general and is antagonistic to a Personal God and the Biblical revelation in particular. We are told that the ultimate faith is not *in* or *upon* anything at all. According to Kierkegaard, the very idea of order in this objective world was the source of the slavery of man. This marks a shift or reaction in the trend of Western thought. This is a turning toward "inwardness" and makes the "mind" its own master.

This process of turning was called Dhyana in Sanskrit or Jhana in Pali; or Chan-na (or Ch'an) in Chinese and better known to Westerners as Zen. This turning to "inwardness" has been the mainspring of all philosophy down through the ages in India. According to the Upanishads, to know "Other is self" ("other" is but the objectification of the self) is the ultimate wisdom of the highest joy. If one could comprehend "Tat Tvam Asi" as expressed in the "Mahavakya" (which means "that thou art" or "the other is yourself," "the eternal is in oneself," "thou art the Eternal"), he is delivered from bondage to freedom. But this is simply an attempt to absolutize or deify the creature (and make man sovereign) as over against God; thus man becomes his own master and Saviour.[21]

In the matter of the salvation of mankind, never has a generation possessed as many avenues of pseudo-escape as we have today. Now the West is confronted with a new menace. There is a search for the "world within," the "limitless inner space," for the "consciousness expansion" or "transcendental experience"; for "Samedhi" and "Satori." But all these psychological experiences or religious phenomena of natural man without spiritual regeneration are counterfeits and deceptive ways which only lead to eternal destruction and total separation from the God of the Bible!

In fact, as the late renowned psychologist Dr. Carl Jung pointed out, "The great neurosis of our time is emptiness." Modern man is like a sheep without a shepherd, caught in the throes of anxiety and despair, absolutely devoid of any light of hope for the future. For instance, the Beatnik—the follower of "the lunatic way of Zen,"[22] has somehow achieved a manner of life, but the empty expression on his face betrays the vacuum in his soul. His is a way of nihilism; for he has escaped from nothing to nothing. Though he might indulge himself in unlimited freedom in his way of thinking and living, "that freedom is like a prison cell without a roof. Although one might soar high to the sky in his imagination, he is still bounded by all walls. His situation remains the same, he is still deep in the bottom of the cell and finds no way out."[23]

When men knew God but refused to honor Him as God, all their thinking ended in futility and their misguided minds plunged into darkness, changing the truth of God into a lie. Because they did not open their minds to love of the truth, so as to find salvation, God puts them under a strong delusion which works upon them to believe in pseudo-religion and worship a false god.[24]

For this reason, since the beginning of this century, Zen has had a profound impact on the West, especially among the intellectuals. Even God's own people are misled and intoxicated. They are fascinated with the spirit of Zen and think they have found the very key to unlock their problems. R. H. Blyth contends that "Zen is the most precious possession of Asia" and even feels that "it is today the strongest power in the world."[25] But, after all, what is Zen? The author, a former advocate of Zen, speaking from his own bitter experiences,[26] believes it an utter fraud, only an avenue of psuedo-escape. It is not only religiously and logically unsound, but psychologically and socially detrimental. Zen is "a technique by which to achieve a mental breakdown." The so-called "satori" is simply "the final critical collapse under the accumulative pressures of stress.' It is "a mental catastrophe," "a piling up of intellectual frustrations that lead to the crumbling of the edifice of logical thought." Although it is labeled as "the way of liberation," it is rather a cult of iconoclasm, a disastrous surrender to Nihilism, a kind of mystical "self-toxication"; "a childish dependence upon magical omnipotence," a ridiculous substitution of "fire cracker-propelled garbage cans for space rockets."[27]

III. THE "OPIATE" BECOMES A RELIGION OF THE PEOPLE

— The Drug Induced Mysticism —

("Mystic Cult of the Feelings")[28]

We are not surprised by this new trend in the Western mentality, for it was revealed by God nearly 2000 years ago that this must happen in the latter days.[29] In recent decades, Zen has aroused the curiosity of many in the West and it is exercising a great influence among intellectuals and students. While the truth of God has been changed into a lie and the pseudo-religion has become "the opiate of the people," it is interesting to note that there is a tendency to make "the opiate" the "religion of the people." Now the minds of the West are being captured by a "new religion"—"the Gospel according to LSD."[30]

Alan Watts, a noted interpreter of Zen Buddhism in the West, relates this current movement to Zen; he says flatly that "LSD is quite emphatically a new religion. The God-is-dead trend is not unconnected . . . This is technological mysticism."[31] When the "apostles of LSD," Drs. Timothy Leary and Richard Alpert were removed from Harvard, a university authority told them "you may be making Buddha out of everyone, but that is not what we are trying to do." Leary and Alpert have published a manual for LSD "trips" based on the "Tibetan Book of Death." Dr. Leary, a former Roman Catholic, now a high priest of the LSD cult, is the leading exponent of "mind-opening substances." Calling himself a Hindu, he uses Eastern symbolism along with psychedelic experience to reject the outward looking "goal-directed" American attitude. According to his own statement, he uses LSD once a week, just as other people go to church. He is now founding a new religion. It is called the League for Spiritual Discovery. He alleges that the use of LSD accomplishes three things: (1) Knowledge of God, (2) Knowledge of self, and (3) Knowledge of a person of the opposite sex. "The present LSD boom is no less than a religious renaissance" says this flamboyant evangelist of the LSD cult. He calls this "the most exciting and inspiring role in society." He claims that a leader is a liberator—one who frees men from their lifelong internal bondage. He spoke at New York Town Hall proclaiming that "more than a million Americans, maybe 20% of the nation's youth, had used the hallucinogenic drug —marijuani, mescaline, psilocybin and LSD. It was too late to attempt to turn back the clock. By 1970, between 10-30 million persons, most of them young, will have embarked on voyages of discovery of their own minds through the limited 'inner space' (of their own minds) and return wiser and more loving than they started out."[32]

Arthur Kleps, Director of the "Neo-American Church" which has 500 members in Florida and California believing that "the sacred biochemicals peyote, mescaline, LSD, and cannobis are the true 'hosts of God' and not drugs," issued a warning "On the day prison doors close behind Timothy Leary... this country will face religious war!" "I would certainly advise my people to use LSD to fight back, to flood the prisons with LSD." Dr. Paul Lee, former Protestant Chaplain at Brandeis University and Prof. of Humanities at M.I.T., now Professor of Philosophy at the University of California, preferred to label the LSD "session" or "trip" "the most profound existential or mystical experience one can have." Lee claims to have new insight into St. Augustine's confessions as a result of LSD intake.

"The mystery of Godliness" is that God humbled Himself and was manifested in the flesh, came down from heaven, dwelt among us, full of grace and truth, that whosoever believes in Him should not perish but have everlasting life.[33] This is Christianity. To the contrary, "the mystery of iniquity" is that man exhalts himself, changes the glory of the uncorruptible God into an image made like unto corruptible man, and changes the truth of God into a lie, and worships the creature more than the Creator by deifying himself as his own Saviour.[34] They knew God but glorified Him not as God, neither were they thankful, and they set their affection not on things "above,"[35] but rather turned *within* seeking so-called "consciousness expansion," believing the absolute oneness of all things and denying the dichotomy between the Creator and the creature, God and man.

As Meister Eckhart, a German mystic wrote: "My eye and God's eye are one and the same...when I have shut the doors of my five senses, earnestly desiring God, I find Him in my soul as clearly and as joyful as He is in Eternity ...Meditation, high thinking, and union with God have drawn one to heaven."[36] William James described his experience with Nitrous Oxide in these words: "It is as if the opposites of the world, whose contradictions and conflict make all our difficulties and troubles, were melted into unity."[37] According to the teaching of Yoga, if one concentrates on one thought "Tadaham," one may attain union with the Supreme Being. Zen also describes its experience of "Satori" as "the bottom of the tub falling off," when that happens, there is a sense of airiness, a newborn sense of flow, a release from all pairs of opposites. Some Yogi and Zen masters even claim that by a single act of will they obtain a sort of magic power, such as the power of telepathy and thought reading, the knowledge of the past and of the future, the ability to make the dead appear and to converse with them, and the ability to transport themselves to any place.

Most experiences of mystical consciousness have come after spartan prayers, fasting, and mortification of the flesh. The spirit of Zen might be described as "ordinary mindness" in that there is nothing unusual that transcends our everyday life. On the other hand, the experience of "Satori" is also described as a kind of "fiery baptism," as the "boiling oil over a blazing fire," or the greatest mental cataclysm, sometimes through the intense pain caused by the harshness of the Zen masters.[38] Now, we are told that through the use of LSD and other psychedelic drugs it is possible to produce the same experiences. Physicians have long suspected that the visions of religious mystics were the result of some change in body chemistry brought on by self-hypnosis, pain, breath-control or intense hunger. It has been reported that LSD may produce an unknown series of metabolic processes which in turn affect the mid-brain. Such experiences are similar to those of the earlier ascetics, Yogi and Zen masters, and are preconditions to "Satori" and the beatific vision over death and life.[39] Dr. Marvin Ziporyn, a Chicago psychiatrist, who sees LSD as instant mysticism, says that "LSD is a psychiatric X-ray. With LSD, you have no greater vision of the universe than you did before." But this is nothing new. It has been recognized that mystical conditions may be induced by certain agencies. In the lowest stage, certain narcotics may be employed, but this was utterly rejected even by higher mysticism.

In our age of crisis this practice has a peculiar fascination for minds of millions weary of conventional religion and philosophy; but it only leads the unwary to the way of perdition. Just like an alcoholic, seeking the pleasures of sin for a season in drinking, only indulges for his own disaster. As one of the leading experts psychiatrist-pharmacologist Dr. Sidney Cohen warns: "If we can tolerate unsupervised use of LSD, . . .why not let children play with hand grenades?" According to his view, Leary is a menace! In the report of Dr. Leszek Ochota of the Food and Drug Administration we see: "There is some uniform agreement among the investigators of LSD, namely: that LSD can be extremely dangerous when used improperly. . . . Some prolonged psychoses resulted from this abuse. Some of these terminated in suicide, others in psycho-social deterioration." "The more evident dangers of the prolonged adverse reaction from hallucinogens are:

1. Mood swings, including depression, which may lead to suicide and emphoria which may lead to socially embarrassing situations.
2. Time and space distortion, presenting obvious traffic dangers.
3. Hallucinations which are perilous out-of-doors.
4. Impulsive behavior, wandering and absent-mindedness. All of which may endanger the user and those with him."[40]

As *Time* magazine reported: "under the influence of LSD, non-swimmers think they can swim and others think they can fly. One young man tried to stop a car on Los Angeles' Wilshire Boulevard and was killed. A magazine salesman became convinced that he was the Messiah. A college dropout committed suicide by slashing his arm and bleeding to death."[41]

The testimony of a space physicist of Stanford University deserves our serious consideration:

> The four weeks which followed my LSD session gradually became a living hell. I was aware of a strange, immense spirit world all around me. There were visions of the universe so overwhelming and overpowering that I was sure I would never come back to life on earth. I was obsessed with haunting, seductive voices suggesting suicide or strange behavior! Gradually I became aware that something was very wrong, and gripped by overwhelming fear I called my pastor. . . . As we prayed together, I gained an immediate sense of the presence of God and a restored relationship of love with Jesus Christ. I became aware for the time

of my serious error in taking drugs, my disobedience to God, and the subtlety of temptation. I had a terrible vision of hell and heard the screams of torment of the lost! I saw that the indirect effects of the drug had brought great inner damage[42] which only time and God's spirit could heal. Today. . . I have been greatly concerned for the growing number who take such drugs. The serious dangers and problems which mind-distorting chemicals present to individuals and to society should be made fully known to everyone. Drugs which open the mind and expand human consciousness are not new. Religious cultists have for centuries made use of drugs in their rites and mystical ceremonies. Thus, every generation has had to deal with similar phenomena and to answer arguments from the authoritative and trustworthy Word of God. God's warning against sorcery, divination and spiritism date to the time of Moses (Ex. 22:18; Lev. 20:6, 27; Deut. 18:9-14). From these passages we are made aware that modern idolatries often come in new guises, but seen in the light of Eternal truth, are nothing more than the age-old deceptions of the devil. The modern use of consciousness-expansion drugs is nothing but a new wile of the Wicked One. While LSD 'trips' bring greater insights into natural man and access to the deeper layers of human consciousness, apart from spiritual regeneration there is no true knowledge of God. . . Large doses of LSD do produce experiences similar to rebirth, tongues phenomena, changes in personality and attitude, 'cures' from alcoholism and other emotional disturbance, but a careful check with scripture reveals that these drug religious phenomena are counterfeit and relative.[43]

From numerous sources we learn that most users of LSD are on college campuses or in beatnik dives. Thus most users are young and directionless. Dr. Leary estimated that possibly 20% of the nation's youth have used the hallucinogenic drugs. According to Dr. Gerald Klerman of

Harvard, 10% of the students on his and other major campuses are "chronic users" of narcotics. In January 1966 staff writers of the *Washington Post* spent two days exploring the "chemical escapism" on college campuses. Judging from the strategic importance of the campus, we see a grave problem in America! Campuses mold the minds and lives of countless citizens. As go the colleges, so goes the nation. The students exercise decisive influence in different walks of life of a nation. Five or ten years later they become the nation's leaders. If the "Opiate" (LSD) becomes the religion of the students, the future of the nation is doomed to decline and fall. History teaches that the decadence of the people and the decay of religion were, as Edward Gibbon pointed out, the chief reasons for the decline and fall of the Roman Empire. The history of China offers a similar parallel. When Buddhism came to China, and especially after the development of Zen, this great empire also began to decline. For this reason, Han Yu, an eminent scholar and statesman of T'ang dynasty presented a petition to the Emperor regardless of the jeopardy to his own position and safety in order to turn the tide at that time.[44]

IV. THE ROOT OF THE HUMAN PROBLEM

("History Passes over into Theology")[45]

Modern man is fascinated by the experience of psychotomimetic, hallucinogenic, illusionogenic, psychotogenic, mysticomimetic, psycholytic, psychodysleptic, psychotropic, psychodelic (mind-manifesting) chemicals on human life. Seeking for "inner space of mind," "consciousness expansion," "superior activities of brain-mind-function," "chemical escapism," "Samedhi," "Satori," "Beatific Vision," he even believes that the sacred biochemicals such as LSD and cannobis are "hosts of God" and "sacraments of psychedelic religion," which take refuge in "technological mysticism." Just as the surgeon used drugs to kill or dull physical pains, false prophets try to apply drugs or ways of special dis-

INTRODUCTION 17

cipline to intoxicate the mind so as to relieve mental sufferings, including the fear and anxiety of death. But in fact, it is a venture of "mystical self-intoxication" or "mind-murder"![46]

However, temporal release does not heal the disease, nor will psychotherapy save the soul. Although Dr. Suzuki claimed to have the courage to plunge into the abyss of Tathata without fear (as he wrote: "Zen does not find anything frightening in infinite possibilities and unlimited freedom"),[47] he is like the LSD user who thought that he could fly, but was dashed to pieces! The roots of our problems are not in the mind, but in the soul. As one noted missionary working among the Buddhists observed, "the attainment of 'satori' does not touch the deepest levels of human life. It does not reach down to the depths of conscience in its relation to God. Although a 'cosmic awakening' may bring a certain clarity and peace of mind to man, the life of faith has not been kindled at all."[48] Zen is known as the way of full realization of the mind and "Koan" exercise is devised to discipline the mind and to stimulate the will. But without the supernatural power, the will of man is a slave and is subject to "the law of sin." So it is futile to discipline the mind through the "Koan" exercise, or to take drugs to trigger metabolic processes and to have so-called "transcendental experience." Without a complete change of human nature by the supernatural power, one's "transcendental experience" is never genuine. For either "Koan" or "LSD" are natural means which might be able to produce psychological or chemical reactions. But to expect supernatural experiences from natural means is entirely illogical. The flesh is flesh, the Spirit is Spirit. The and enthroned in heavenly realms in union with Christ Jesus.[50] Our hope is only in the One Great Physician, in One Great Psychiatrist from heaven. Only His supernatural work and divine power can set us on safe ground and fully And only those who are saved by His grace are raised up again in the Spirit, he cannot see the heavenly things.[4] difference, is in kind, not in degree. Except a man be born answer the restless strings of our psyche and heal the disorder which results therefrom.[51]

Historian Arnold Toynbee pointed out that there is no reason to expect any change in unredeemed human nature, while human life on this earth goes on. Since there has been no perceptible variation in the average sample of human nature in the past, there is no ground, in the evidence afforded by history, to expect any great variation in the future. Nor is there any warrant for supposing that within "historical times" there has been any progress in the evolution of human nature itself." "Western man, at the present high level of his intellectual powers and technological aptitudes, has not sloughed off Adam's heirloom of original sin." "History passes over into theology." "The central and dominant feature in the soul's spiritual landscape is its relation to God."[52] D. R. Davies suggested that Toynbee's monumental work, *A Study of History* could be renamed as *The Science of Original Sin* since 6000 years of historical facts prove the Biblical truth that "the wages of sin is death" (Rom. 6:23). Without the removal of sin, mankind has no hope.[53] And without shedding of blood, there is no remission of sin.

"The drug experience leads the unwary to believe that the reconciliation of the fallen world can be accomplished simply by conscious (or unconscious) expansion. However, true reconciliation occurs solely when a man faces up to his sin and accepts the atoning work of the historical Christ in his behalf. LSD offers a deceptive possibility of bypassing the Cross while achieving harmony within and without. Like Altizer's chimerical endeavor to gain the "conjunction of opposites" through the substitution of a mystical fully kenotic "Christ" for the historical Jesus, psychedelic mysticism tries to reconcile all things apart from the only Reconciler."[54]

This is a senseless speculation which will plunge the nations into pagan darkness. Now the Bible has been distorted and mocked; Christianity has been misinterpreted or diluted with humanistic and pagan doctrines. Those who blasphemously pronounce "God is dead" still occupy the chairs in seminaries and want to retain the title of "Christian Atheist"—a totally illogical and irrational term. But God is not mocked (Gal. 6:7). "Blessed is the nation whose God is the Lord; and the people whom he hath chosen for his own inheritance" (Ps. 33:12). "If ye forsake him," it means you are forsaking the foundation of living waters (II Chron. 15:1, 2; Jer. 2:13). You are cutting off your life-line. This is a basic spiritual law in the history of mankind.

There was a time when Asia Minor, Greece, and North Africa were full of professing Christians, while England and America were heathen lands. But when they turned off the true light and accepted Islam, the churches of Africa and Asia fell into complete decay[55] and their peoples have suffered miserably. On the other hand, after Europe and America became Christian nations, God showered down special mercies upon them, and their peoples have received distinguishing favor of God. When America was tossed by the winds of atheism from France, George Washington warned his people that it would be a "suicidal policy," if America should revolt against God's authority and deny His existence. Indeed American people have received countless blessings from the hands of God and they are enjoying them so abundantly, yet they are now kicking away the "ladder" which has exhalted their nation, departing from the faith, "giving heed to seducing spirits and doctrines of the devils." This is literally committing suicide and will surely bring this nation to destruction!

But our present crisis had its root in theology—our proper relation to God. Modern theologians have been misled by Schleiermacher.[56] According to him, religion is essentially a sense of the infinite, more than trust in a personal God. In religion, man feels himself one with the Absolute. Religion is pure feeling. It is true that feeling has an important place in religion, but, it is a grave mistake to regard it as the exclusive seat of religion. It is more incorrect to regard it as the source of religion. Schleiermacher's conception of religion makes it entirely subjective, a product of human factors and ignores its relation to absolute truth.[57]

Thus, men are apt to be tossed to and fro and carried about with every wind of doctrine and deceived by seducing spirits. One can be a "Christian" with his feeling and a heathen with his head. This is why an Episcopal priest, like Alan Watts can be a Zen Buddhist. This is why Thomas Altizer, while occupying his position in a Christian institute, could consider Buddhism as the most challenging religion, and contemplation as the highest of man's activity for therein can he become God, and Nirvana and the kingdom of God are parallel and not contrary to each other.[58] But true religion is not a matter of feeling. It embraces the entire man with all his thoughts, feeling and volitions. It has its seat in the heart, where all the faculties of the human soul are seen in their unity. The heart in the language of Biblical psychology means "the focus of the personal and moral life." All the soul's motions of life proceed from it and react upon it. It is the central organ of the soul. Religion is rooted in the image of God in man; man's relation to God is central and involves the whole man.[59] The heart of man was created for God and it cannot find rest until it rests in his Father's heart. "Man, captive in the world, arises and says to himself: I shall go to my Father."[60] This is true religion and this is the only way of salvation for "God so loved the world, that he gave his only begotten Son, that whosoever believes in him should not perish but have everlasting life" (John 3:16). So shun "vain deceit after the tradition of man, after the rudiments of the world"; and go back to God, for history centers in Jesus Christ and "passes over into theology. 'To Him return ye every one.' "[61]

---

[1] Cf. O. Spengler: *The Decline of the West*, I pp. 367, 424.

[2] Abraham Kuyper: *Calvinism*, pp. 10, 11, 18, 23; cf., Part Two, Chapter Four of this volume.

[3] *Ibid.*, pp. 180, 181, 182.

[4] Cf. Carl G. Jung: *Modern Man in Search of a Soul*, pp. 235-7, 241, 245.

INTRODUCTION 21

⁵ In the last century in America, mysticism was associated with the "Transcendental" movement in New England. More recently, the psychological phenomena of mysticism are receiving more and more attention; and experiments with various kinds of intoxicants have been made with a view to ascertaining how far these are similar to mystical states. But in fact, to employ certain narcotics to induce mystical conditions is the mysticism of the lowest stage which has been utterly rejected even by higher mysticism. In South America, witch doctors take 'Cohoba' snuff to consult with familiar spirits and converse with gods, and Indian tribes in Venezuela and Brazil take 'Parica' or 'Epena' snuff to induce intoxication and, as reported, to talk with the "angels"; in India, the Hindus believe that they can attain immortality by drinking Soma; in China, Taoists believe that some special herb transmuted by alchemy into elixir can prolong life indefinitely and the Boxers in 1900 believed that they are filled with magic power and immune to bullets and could banish away all foreign powers, but instead caused great national humiliation.

⁶ C. Humphreys, *Zen Buddhism*, p. 208.
⁷ Alan Watts, *Spirit of Zen*, p. 121.
⁸ Wm. Barrett (ed), *Selected Writings of Suzuki*, pp. 232-234.
⁹ Cf. Alan Watts: *Beyond Theology, The Art of Godmanship*, pp. 34, 35, 75, 76, 81, 82.
¹⁰ C. Humphreys, *Zen Comes West*, pp. 74, 203.
¹¹ John A. T. Robinson: *Honest to God*, pp. 7, 8, 11,16, 55, 56, 140, 141. His position has been attacked even by secular newspapers *(Manchester Guardian and London Daily Mails)* as very dangerous!
¹² Paul Tillich: *The Courage to Be*, p. 185.
¹³ Paul Tillich: *The Shaking of the Foundations*, pp. 63, 64.
¹⁴ Altizer: "Creative Negation in Theology," *The Christian Century*, July 7, 1965, p. 865.
¹⁵ The Sayings of Master Linchi; cf. Ogata: *Zen for the West*, p. 12.
¹⁶ Altizer: *Oriental Mysticism and Biblical Eschatology*, pp. 11, 43, 107.
¹⁷ Watts: *op. cit.*, pp. 115, 162.
¹⁸ Watts: *ibid.*, pp. 164-165.
¹⁹ Cf. Ephesians 2:1-16.
²⁰ Watts: *op. cit.*, pp. 212.
²¹ Cf. Guru K. Dutt: *Existentialism and Indian Thought* pp. 57, 62; Radhaknishnan: *East and West*, p. 20; *Eastern Religions and Western Thought*, pp. 20-33; 97-102.
²² Cf. Jack Kerouac: *The Dharma Bums*.
²³ Surgit Singh: *Christology and Personality*, p. 166.
²⁴ Cf. Romans 1:21, 25; II Thess. 2:10, 11.
²⁵ R. H. Blyth: *Zen in English Literature and Oriental Classics*. p. vii.

[26] See Appendix of this volume: *From Zen to Christ*.
[27] Griffis: *Religion in Japan*, p. 255 Reischauer: *Studies of Buddhism*, p. 118; Ernest Becker: *Zen: A Rational Critic*, pp. 14, 16, 17, 57, 81, 92, 140.
[28] Kuyper, *op. cit.*, p. 180.
[29] I Timothy 4:1, 2.
[30] John Warwick Montgomery: "The Gospel According to LSD," *Christianity Today*, Current Religious Thought, July 8, 1966.
[31] *Time*, June 17, 1966.
[32] Tom Buckley: "The LSD Trigger, Crystal Palace and Absolute Horror," *The New Republic*, May 14, 1966.
[33] Cf. I Tim. 3:16; John 1:10-14; 3:16.
[34] Cf. II Thess. 2:7; Rom. 1:23, 25.
[35] Cf. Romans 1:21; Col. 3:1, 2.
[36] Raymond B. Blakney (Tr.) Meister Eckhart — A Modern Translation, pp. 206, 252.
[37] Varieties of Religious Experiences, Lectures 16, 17.
[38] Cf. Part One, Chapter Two, II.4, of this volume.
[39] The author's father had this beatific vision almost daily which had caused the author to practice Zen in his early 40's.
[40] Leszek Ochota: "What is The Clinical Evidence?," *The New Republic*, May 14, 1966.
[41] *Time*, June 17, 1966.
[42] According to recent reports, LSD "trips" may produce chromosomal damage and also cause genetic defects, *Time*, March 24, 1967.
[43] Lambert Dolphin, Jr., " The Christian and LSD or my LSD 'Trip' Nearly Crashed," *Christian Reader*, Feb.-March, 1967.
[44] Han's petition to the Emperor against Buddhism, Entitled, *"Chʻien Ning Fu-Kuo Piao,"* has been widely read through generations of Chinese people and is also included in textbooks as a masterpiece of Chinese literature.
[45] Arnold Toynbee: *Civilization on Trial*, Preface p. v.
[46] Griffis: *Religions in Japan*, p. 255; and Reischauer; *Studies of Buddhism*, p. 118.
[47] Wm. Barrett (ed), *Zen Buddhism Selected Writings of Suzuki*, pp. 265-266.
[48] Reichelt: *Meditation and Piety in the Far East*, pp. 16, 17.
[49] Cf. John 3:3, 27.
[50] Ephesians 2:5, 6.
[51] Cf. Murray: *Introduction to Christian Psychotherapy*, pp. 148, 270, 271.
[52] Toynbee: *Civilization on Trial*, pp. 248, 260, 261, Preface p. v.
[53] Cf. D. R. Davies: *Down; Peacock's Feathers*, MacMillan 1944. pp. 95-104, also Arnold Toynbee: *A Study of History*, Vol. V. pp. 16, 17.

[54] John Warwick Montgomery: "The Gospel According to LSD," *Christianity Today*, July 8, 1966.
[55] Cf. Bishop J. C. Ryle: *Expository Thoughts on the Gospels-Mark*, pp. 214, 247.
[56] Cf. Part Two. Chapter 4 of this volume, "Theology in Crisis."
[57] L. Berkhof: *Introductory Volume to Systematic Theology*, p. 108.
[58] Cf. Altizer: *Oriental Mysticism and Biblical Eschatology*, pp. 11, 43, 178.
[59] Berkhof: *op. cit.*, p. 109; Laidlaw: *The Bible Doctrine of Man*, p. 225.
[60] J. H. Bavinck: *Inleiding in de Zielkunde*, p. 277.
[61] Arnold Toynbee *"Civilization on Trial,"* Preface, p. v.

PART ONE

FANTASY OF THE EAST
—THE SPIRIT OF ZEN—

CHAPTER ONE

HISTORY AND NATURE OF ZEN

I. THE HISTORY OF ZEN

1. Its inception in India. According to tradition, Zen originated with certain esoteric teaching allegedly expounded by the historical Buddha to his disciples. It is said that once when Buddha was seated with his Bhikhus (mendicant monks, members of the Order) on the Mount of Holy Vulture, a Brahma-Raja came to him offering him a golden flower, and asked him to preach Dharma (Law, Truth). Instead of delivering a sermon, upon receiving the flower, Buddha simply held it aloft and gazed at it with perfect silence. No one understood his silence except the disciple Mahakasyapa who responded to his Master with a smile. It is further said that "the most precious treasure," spiritual and transcendental, was handed to Mahakasyapa. Thereafter the Wisdom was transmitted without the use of written texts, from mind to mind, through the centuries by twenty-eight successive Patriarchs, Buddha himself being the first. Finally the twenty-eighth of these Patriarchs, the famous Bodhi-Dharma (A.D. 480-528) came to China about A.D. 520 during the reign of Emperor Wu (A.D. 502-549) of the Liang Dynasty and thus became the founder of the Zen school of Buddhism in China.

2. Its Development in China and Japan. After the death of Bodhi-Dharma, the school was successively headed by his disciple Hui-K'o (487-593) as the second Chinese

patriarch; by Seng-T'san (606) as the third; by Tao-Hsin (580-651) as the fourth; and by Hung-Jen (605-675) as the fifth.

After Hung-Jen's death, a schism split the school into two branches: (1) The Northern sect, headed by Shen-Hsiu (c. 606-706); and (2) the Southern sect, headed by Hui-Neng (638-713). The Northern sect, known as the school of "gradual" enlightenment, did not survive more than a hundred years after the founder's death. The Southern sect, known as the school of "instantaneous" enlightenment, gained increasing popularity and became a genuinely Chinese form of Buddhism by reason of the founder's famous gatha and his famous Tan-Chin (Platform Sutra) which we will discuss later.[1]

By the thirteenth century, Zen in China began to lose its initial popularity. As early as the seventh century, Zen had reached Japan but it was not until the twelfth century that a Tiendai monk called Eisa crossed into China to study Zen and returned to found a Zen monastery in Kyoto. Consequently, Zen took root in Japan. Eisa founded the Japanese branch of Linchi (Rinzai in Japanese pronunciation) Zen. While the Tiendai and Kegon sects of Buddhism were too philosophic for the Japanese knights of the middle ages, Zen was seized by the Japanese military class and became a warrior creed. It called for action, for the most rigorous self-discipline, for self-reliance, for contempt of death,[2] and thus Zen was able to reach the culminating point of its development under the influence of Shintoism[3] and was used by Japanese militarists as an incentive for their aggressive wars.

3. Its Impact on the West. Zen was first introduced to the West in the "Sermons of Buddhist Abbot" translated by Dr. Suzuki in 1906 (Open Court Publishing Company of Chicago). In the following year, Dr. Suzuki's paper in the Journal of the Pali Text Society of London was the first presentation of Zen to England. After 1930 books and articles on Zen began to increase in quantity.[4] The result of these works has been a swiftly increasing Western interest

in Zen. In the past twenty years or so, it has become very widely known in Europe and America, where it is exercising great intellectual and artistic influence. Zen finds its place in the West as a study of serious interest for three principle groups as Alan Watts observed: (1) In philosophical circles, it is being found of special relevance to those who are looking for a step beyond the impotent insights of logical positivism and scientific empiricism, (2) Among scientists, its interest has been chiefly for psychotherapists, and (3) In the world of art, the influence of Zen is more indirect and is seen in the great indebtedness of contemporary American architecture and ceramics to Japanese feelings for space and texture. Since Zen is so markedly different from any other form of Buddhism, and from other religions as well, it has aroused the curiosity of many who would not ordinarily look to the impractical East for practical wisdom. Once such curiosity is aroused, it is not easy to set it at rest, for Zen has a peculiar fascination on minds weary of conventional religion and philisophy.[5]

R. H. Blyth contends that "Zen is the most precious possession of Asia. With its beginning in India, development in China, and final practical application in Japan", he permits himself to exaggerate, "it is today the strongest power in the world. It is a world-power, for in so far as man lives at all, he lives in Zen. Wherever there is poetical action, a religious aspiration, a heroic thought, a union of the Nature within a man and the Nature without, there is Zen."[6]

II. THE MEANING OF ZEN

1. Its Etymological Rendering. Ch'an, better known to Westerners under its Japanese pronunciation of Zen, is an abbreviation of the original phrase Ch'an-na, which is the Chinese phonetic rendering of the Sanskrit word Dhyana or the Pali Jhana. Dhyana comes from the root "dhi," meaning "to perceive," "to reflect upon," "to fix the mind upon"; while "dhi" etymologically may have some connection with "dha," "to hold," "to keep," "to maintain." Dhyana thus

means to hold one's thought collected, not to let thought wander away from its legitimate path; that is, it means to have the mind concentrated on a single subject of thought. By Dhyana is generally understood a kind of meditation or contemplation. But, though the term Zen is derived from the Chinese transliteration (Ch'an-na) of the original Sanskrit, it must not be identified with it. Zen is more than Dhyana in its primitive sense. Dhyana is merely a quieting exercise of mind, while Zen purposes to discipline the mind itself, to make it its own master, through an insight into its proper nature.[7]

2. Its Different Interpretations. What is Zen? Perhaps this is the most difficult question to answer. Zen is considered to be "extremely elusive" and as a "bottomless abyss." It is beyond perception, description, definition and grasping. Dr. Suzuki says, "The only truthful answer is 'that's it.' "[8] "Zen is more than meditation and Dhyana in its ordinary sense. The discipline of Zen consists in opening the mental eye in order to look into the very reason of existence."[9] "Zen in its essence is the art of seeing into the nature of one's own being and it points the way from bondage to freedom."[10] "It liberates our natural energies and compels us to express our faculty for happiness and love."[11] Someone says, "If Zen is to be translated at all, the nearest equivalent is Enlightenment, but even so, Zen is not only Enlightenment, it is also the way to its attainment."[12] "Zen can be defined as the unity of man and the universe, as the rhythm of the mind with the changing forms, as a state of Oneness in which all distinction of "I" and "Not I," "Knower" and "Known," "Seer" and "Seen" are set aside."[13] Zen is also known as 'Hsin Tsung' (Mind Doctrine or the teaching of the Mind). "This term is probably the best summary of what Zen stands for, for what it teaches is the way of full realization of the Mind. Enlightenment is merely another name for the complete unfolding of the 'inner mind.' "[14] However, it is not the logical rational Enlightenment of eighteenth century France, but is to be understood as irrational and inconceivable. We are told that

Zen was not subject to logical analysis or intellectual treatment.[15]

III. THE ELUSIVE NATURE OF ZEN

1. Is Zen Philosophy? Zen is not a mere system of thought and philosophy. It would be a great mistake to think that Zen can be grasped by intellectual study. Zen teaches nothing. They say, "We teach ourselves; Zen merely points the way." "Unless this pointing is teaching, there is nothing in Zen purposely set up as its cardinal doctrines or as its fundamental philosophy."[16] The term philosophy generally does not exist in Buddhist texts, and in Zen it is even harder to find. Both disdain metaphysical speculation. They require us to free our mind from the general preoccupations which usually form the basis of all our philosophies.[17]

2. Is Zen Religion? Zen is the spirit of man, Zen is not a religion, for Zen has no God to worship, no ceremonial rites to observe, no future abode to which the dead are destined, and last of all, Zen has no soul! Zen is free from all those dogmatic and religious encumbrances. It boldly declares that the immaculate Yogins do not enter Nirvana and the precept-violating monks do not go to hell. Zen believes in its own purity and goodness. Zen is emphatically against all religious conventionalism.[18]

3. Is Zen Buddhism? While Zen claims to be the "pinnacle of Buddhism"[19] or the "inmost essence of Buddhism,"[20] it represents a teaching that is most direct, profound and practical, capable of bringing one to thorough liberation and perfect Enlightenment, [21] yet, on the other hand Zen is not considered classical Buddhism, but a "Chinese anomaly of it."[22] As some Chinese scholars have observed: in actual fact, its development in India may safely be regarded as entirely imaginary, and even Bodhi-Dharma, its alleged transmitter to China, looms uncertainly through the mists of tradition as a half legendary person. All that we can say with assurance is that in China itself, as early as the Period of Disunity (396-588), the theory of instantaneous enlightenment had been developed.[23] "All the

Buddhist teachings as propounded in the Sutras and Sastras are treated by Zen as mere waste paper."[24] "The Buddha cannot save us," says Hui-Hai, "strive diligently, practice the method for yourselves, do not rely on the strength of the Buddha."[25] It is interesting to note that Buddha is often spoken of as a "dry stick of dung" and it is also a very popular saying among Zen, "When you have mentioned Buddha's name, wash your mouth!" The attitude of Yun-men; (Ummon, the founder of the Ummon school) was even more radical: "When Sakyamuni was born it is said that he lifted one hand toward the heaven and pointed to the earth with the other, exclaiming, 'Above the heavens and below the heavens, I alone am the Honoured One.' Yun-men comments on this by saying, 'If I had been with him at the moment of his uttering this, I would surely have struck him dead with a blow and thrown the corpse into the maw of a hungry dog'."[26]

Thus we might say that Zen is not Buddhism, but a Chinese anomaly of it. Prof. Fung Yu-lan asserts with assurance that the theory of instantaneous enlightenment has been developed as early as the Period of Disunity and gained wide currency during the T'ang Dynasty (618-905). Dr. Hu-Shih describes Zen as a Chinese revolt against Buddhism. He accepts neither the historical reality of Bodhi-Dharma nor the authenticity of the earlier Zen works.[27] Even Suzuki acknowledged "Zen was the Chinese revolt against Buddhism."

4. Is Zen Taoism? Zen grew out of a combination of mahayana Buddhism and Taoism. "From Hui-Neng, Zen lost all its distinctively Indian characteristics, it became thoroughly transformed by the more practical Chinese mentality."[28] "It was actually more deeply influenced by Taoism. In Taoism, Reality is termed Tao which has a rather more dynamic connotation than Dharma, Tathata, or Sunyata. Tao is life considered as flowing power. If man ceases from self-assertion and lets go of life, the Tao will have a chance to operate freely within him. His life will be lived not by his own ego but by Tao."[29] The central theme of Taoism

is "Wu-Wei" (non-action). According to the teaching of Lao-Tzu, Tao is the mighty stream of life flowing on from eternity to eternity. He looks with scornful disdain upon the wisdom of man, the busy-body, the self-deceived prophets who try to improve their situation by much ado which is worse than useless; and therefore advises mankind to know the Tao, to conform to the Tao and to be subject to the Tao. Tao is non-action; and non-action prevails over all things. Zen also teaches "Wu-Chu" (non-abiding) and "Wu-Nieng" (no-thought), etc. which might be considered as the exegesis of the notion "Wu-Wei."[30] "In the sayings of the later Masters, the word Tao is often used synonymously with Buddha, nature, or the Dharma."[31] Therefore, Humphreys asserted more affirmatively, "The Taoist doctrine of 'Wu-Wei' is excellent Zen." According to him, "Taoism is 'The godmother of Zen.' "[32]

5. Is Zen Atheism, etc? Aside from the above considerations, one might also discuss whether Zen is atheism, pantheism, mysticism, or existentialism. But since these raise questions of Western philosophy, such comparisons will be postponed to later chapters.[33]

IV. THE ICONOCLASTIC STANCE OF ZEN

1. A Revolt Against Language. The following statement ascribed to Bodhi-Dharma, the founder of Zen in China, is most clear on this point:

A special transmission outside the scriptures,
No dependence upon words and letters,
Direct pointing to the soul of man,
Seeing into the nature and attainment of Buddhahood.

To Zen, scriptures are only so-called "fingers pointing to the moon" or a "ferry boat in which to cross a stream." As finger and boat are simply the means and not the end, so are the scriptures or words. They never take them as the canon of truth. Therefore, to Zen, neither logic nor metaphysics is to be relied upon for insight, theoretical instruction may be positively harmful. The trust of books can be at best but a "finger pointing at the moon." "If we fix our gaze on the finger, we miss the heavenly glory."[34]

2. A Revolt Against Reason. Zen is not only a wordless sect, but also a revolt against reason, a breaking down of the mere intellectual images of the living reality knowable only by personal experience. Anyone who attempts to write about Zen has to encounter unusual difficulties. The moment he attempts any fixed definition, the thing slips away. Zen cannot be made to fit any "ism" or "ology."[35] To understand Zen, we have to get away from the abstract and dead realm of concepts, and come face to face with reality as it stands quite clearly before us here and now. In essence, Zen involves no doctrine. It is an experience of Reality beyond doctrine.[36] As a Belgian scholar says, "Zen is the science of the Real, and the nature of the Real forbids all mental representation or attribution. Reality transcends dualistic intellectual analysis."[37] "Zen is the most irrational and inconceivable thing in the world. Zen was not subject to logical analysis or to intellectual treatment. It must be directly and personally experienced by each of us in his inner spirit."[38] "Zen is ex-hypothesis, beyond the intellect and the chains of intellectual usage. . . ."[39]

3. A Revolt Against Authority. According to the saying of Linchi (Rinzai), "Dharma is no other than the Mind." "Only keep the Mind from being stirred up, having no longing for the outside. There is no Dharma as long as you seek it outwardly." "O brethren, if you wish to grasp the correct view of the Dharma, be mindful not to be led astray by human temptation. Smash whatever you come across, regardless of whatever it is from within or without. Smash the Buddha, Patriarchs and Arhats, if you come across them; smash your parents and relations, if you come across them. You will be in real emancipation."[40] "Zen purposes to discipline the Mind itself, to make it its own master through an insight into its proper nature." "Anything that has the resemblance of an external authority is rejected by Zen. Absolute faith is placed in a man's own inner being." "Zen

wants to live from within, not to be bound by rules, but to be creating one's own rules."[41]

---

[1] Cf. Fung Yu-lan, *A History of Chinese Philosophy*, II, pp. 387-388; Robert Linssen, *Living Zen*, pp. 40-41; Suzuki, *Essays*. I, p. 165, etc.
[2] Cf. Humphreys, *Zen Buddhism*, pp. 37-39.
[3] Cf. Dr. Chikao Fujisawa, *Zen and Shinto*, p. 69; also cf. Harrison, *The Fighting Spirit of Japan*.
[4] Cf. Humphreys, *ibid*, pp. 39-42.
[5] Cf Watts, *The Spirit of Zen*, pp. 14, 15, 17, also Part III, Chapter one of this volume. Men like Martin Heidegger and Paul Tillich are admirers of Zen.
[6] Cf. R. H. Blyth, *Zen in English Literature and Oriental Classics*, p. vii.
[7] Suzuki, *Introduction to Zen Buddhism*, pp. 32, 40, 96, 100, 101.
[8] Suzuki, *Essays, III*, p. 7.
[9] Suzuki, *op. cit.*, p. 40.
[10] Suzuki, (Barrett ed.), *Zen Buddhism—Selected Writings* p. 1.
[11] Fromm and others, *Zen Buddhism and Psychoanalysis*, p. 115.
[12] Watts, *Spirit of Zen*, p. 24.
[13] *Ibid.*, p. 121.
[14] Chang, chen-chi, *The Practice of Zen*, p. 25.
[15] Suzuki, *Selected Writings*, pp. 3-13.
[16] Suzuki, *Introduction to Zen Buddhism*, p. 38.
[17] Linssen, *Living Zen*, pp. 46-51.
[18] Cf. *ibid.*, pp. 52-67; Suzuki *op. cit.* 34, 40.
[19] Linssen, *ibid.*, p. 44.
[20] Suzuki, *Selected Writings*, p. 59.
[21] Chang, Chen-chi, *The Practice of Zen*, pp. 1, 2.
[22] Suzuki, *ibid.*, *op. cit.*, p. 27
[23] Fung Yu-lan, *History of Chinese Philosophy II*, p. 388. Cf. also Dr. Hu-Shih, *The Development of Zen Buddhism in China-Chinese Social and Political Review*, Vol. 15, pp. 475-505, 1931.
[24] Cf. Suzuki, *Introduction to Zen Buddhism*, p. 38.
[25] Hui-Hai, *The Path to Sudden Attainment* (tr. John Blofled), p. 41.
[26] Cf. Suzuki, *op. cit.*, p. 40; also Humphreys, *Zen Buddhism*, pp. 46-49.
[27] See note 17.
[28] Watts, *Spirit of Zen*, p. 38.
[29] Watts, *Zen*, pp. 18, 19.
[30] Cf. Tao Teh-chin, and Part III chap. Two 1, 2, of this volume.
[31] Cf. Watts, *Zen*, pp. 33-38.

[32] Humphreys, *Zen Buddhism*, Preface, ix, p. 217; cf. Ogatu, *Zen for the West*, pp. 29-31.
[33] Cf. *ibid.*, Chap. III, and Suzuki, *Selected Writings*, pp. 265, 266, also part two, chapter IV; part three, chapters I, II, III of this volume.
[34] Pratt, *The Pilgrimage of Buddhism*, p. 624; Cf.; also *Tan-Chin* and *Chih-Yueh-Lu*.
[35] Cf. Watts, *Spirit of Zen*, pp. 18-20.
[36] Cf. Watts, *The Way of Liberation in Zen Buddhism*, pp. 28, 38.
[37] Cf. Linssen, *Living Zen*, pp. 76, 79, 81, 131.
[38] Suzuki, *Selected Writings*, pp. 7-13
[39] Humphreys, *Zen Buddhism*, pp. 2, 3.
[40] The Sayings of the Master Linchi (Rinzai), cf. Ogata, *Zen for the West*, p. 12.
[41] Cf. Suzuki, *Introduction to Zen Buddhism*, pp. 40, 44, 45, 64, 131.

CHAPTER TWO

TEACHINGS AND PRACTICE OF ZEN

I. THE TEACHINGS OF ZEN

1. The Method of Teaching. As pointed out in a previous section, Zen is a wordless sect; so, strictly speaking, it has no doctrinal teachings. Whatever teaching it does possess, is unique. Apart from a few collections of sermons by the earlier Zen masters, almost all records of Zen instruction are a number of dialogues between the masters and their disciples which seem to pay so little attention to the usual standard of logic and sound reasoning as to appear at first sight to be nonsense. The aim of Zen is to focus the attention on reality itself, rather than intellectual and emotional reactions to reality.[1]

While the next section deals with the practice of Zen, some striking examples of their unique way of teaching might be mentioned at this point. It is said that, "Bodhi-Dharma, after having introduced in his inimitable style the teaching and technique of Zen, meditated in silence for nine years. Finally, there came to him a former Confucian scholar by the name of Shen-Kuang, who asked to be instructed in the Dharma. The Master took no notice. For seven days and nights the petitioner waited in the snow; finally, to prove the life-and-death sincerity of his demand, he cut off his arm and sent it in. The Master saw him. "Pray," said the exhausted student, "purify my mind." "Let me see your mind," said the Master, "I will purify it." "I cannot produce this mind which troubles me so much," said the would-be pupil." "Then I have purified your mind," said Bodhi-Dharma, and the pupil was at last enlightened."[2] Another story that is related is about the fourth Chinese Patriarch, Tao-Hsin (A.D. 580-651) who asked his previous Master, "Pray show me the way to deliverance." Said the Master, "Who has put you under restraint?" When the enquirer answered, "No one," the Master inquired in return, "Then why do you seek deliverance?"[3]

"Zen's way of teaching is to demonstrate Reality rather than to talk about it, and to avoid formally religious terminology and conceptual statements. When Zen speaks, it expresses Reality, not with logical explanations and doctrine, but with every day conversation or with statements that upset the normal conceptual mode of thinking so violently that they appear as utter nonsense: it employs a thoroughgoing iconoclasm."[4] So "Zen teaches nothing," as Suzuki asserted, "Whatever teachings there are in Zen, they come out from one's own mind. Zen merely points the way. There is nothing in Zen purposely set up as its cardinal doctrine or as its fundamental philosophy."[5]

Therefore, Zen masters do not always teach with their mouths, but with their actions. "They shout, strike, and push; and when questioned, they sometimes run away or simply keep their mouth shut and pretend to be dumb. Such actions have no place in Rhetoric, Philosophy or Religion." For instance, "a monk called Hung Chou came to visit Ma Tsu, and asked: 'What is the meaning of Bodhi-Dharma's coming from the West?' Ma Tsu said: 'Bow down to me first.' As the monk was prostrating himself, Ma Tsu gave him a vigorous kick in the chest."[6]

2. The Schools of Teaching. Although Zen teaches nothing, nevertheless it was split into two schools so far as the doctrines or views are concerned.[7] The one is the so-called "gradual school," holding a view of continuous movement, also known as the "dust wiping" school, represented by Shen-Hsiu (A.D. 605-706) in his gatha:

> The body is like unto the Bodhi-tree,
> And the mind to a mirror bright.
> Carefully we cleanse them hour by hour,
> Lest dust shall fall upon them.

This school is no longer in existence. The other is known as the "abrupt or instantaneous school," represented by Hui-Neng with his famous gatha which is antagonistic to the former one:

> Originally there was no Bodhi-tree,
> Nor was there any mirror.
> Since originally there was nothing that has real existence,
> How then could the dust settle thereon?

This school advocates that the movement from Mayoi (Mi, in Chinese) to Satori (Wu) is abrupt and not gradual; discrete and not continuous, altogether beyond calculation. There is a leap, logical and psychological, in their experience. It teaches "seeing into one's own nature." "There is no enlightenment whatever which you can claim to have attained. If you have attained something, that is the surest proof that you have gone astray."[8]

3. The teachings on Original Nature. According to Hui-Neng, Zen is "the seeing into one's own nature." The nature is Mind, (Hsin) and the Mind is the Buddha, the Buddha is the Way, and the Way is the Zen. To see directly into one's original Nature, that is Zen.[9] They do not use the term God, but rather prefer to talk of the "Absolute" or the "One Mind." The aim of Zen is to take hold of the truth of Non-duality, which is the Absolute or the One Mind. In Zen, there is nothing to gain, nothing to understand. The truth of Zen opens by itself within.[10] So "the followers of Zen hold that the Absolute or union with the Absolute is not something to be attained; one does not enter Nirvana, for entrance to a place one has never left is impossible. The experience commonly called "entering Nirvana" is, in fact, an intuitive realization of the Self Nature which is the Nature of all things.[11] This is called

in Chinese "Ming-Hsin Chien-Hsing." They believe the truth lies in our "inner being." "Zen trains the Mind to see this truth; it opens one's eye to see the greatest mystery as it is daily and hourly performed, it enlarges the heart to embrace eternity of time and infinity of space."[12]

4. The Teachings on Non-duality. According to the teaching of Hui-Neng, "As long as there is a dualistic way of looking at things, there is no emancipation. Light stands against darkness, the passions stand against enlightenment. Unless these opposites are illuminated by Prajna, so that the gap between the two is bridged, there is no understanding of the Mahayana. The Buddha nature knows neither decrease nor increase. The Buddha nature is above birth and death."[13] "Reality transcends the duality. Reality is in itself entirety, it is beyond the traditional opposition of mobility and immobility. The experience of Satori is a result of emancipation from the arbitrary practice of partitioning our mind."[14] Zen signifies the mystical experience in which subjectivity and objectivity merge. To be Buddha means that one has realized one's identity with Tathata, with the one true self which is not conditioned by distinction between "I" and "you," "this," and "that."[15] They even assert that Enlightenment and darkness are substantially one and the same thing from the very beginning; the change from one to the other has taken place only inwardly or subjectively. Therefore, the finite is infinite and vice versa. There are not two separate things, though we are compelled to conceive them so intellectually. The mistake consists in our splitting into two what is really and absolutely one.[16] The ultimate standpoint of Zen is that we have been led astray through ignorance to find a split in our own being, that there was from the very begining no need for a struggle between the finite and the infinite, that the peace we are seeking so eagerly has been there all the time.[17] "Zen is at once the knower and the known. It is also the factor which unites the two in one. Zen seeks that which lies beyond antithesis."[18] "Zen takes us to an absolute realm wherein there

is no antithesis of any sort." "Unless we break through the antithesis of 'yes' and 'no,' we can never hope to live a real life of freedom." "To be free, life must be an absolute affirmation."[19]

5. The Teachings on Egolessness. Zen, teaches that we are living in an "ego-shell" which is the hardest thing to outgrow, and which we seem to carry from birth to death. So Zen is considered as a "complete revolution of our spiritual values, which should inevitably be expressed by a new social order free from egoism."[20] Where individualism is emphasized, the mutually restricting feeling of tension prevails. There is no freedom here, no spontaneity, but a deep, heavy atmosphere or inhibition. Suppression and oppression overpowers one and the result is psychological disturbance in all its varieties.[21] When Wei-Kuan was asked by a monk "What is Tao?" "Right before you," he replied. "Why don't I see it?" the monk wondered. To this Wei-Kuan explained, "Because of your egoism." The real disciple of Zen begins only at the point where the ego has altogether stopped trying to improve itself. In the words of Linchi, "If you seek deliberately to become Buddha, your Buddha is just 'samsara.' If a person seeks Tao, the person loses the Tao."[22] The essence of Zen consists in suppressing the activity of Ego, in emerging from the cocoon of self-centered thought and feeling. Our straining to possess, to become, to improve, to dominate and even to purify creates attachment and, therefore, bondage. So enlightenment means egolessness.

6. The Teachings on Voidness. Furthermore, enlightenment lies in unconsciousness. Unconsciousness does not mean the loss of consciousness. In the Prajnaparamita and other Mahaya Sutras it is stated: "To be unconscious in all circumstances is possible because the ultimate nature of all things is emptiness; and because there is after all not a form which one can say one has laid hands on. This unattainability of all things is Reality itself which is the most exquisite form of the Tathagata." "The Unconscious is thus the Ultimate reality, the true form."[23] Form is void, and

void is form. "Since all is void, originally there was nothing" (Pen-Lai-wu-i-wuh); this is the inmost essence of Zen teaching as expressed in the famous 'gāthā' of Hui-Neng, who is distinguished most conspicuously from his predecessors and whose doctrine was considered revolutionary in the history of Zen thought.[24]

The whole system of Zen discipline is a series of attempts to be free from all forms of bondage. In this respect even the "dust wiping," or "to keep the eye on purity" are considered to be another form of bondage. Tachu Hui-hai of the T'ang Dynasty said, "The unconscious means to have no mind in all circumstance, . . .to be eternally free from any form of string. Not to abide in goodness, evil; being, non-being; inside, outside, or in the middle; nor in void, non-void; abstraction or non-abstraction—that is not abiding anywhere. Whoever attains to this is said to have a non-abiding mind. The non-abiding mind is indeed the mind of Buddha."[25] "The absolute is that which is not affected. Because the mind is the ultimate reality, it is called the absolute." "When nothing is loved, that is called possessing a mind free from defilement. This implies the voidness of the nature of phenomena which (if comprehended) results in breaking the myriad chains of causation. The breaking of the myriad chains of causation leads naturally to deliverance."[26]

As Huang-Po Hsi-Yun (A.D. 850) pointed out, "If you fail to comprehend how to be devoid of mind, your attachment to objects will all be those of devil-Karma. Even if you do things with a view to the Pure Land, these too produce a Karma which is called the Buddha-hindrance, because it hinders the mind. Thus you will be bound by cause and effect and have no degree of freedom in your dying and living."[27] To be unconscious is to have no thought. Hui-Neng points this out in his famous Tan-Chin (Platform Sutra): "In the teaching of Zen, first of all, we have established "No thought" (Wu-Nien) as the essential; "No phenomenon" (Wu-hsian) as the substance; and "No abiding" (Wu-chu) as the basis. Again, "To think of all things without abiding in them, this is to be free of the bonds. But what is called here no thought does not mean 'not to think of anything at all,' nor does it mean 'the complete expulsion of thought,' for this would in itself be a case of being 'bound by things.' "[28]

7. The Teaching of Nothing. But after all, Zen teaches nothing. All cosmological and psychological theories of original Buddhism are regarded, according to the phrase of Hui-Hai as arguments which are of the order of nonsense.[29] As Ching-Yuan remarks, "My late teacher used to say that the practice of Zen is to be described as the gold and ordure method. Before it is comprehended, it is all like gold; after it is comprehended it is all like ordure."[30] The Zen school often describes enlightenment as "the bottom of the tub falling out" (Tung-ti-tuh-loh). When that happens, all its contents are suddenly gone; he finds his problems suddenly solved. They are solved not in the sense that he gains positive solutions for them, but in the sense that all his problems have ceased any longer to be problems. As Tao-Yi (Matsu) says, "We speak of enlightenment in contrast to delusion. But since there is originally no delusion, enlightenment also cannot stand. This is what is known as 'an obtaining which is not an obtaining' and also 'in the last resort nothing gained'."[31]

II. THE PRACTICE OF ZEN

1. The Object of Zen Practice. The object of the practice of Zen is to attain[32] "Satori" (Enlightenment, "Wu" in Chinese) which is a sort of inner perception of Reality itself. According to Hui-Neng, Zen was the "seeing into one's own nature." The ultimate destination of Satori is to be "back within oneself." Zen calls that to "return home." In order to achieve this object one should acquire a new viewpoint and break the rules of the dualistic logical analysis, for the Reality transcends the duality.[33]

Satori is the heart of Zen. There can be no Zen without Satori. Satori is the measurement of Zen in particular, and of Buddhism in general. For Buddhism springs from the Buddha's Satori—enlightenment. Satori is the world of non-discrimination, non-differentiation, or two-ness become one-ness and yet equally seen as two. The self, with its pride and regret of the past; its fears and boasts and desires of the moment, its hopes and ambitions for the days unborn, must be transcended.[34]

2. The Ways of Zen Practice. In order to attain the ultimate destination, the essential task is to discipline and therefore to master the Mind. To this end the Zen Master has evolved a technique of Dhyana (Za-Zen; Tso-Ch'an, in Chinese) which enables the disciple to relax the body, banish wandering thoughts and preserve his nervous energy so that he may devote his entire strength to the Koan (Kung-an, in Chinese). But Za-Zen and Koan are not the objectives of Zen life, they are ways of discipline aiming to attain the experience of Satori.[35]

While Zen has often been mis-interpreted as meditation properly speaking Zen is not merely meditation. A story is told of Hui-Neng's famous disciple Huai-Jang (A.D. 677-744), in the record of the latter's sayings: "Matsu lived in the Ch'uan-fa Monastery on the Southern Peak. There he occupied a solitary hut in which all alone he practiced meditation, paying no attention to those who visited him. One day Huai-Jang kept grinding a brick in front of the hut; and after having continued for a long time, Matsu finally asked: 'What are you doing?' Huai-Jang replied that he was grinding to make a mirror. 'How can a mirror be made by grinding bricks?' asked Matsu. Replied Huai-Jang, 'If a mirror cannot be made by grinding bricks, how can a Buddha be made by practicing meditation?' "[36]

As Hui-Hai pointed out, walking, standing, sitting or lying, whatever you are doing, and at all times, continually exert yourselves without interruption. This is called forever dwelling (on Enlightenment).[37] "Good morning, how are you today?" "Thank you, I am very well," here is Zen. "Please have a cup of tea," this again is full of Zen, as Suzuki writes.[38] A monk asked Chao-chou Tsung-shen (A.D. 778-897) to be instructed in Zen. "Have you had your breakfast?" "Yes, I have," answered the monk. "If so, have your dishes been washed?" It is said this answer at once enlightened the monk's mind to the truth of Zen.[39] In a hymn of the eighth century, the Buddhist layman P'ang-Yun writes, "Spirit, like understanding and divine functioning lies in carrying water and chopping wood."[40] This has become a popular saying among the Zen followers: "In carrying water and chopping wood, therein lies the wonderful Tao."[41]

3. The Means of Zen Practice. Toward the end of the T'ang dynasty, the Koan (Kung-an, in Chinese) exercise was devised and came into vogue during the Sung dynasty, it was used as a means of Zen practice, and took its systematization in Japan in the twelfth century. This is known as the Linchi (Rinzai) approach. By Koan is understood a paradoxical question, expression or action of the Master. The Koans are submitted to the students for meditation. They are of great variety, ambiguity and above all of an overwhelming by paradoxical nature.[42] The number of Koans is traditionally estimated at 1700. But for all practical purposes, less than ten, even less than five, or perhaps just one may be sufficient to open one's mind to the ultimate truth of Zen.[43]

Koans are the principal means used by Zen masters to assist the disciple clean his mind of the fetters of logical ratiocination, to get rid of different types of conceptualism and mental fixation, which are the barriers that shut off all possible avenues to rationalization.[44] The worst enemy of Zen experience, we are told, is the intellect which consists of and insists on discriminating the subject from the object. The discriminating intellect must be cut short if Zen consciousness is to unfold itself and Koan is constructed to serve its end.[45] As Carl Jung observed, "The conscious is only a part of the spiritual and is never capable of spiritual completeness, for that the indefinite expansion of the unconsciousness is needed. The latter can neither be captured with skillful formulas nor exercised by means of scientific dogmas."[46] Zen deals with something going beyond the logic of things. In Zen, will is more basic than the intellect because it is the principle that lies at the root of all existences and unites them all in the oneness of being. The one great will from which all infinitely varied wills flow is "Cosmic Unconscious,"[47] which is the Zen's reservoir of infinite possibilites. The intellect only serves varied purposes in our daily living, but it does not solve the intimate problem of life and death.[48] When we face it, the intellect has to confess its inability to cope with the problem. The intellectual blind alley to which we are now driven is like the "silver mountain" or the "iron wall" standing right in front of us. Not intellectual maneuver or logical trickery, but the whole of our being is needed to effect a penetration. This is like climbing up to the end of a pole one hundred feet long and yet being urged to climb on and on, until you have to execute a desperate leap, utterly disregarding your existential safety.[49]

Zen's method of discipline generally consists in putting one in an insoluble dilemma out of which one must contrive to escape, not through accustomed logic, but must pass beyond logic to a "mind of higher order." There are many impossible demands, such as: "(1) Talk without tongue; (2) Play your stringless lute; (3) Clap with single hand; (4) A long time ago, a man kept a goose in a bottle. It grew larger and larger, until it could not get out of the bottle any more; but he did not want to break the bottle, nor did he wish to hurt the goose; how would you get it out? (5) Suppose a man climbing up a tree takes hold of a branch by his teeth and his whole body is thus suspended beyond a precipice. His hands are not holding anything and his feet are off the ground. Now another man comes along to ask the man as to the fundamental principle of Buddhism. If the man does not answer, he is neglecting the question; but if he tries to answer he will lose his life, how can he get out of his predicament? (6) Chao Chou was once working as a cook in the monastery. One day he barred the kitchen door from the inside, and started a fire. In a short time, the room filled with smoke and flames. He then cried out:

'Fire, Fire! Help, Help!' All the monks in the monastery immediately gathered round, but they could not get in, because the door was locked. Chao Chou said: 'Say the right word and I will open the door, otherwise, I won't'. Nobody could answer."[50]

The Koan exercise is so devised to concentrate the mind and to stimulate the will to the highest degree. It is a way of presenting the care of life in an intensified form. Like the man hanging beyond the precipice, he is completely at a loss as to what to do next. Suddenly, he finds his mind and body wiped out of existence together with the Koan. This is what is known as "letting go of your hold." This "letting go" is the acceptance of life as life which is always free and spontaneous and unlimited. "At this moment the Zen disciple attains freedom of the spirit, for he realizes the suffering inherent in man's attempt to shut the wind in a box, to keep life alive without letting it live."[51]

4. The Experience of Zen Practice. The experience of Zen can be viewed from two respects: On the one hand it is often said that Zen is our "ordinary mindness," "in carrying water and chopping wood, therein lies the wonderful Tao." There is nothing unusual or supernatural that transcends our everyday life. When you feel sleepy, you retire; when you are hungry, you eat. This is the spirit of Zen. "In Zen there is nothing to explain, nothing to teach. Unless it grows out of youself, no knowledge is really of value to you." "In fact, all the causes of Satori are in the mind. When the clock ticks, all that has been lying there bursts up like a volcanic eruption or flashes out like a bolt of lightning. Zen calls this returning to one's own home."[52]

But, on the other hand, "it is no easy task; it is the greatest mental cataclysm. It is a kind of fiery 'baptism' and one has to go through the storm, the earthquake, the overthrowing of the mountain and the breaking in pieces of the rocks."[53] To the question, "What is Zen?" a master gave this answer: "Boiling oil over a blazing fire." We have to go through with this scorching experience before Zen smiles on us and says, "Here is your home?"[54]

The Zen Masters, while sometimes puzzling a disciple by using a "jargon" or by poking fun, in a cynical manner often gave a slap, blow or kick without any instruction. The poor questioner was often stopped, kicked, and beaten. A classical example was that of Linchi, a great Zen master, the founder of the school that bears his name. Once he saw his master, Huang-Po, and asked "What is the principle of Buddhism?" Before he could finish, his master gave him several blows. This is why, in the monastery, the monk or student, when he is not yet at 'determination,' frequently refuses to see the master; and why, for the compulsory Sa-Zan visits, he has sometimes to be beaten, pulled, dragged or forcibly carried by other monks out of the meditation hall and into the interview."[55]

Yun-man (Ummon), great master of Zen at the end of the T'ang Dynasty, had to lose one of his legs in order to get an insight into the life principle. He had to visit his teacher Bokupu (Mu-Chou), who was a senior disciple of Rinzai (Linchi) under Obaku (Huang-Po) three times before he was admitted to see him. When the truth-seeking monk was allowed to go inside the gate, the master took hold of him by the chest and demanded: "Speak! Speak!" Ummon hesitated, where upon the Master pushed him out of the gate, saying, "Oh you good for nothing fellow!" While the gate was hastily shut, one of Ummon's legs was caught and broken. It is said that the intense pain resulting from this apparently awakened the poor fellow to the greatest fact of life. This realization, more than enough recompensed for the loss of his leg. However, this is not a solitary instance in this respect. There have been many such individuals in the history of Zen who were willing to sacrifice a part of their body for the so-called "truth."[56] This is evidently a sheer absurdity. At this point, it is hard to refrain from some contrast and comparison between the harshness of the Zen Masters and the meekness of the Lord Jesus Christ.[57]

5. The Result of Zen Practice. The Zen school commonly describes its experience of Satori (Enlightment, Wu, in

Chinese), as "the bottom of the tub falling off." When that happens, all of its contents are suddenly gone. So with the man who has gained Satori; he finds all his problems suddenly solved, in the sense that all his problems have ceased to be problems. Nothing is left, but to burst out into a loud laughter! Then, as it is described, there is a source of certainty, a sense of airiness which comes from dropping the burden of self and its desires. There is a sense of returning from the recovery of our essence of mind. There is an increasing serenity and an increasing balance combined with a refusal to rest the mind in any of the pairs of opposites. There is a new-born sense of flow, a refusal to let mind rest anywhere at all. The Mind (Hsin) becomes no-mind (Wu-Hsin), without thought of security or achievement or any purpose, much less ultimate goal. And there is a sense of a rightness in all actions. All that happens is right. There is a willingess to let things happen and a diminishing desire to control the universe. Action is done without haste and delay, without thought of self, without thought of merit and reward. As self dies out, the true self grows.[58]

Despite the favorable sympathetic picture of Zen as seen by its adherents, Zen practice may be viewed from a different angle. It is "a technique by which to achieve a mental breakdown of people so that they can be made to accept a new ideology." The so-called "Satori" is simply "the final critical collapse under the accumulative pressures of stress." It is "a mental catastrophe," "a piling up of intellectual frustration that leads to the crumbling of the edifice of logical thought." "There has been a good deal of misgiving about the use of Koan. The coercive aspect of the discipline is painful. It has been called largely artificial and been accused of harboring grave pitfalls." It is "a childish dependence upon magical omnipotence," "a submission to the master's psychological dominance." "The cure is supplied with the disease."[59] This is why many Zen masters in China got very odd qualities and are called "Mo-Wong" (literally means "demon-king") which proves that they

TEACHINGS AND PRACTICE OF ZEN 49

have become mentally deranged. This will be further discussed in the latter past of this volume.

---

[1] Cf. Watts, *Spirit of Zen*, pp. 18, 19; Cf. also Chu Chan, *The Huang Po Doctrine of Universal Mind;* Hui Hai, *The Path to Sudden Attainment*. (Tr. by John Blofeld).

[2] Cf. Humphreys, *Zen Buddhism*, p. 34.

[3] *Ibid.*, p. 35.

[4] Watts, *Zen*, p. 24; *Spirit of Zen.* pp. 30, 31.

[5] Suzuki, *Introduction to Zen Buddhism*, p. 38.

[6] Chang, Chen-Chi: *The Practice of Zen*, pp. 13, 14.

[7] Cf. Chapter I, Section 1, 2, of this volume.

[8] Suzuki, *Selected Writings*, pp. 184-186, 195.

[9] Cf. Blyth, *Zen in English Lit. and Oriental Classics*, p. 68.

[10] Cf. Fung Yu-lan, *History of Chinese Philosophy*, pp. 390-406. Barret, Ed., *Zen Buddhism*, pp. 73-78.

[11] Cf. Hui-Hai, *The Path to Sudden Attainment*, p. 16.

[12] Suzuki, *Introduction to Zen Buddhism*, p. 45.

[13] Suzuki, *Selected Writings*, pp. 169-170.

[14] Linssen, *Living Zen*, pp. 76, 79, 81, 131.

[15] Watts, *Spirit of Zen*, p. 29.

[16] Cf. Suzuki, *Selected Writings*, p. 15.

[17] Cf. *ibid.*, p. 13; Humphreys, *Zen Buddhism*, pp. 8, 9.

[18] Humphreys, *ibid*, p. 2.

[19] Suzuki, *Introduction to Zen Buddhism*, pp. 66, 68.

[20] Linssen, *Living Zen*, p. 205.

[21] Cf. Suzuki, Fromm, et al., *Zen Buddhism and Psychoanalysis*, p. 31.

[22] *Sayings of Linchi.*

[23] Suzuki, *Selected Writings*, p. 193.

[24] Cf. *ibid.*, pp. 157-160.

[25] Hui-Hai, *The Path to Sudden Attainment* (Tr. by J. Blofeld), p. 11.

[26] *Ibid.*, pp. 11, 27, 46.

[27] *Saying of Ancient Worthies*, 3:95.

[28] *Tan-chin*, Chap. IV; cf. Fung Yu-lan, *History of Chinese Philosophy* II, p. 395.

[29] Cf. *Saying of Ancient Worthies* 2:87; *Transmission of the Lamp*, 12:290.

[30] *Sayings of Ancient Worthies*, 32:288.

[31] Cf. Fung Yu-lan, *A History of Chinese Philosophy* II, pp. 399-402.

[32] This is only an expression of expedience; strictly speaking, as Zen teaches, there is no object or goal to be obtained or achieved.

[33] Cf. Suzuki, *Introduction to Zen Buddhism*, pp. 88, 93.
[34] Cf. Humphreys, *Zen Buddhism*, pp. 144, 145.
[35] Cf. Watts, *Spirit of Zen*, pp. 79-81.
[36] *Sayings of Ancient Worthies* 1:79, 80; cf. Fung, Yu-lan, *History of Chinese Philosophy* II, pp. 391, 392; and *Tao-Yin*, II, pp. 94, 95.
[37] Cf. Hui-Hai, *Path to Sudden Attainment*, p. 21.
[38] Suzuki, *Introduction to Zen Buddhism*, p. 85.
[39] Suzuki, *Selected Writings*, p. 91.
[40] *Transmission of the Lamp*, 8:263.
[41] Fung Yu-lan, *History of Chinese Philosophy* II, pp. 402-406.
[42] Cf. Carl Jung, Foreword in Suzuki's *Introduction to Zen Buddhism*, pp. 19-21.
[43] Cf. Suzuki, *Introduction to Zen Buddhism*, p. 115.
[44] Cf. Watts, *Zen*, p. 34; Suzuki, *Introduction to Zen Buddhism*, p. 108; Fromm, et al, *Zen Buddhism and Psychoanalysis*, pp. 126, 156.
[45] Cf. Suzuki, *Selected Writings*, pp. 136, 137.
[46] Cf. Carl Jung, Foreword in Suzuki's *Introduction to Zen Buddhism*, pp. 27, 28.
[47] According to Richard R. Buck, in his *Cosmic Consciousness—A Study in the Evolution of the Human Mind*, man has progressed from animal "simple consciousness" to "human self-consciousness" and is now on the threshold of developing "cosmic consciousness." What Buck describes as "cosmic consciousness" is, according to Dr. Fromm, precisely the expression which is called "Satori" in Zen Buddhism, and Dr. Suzuki's term as cosmic unconsciousness. Cf. Fromm, et al., *Zen Buddhism and Psychoanalysis*, p. 134.
[48] But no one is worthy to solve the problem except the Prince of Life, our Saviour, who said: "I am the resurrection and the life; he that believeth in me, though he were dead, yet shall he live. And whosoever liveth and believeth in me shall never die" (John 11:25).
[49] Cf. Suzuki, Fromm and others, *Zen Buddhism and Psychoanalysis*, pp. 50, 51.
[50] Chang, Chen-Chi, *The Practice of Zen*, p. 23.
[51] Watts, *Spirit of Zen*, pp. 73-77.
[52] Suzuki, *Selected Writings*, p. 97.
[53] *Ibid.*, p. 83.
[54] *Ibid.*, p. 18.
[55] Fromm, et al., *Zen Buddhism and Psychoanalysis*, pp. 160, 161.
[56] Cf. Suzuki, *op. cit.*, pp. 11, 12.
[57] The Lord Jesus Christ says: I am "meek and lowly in heart," and "Ye shall find rest unto your souls. For my yoke is easy, and my burden is light." Jesus says: "Come unto me, all ye that labor and are heavy laden, and I will give you rest... for I am meek and lowly in heart and ye shall find rest unto your souls. For my yoke is easy, and my burden is light" Matthew 11:28-30.

[58] Cf. Humphreys, *Zen Buddhism*, pp. 74, 80; Linssen, *Living Zen*, pp. 168-173.
[59] Cf. Ernest Becker: *"Zen: A Rational Critique,"* pp. 14, 16, 57, 81, 140.

PART TWO

CRISIS IN THE WEST

—THE IMPACT OF ZEN—

CHAPTER ONE

CRISIS IN CULTURE
—CULTURAL BACKGROUND OF ZEN'S IMPACT—

I. THE FAILURE OF HUMANISM

Why then has this phantasy of the East had such an impact on the West? This is not necessarily a resurgence from the East, we have to search its root cause which lies deep in the Crisis of the West. First, let us examine it culturally. With its alienation from the Christian faith and its negligence in spiritual things, modern western civilization is breaking down. This is not only the cry of many noted scholars, but rather the ominous sign of our age.

In Civilization on Trial, historian Toynbee pointed out that "man has been a dazzling success in the field of intellect and 'knowhow,' but a dismal failure in the things of spirit."[1] A noted authority in sociology, Dr. P. A. Sorokin also said that the history of human progress is a history of incurable stupidity. In the course of human history, several thousands of revolutions have been launched with a view to establish a paradise on earth. Practically none of them has ever achieved its purpose.[2] During the last four centuries, the main pattern of the Western culture is sensate culture. Modern man entirely disregards the truths and facts that human societies were preserved from dissolution not so much through the practical and expert manipulation of economic, political, and genetic or other factors, but mainly through the transmutation of values and the spiritualization of mentality.³ Without the Kingdom of God, we are doomed to weary and torturing pilgrimages from calamity to calamity, from crisis to crisis, with only brief moments of transitory improvement for regaining our breath.⁴

Owing to its deviation from the Christian truth and faith in God, modern sensate culture is in the process of disintegration. Although Christianity is primarily a religion of divine revelation, it owes its origin neither to art nor to science, yet it permeates and pervades them with its heaven-like nature and inspires them with a higher and nobler aim. As Dr. Philip Schaff pointed out, throughout the middle ages, the Church was almost the sole vehicle and guardian of literature and art, and she is the mother of the best elements of modern culture.⁵ We remain at all times aware of the immense debt of gratitude that Western civilization owes to St. Augustine. He was raised by God at time when the dying empire in the West was passing on to the Barbarians. It was Augustine who shifted the center of gravity and set Western culture on its God-given course. It was Augustine's vision that gave meaning and orientation to the new social order. The "City of God" laid the foundation of Christian sociology and Western civilization.⁶ For instance, before the Scandinavian peninsula was evangelized, the people there were living in the shadow of darkness and terror. As Philip Schaff recorded: "In his passion, the old Scandinavian was sometimes worse than a beast. Gluttony and drunkenness he considered as accomplishments. In his energy, he was sometimes fiercer than a demon. Revenge was the noblest sentiment and passion of man; forgiveness was a sin. The battlefield reeking with blood and fire was the highest beauty the earth could show; patient and peaceful labor was an abomination. They slew the missionaries and burnt their schools and churches. After a contest of more than a century, it became apparent that Christianity would be victorious; the pagan heroes left the country in great swarms as if they were flying from some awful plague."⁷ From these illustrations we would readily see the real foundation of the Western culture.

Since the Reformation, however, Christian thinkers failed to take positive leadership in the realms of philosophy and culture. They burned, as it were, the bridge between the Church and the secular world which is her own mission field. They serve the Creator by ignoring His creation. Since they could not offer guidance and provide a frame of reference for culture, the dichotomy and cleft between the Christian faith and culture became more and more acute in the spheres of education, social philosophy, and politics.[8] Thus philosophy was left in the hand of secular scholars. Descartes reasserted the ontological axiom—*cogito, ergo sum;* only what was completely intelligible would henceforth be taken as true. And Kant's antagonism to the Christian notion of a person-to-person relationship with God, locked and barred the God of Scripture out of his world. Since the advent of the Darwinian revolution, humanism has introduced a new paganism, so that Christianity no longer controls the media of culture and it is no longer the motivating power in the cultural urge of the West.[9] Facing such a situation, even a liberal Christian like Dr. Albert Schweitzer cried out: "It lifted up its voice but only to protest. It cannot command. The spirit of the age does not listen. It goes its own way."[10] While theology, the keystone of the edifice of human knowledge under God, became obsolete and empty logicism, our culture has grown unevenly in distorted and even monstrous ways without proper guidance and integration under God.[11]

Today the divorce of Western culture from Christian ideology is general.[12] While European culture is based on Christianity, it no longer believes in it; though it tries to keep the moral cultural concepts built on it, there is no real relationship between what the Western world is trying to keep and what it believes.[13] As Dr. Elton Trueblood puts it: "We live in a 'cut flower' civilization." Diagnosing the modern malaise of our so-called Christian culture, he compares us to a bouquet of flowers that may be radiant, fragrant and lovely, but will soon wither and die because the flowers have been severed from their roots. We have forgotten that the qualities and ideals we admire and revere did not just happen; they grew from the root of a personal faith in God and in Jesus Christ.[14] The dominant scientific man of the West is to a large extent alienated from the historic Christian faith. Its unity with the supernatural faith in which it was begotten and formed has disintegrated.[15] Secularism and naturalism rule supreme. Standards of spiritual values, normative principles, social order are all voided of any absolute character or significance. Religion became irrelevant in modern life, because God has been shut out of man's mind and banished from the center of the modern world. As a result, Gothic terror novels, popular demonology, romantic self-pity, Nietzsche self-deification, the nightmare cult of decadence practiced by Baudelaire and de Maupassant, an anti-puritanical mood of hedonistic and detached existence—a philosophy of a subculture, "hippiedom," and over-all a deepening pessimism and a growing weariness have become prevailing symptoms in the West. Now the West faces a cultural crisis of the first magnitude, because its culture has been uprooted. For most men, "God is dead," and the gods which they manufactured for themselves have failed. This is the tragic cry not only of the Existential philosophers but of the masses as well.[16] Western man, at the present high level of his intellectual powers and technological aptitudes, has not sloughed off Adam's heirloom of original sin. We now have an unprecedented power of production side by side with unprecedented shortages and frustrations. We have invented machines to work for us, but we have less spare time than ever before for human service.[17] Albert Schweitzer also pointed out that without a moral factor or foundation, all human endeavors, scientific inventions, cultures, and civilizations are doomed to decline and corruption as already manifested in the symptoms of over-labor, spiritual insecurity, moral nihilism, weariness and disquietness, lack of profound thinking and meditation, and lack of spiritual freedom and humanity.[18]

In the preceding centuries, modern man "thought that in science and technique, human reason could rule the world and solve its problems. The future promised progress and prosperity. However, various factors have radically abolished this optimism in the last decades. The enlightened culture has ended in wars and crises, the scope and horror of which were previously unknown. . . Problems have arisen which seem to transcend the power of the human mind. . . Humanist culture has miserably failed; progress has ended in defeat."[19] Indeed, as Spengler predicted in his noted book *The Decline of the West*, "the world-city has definitely overcome the land and now its spirit fashions a theory proper to itself, directed of necessity outward, soulless." "In this very century, the century of scientific-critical Alexandrianism, a new element of inwardness will arise to overthrow the will-to-victory of science. Exact science must presently fall upon its own keen sword!"[20] Now the awful sickness and disease of modern culture is very apparent. Ideological evidences even more persistently declare that the two world wars mark the collapse of the Renaissance ideals. This is the first time that the controlling ideas of a world culture have been contradicted and repudiated by history and experience. The seriousness of the modern man's predicament centers in the fact that reality has thundered "no" to his "yes!"[21]

II. THE AGE OF TENSION

The meaning of culture is twofold: On the one hand, it is the subjection of the world to our purpose—our kingship over the world; but on the other hand, it is the subjection of our hearts to God's purpose—God's kingship over man. This is the order of God. Man cannot break the order of God. The defying of the order of God will surely break man himself, because God is always on His throne.

Modern man, with his materialistic and technical improvements became the "conqueror" of the physical world, totally overlooking his subjection to God's purposes. The root of the great tragedy of mankind today is located deep in its ontological deviation by making man's intellectual understanding the measure of all truths, even the truth about God, and thus reducing a living God to a meaningless abstraction according to his vain imagination (cf. Romans 1:21). In fact, modern man is now destroying himself by trying to overrule God and destroy God!

Seismology has taught us how strains of increasing intensity may bring about in the crust of the earth a fault along which earthquakes are likely to occur. So also psychology tells that increasing tensions may disrupt the human organism.[22] Contemporary thinkers have remarked that the seventeenth century was the century of rationalism; the eighteenth century was the century of enlightenment; the nineteenth century was the century of science; and now the twentieth century is the century of tension! Indeed, the great tensions which Western civilization has to endure are becoming more evident, while the inner disintegration is aggravated by the obvious crisis of the Western sensate culture. Modern man has lost any concept of certainty and no longer has a feeling of safety and stability. New calamities and disasters and catastrophies threaten all of humanity. Anxiety and dread fill the hearts of modern man.[23]

As Billy Graham pointed out: "Historians will probably call this present era 'the age of anxiety!'" Though we have it easier than our forefathers, we have more uneasiness. Calloused hands were the badge of our forefathers, but a furrowed brow is the insignia of modern man. This generation is dying, not from external pressure, but from internal combustion. Modern man has fled to his "Ivory Tower," and there, surrounded by his luxuries, his gadgets, his false sense of security, he hides away from reality, his conscience and from God. He is frustrated and overwhelmed by a sense of futility. He has tried to fill the vacuum of his empty soul with all sorts of snythetics, but they have proved inadequate to satisfy his deeper longings and hungers. Anxiety then is the natural result when our hopes are centered in anything short of God and His will for us.[24] Man in the nuclear age is painfully and agonizingly aware that something is wrong with him. He is nervous. He is afraid. On one hand, he is slave to schedule; on the other hand, he is bored and lonely in his leisure. Our playwrights by the dozens, our poets, novelists, philosophers and artists, our sociologists and our psychologists, no less than our men of religion, have been literally screaming the weakness of modern man. Evidence is piled up on top of evidence that man is sick. So exhaustive has been our analysis that even our symptoms have symptoms and our analysts rush to consult their analysts. But what is really wrong with the modern man?[25]

In the preceding section, we considered the thought that, since God was thus locked and barred away from the world, the West was consequently doomed to exist in a spiritual vacuum. Hence, modern Western culture despite its strength and growth, is now without spiritual vitality. It has no soul to transmit, no light to shine, and thus has become aimless and lifeless. When man turns away from God, he is destined to end in frustration and defeat.

The late renowned psychologist, Dr. Carl G. Jung has well observed that modern man has lost all the metaphysical certainties of his medieval brother and set up in their place the ideals of material security. But it takes more than ordinary doses of optimism. Material security even has gone by the board, for modern man begins to see that every step in material "progress" adds only so much force to the threat of a more stupendous catastrophe. Science has destroyed even the refuge of the inner life. What was once a sheltering haven has become a place of terror. The rapid and worldwide growth of a psychological interest over the last two decades shows unmistakably that modern man has to some extent turned his attention from material things to his own subjective processes. This psychological interest of the present time shows that man expects something from psychic life which he has not received from the outer world. Since the beginning of the nineteenth century, man has given a more and more prominent place to his psyche. There are many persons to whom Freudian psychology is dearer than the Gospels.[26]

However, the basic cause of much of our anxiety is beyond the reach of the psychiatrist. This is why modern psychiatrists are beginning to realize that psychiatry has its limitations; it cannot give proper cures.[27] For man's problem is basically spiritual, and naturalistic psychology cannot bring man to God. Man is the crown of God's creation and religion by nature must claim to be central in human life; so man's heart still aches for God and hungers for new authority or symbol to give meaning to life to occupy his spiritual vacuum.[28] Unfortunately as the Bible teaches us: "The Light shineth in darkness and the darkness comprehended it not; Light is come into this world and men loved darkness rather than Light" (John 1:5; 3:19) Therefore, modern man, instead of accepting the Lord Jesus Christ, the Light of the World, as his Savior, resorts to demonic and false religions to satisfy his desperate needs.

Moreover with the great upheaval and catastrophe resulting from the two world wars and the rise of the resurgent movement of paganism and fanatical nationalism, the religious leaders in the Orient, including the Zen masters, totally ignoring the fact that Western humanist culture has been divorced from the Christian faith, claim that the unique supremacy of Christianity is simply the result of the military and cultural prestige of the conquering race. They further charge that the two great world wars so devastating and bloody have been fought for the most part in the West, and thus allege the weakness and shortcomings of the Western Christian nations. Refusing to acknowledge the supreme uniqueness of the Christian faith, they distort the truth of Christianity by identifying it with Western culture, and therefore claim universal validity for their philosophic and religious systems and with strong convictions and great vigor assert that the hope of mankind and peace on earth are in the East rather than in the West.[29]

As the human race is living in an age of tension and anxiety, Zen steps in and appeals to Western minds weary of conventional religions and philosophy that Zen can "reduce the tension of all opposites, including the ultimate strain of 'this' and 'that,' by rising above them." The West needs integrity. There are symptoms of a dichotomy in their mind. The conscious and the unconscious wage their civil war and none shall heal them. Only Zen is the answer.[30]

It is true, the basic cause of the crisis today is found in the failure of the secular humanistic idea especially since the time of the Renaissance. The whole movement of existentialism and subsequently the impact of Zen on the West represents a reaction in the trend of Western thought.[31] It is essentially a protest of human nature against the idea of an objective order and the shallow rationalism which played a great role in Western philosophy and humanist culture. Unfortunately, this movement is only a turning inward,[32] and is not motivated by an "affection on things above" (Col. 3:2). Its kernel is in the deification of the historical function of human nature; so this reaction still remains ensnared in the very pit of humanism! This is a pseudo-avenue of escape, not the true way of salvation. Salvation belongs unto the Lord in heaven, not from the human heart "within." The human heart is deceitful above all things and desperately wicked (cf. Jer. 1:9). "For out of the heart proceed evil thoughts, murders, adulteries, fornications, thefts, false witness, blasphemies" (Matt. 15:19). What mankind really needs is total regeneration by the grace of God, not self-deification by the efforts of man. Modern man should stop hewing out "broken cisterns which can hold no water," but go back to God — "the foundation of living waters" (Jer. 2:13), the source of human culture.

---

[1] Arnold Toynbee, *Civilization on Trial*, p. 262.
[2] Cf. P. A. Sorokin, *The Crisis of Our Age*, pp. 318-326.
[3] *Ibid.*, cf. also his works on *Social in Cultural Dynamics and the Reconstruction of Humanity*.
[4] Cf. P. A. Sorokin, *Man and Society in Calamity*, pp. 318, 319.

[5] Cf. Philip Schaff, *History of the Christian Church*, Vol. II, pp. 267, 625, 626.

[6] Cf. Emile Cailliet, *The Christian Approach to Culture*, p. 142.

[7] Philip Schaff, *ibid.*, IV. Vol. IV, pp. 109-110.

[8] Cf. Cailliet, *ibid.*, pp. 24, 59.

[9] Cf. Henry R. Van Til, "Religion and Culture," *Christianity Today*, September 14, 1959.

[10] "Religion in Modern Civilization," *The Christian Century*, November 21 and 28, 1934; cf. Cailliet, *op. cit.*, p. 222.

[11] Cf. Calliet, *ibid.*, pp. 268, 269.

[12] Cf. Lindsell, *A Christian Philosophy of Missions*, Dr. H. Ockenga's Introduction, p. 12.

[13] Cf. F. A. Schaeffer, "Is Nobody Home in the World?," *Christianity Today*, June 20, 1960.

[14] Trueblood, *The Predicament of Modern Man*, pp. 59, 60; Leighton Ford, "A Firsthand Faith," *Decision*, Dec. 1961.

[15] Cf. Dr. L. Newbigin, "Summons to Christian Missions Today," *International Review of Missions*, April 1959.

[16] Cf. Henry R. Van Til, *op. cit.*

[17] Cf. Toynbee, *op. cit.*, pp. 151, 261.

[18] Cf. Albert Schweitzer, *The Philosophy of Civilization* 1923 which won the Nobel Prize with General Marshall in 1952-53.

[19] Cf. J. M. Spier, *Christianity and Existentialism*, p. 15.

[20] Cf. Oswald Spengler, *The Decline of the West*, I. pp. 367, 424.

[21] Cf. Carl H. Henry, *Remaking of the Modern Mind*, pp. 265-270.

[22] Cf. Cailliet, *op. cit.*, pp. 210, 211.

[23] Cf. Spier, *op. cit.*, pp. 15, 16.

[24] Cf. Billy Graham. *The Cure for Anxiety*, pp. 1-3.

[25] Cf. Dr. Chalmer E. Faw: "The Bible and Modern Man," *Christianity Today*. August 3, 1962.

[26] Cf. Carl G. Jung, *Modern Man in Search of a Soul*, pp. 235, 237, 241, 245.

[27] Cf. Billy Graham, *op. cit.*, p. 5.

[28] Cf. Cailliet, *op. cit.*, chapters 3, 4; Toynbee, *op. cit.*, chapter 8.

[29] This was the author's own position and experience before his conversion. This issue will be discussed in the following chapter.

[30] Cf. C. Humphreys, *Zen Buddhism*, p. 208.

[31] This will be discussed in part three, chap. one of this volume.

[32] Cf. K. Gurn Dutt, *Existentialism and Indian Thought*, pp. 57-62.

CHAPTER TWO

CRISIS IN PHILOSOPHY
—PHILOSOPHICAL BACKGROUND OF ZEN'S IMPACT—

I. THE SKEPTICAL FUTILITY OF HUMAN THOUGHT

Non-Christian philosophy is immanent and anthropocentric by its nature; it begins by absolutizing and deifying a created aspect. So it is akin to the spirit of Zen. It is implicitly blasphemous, since it seeks to honor and deify the sovereign man. Originally it stems from the rebellious nature of man and therefore is an apostate religious deed. It was also the root from which liberal Christian theology as well as the Western humanist culture have grown.

Non-Christian philosophers distort our view of the cosmos and its relationship to the Creator. They often give worship in exchange for philosophy and in the temple of the latter bow down before the idol erected to sovereign reason![1]

Plato believed that all knowledge is innate in the mind. His emphasis was on postulations born of intelligibility, making intelligibility the criterion of truth. Plato attempted to transmute the human mind, whose essential function is that of a knower, into a "pseudo-maker." The fallacy involved in this procedure is twofold: (1) the Platonic man colonizes Reality with abstractions; (2) the thinker involved runs the risk of becoming a prisoner of his own mind and no longer sees the things that are truly before him. The higher the flight into the intelligible, the deeper the subsequent dent into the real.[2]

Since the Greek concern is mostly with intelligibility over against the Hebrew-Christian concern with Reality, through Plato and Aristotle, they lost their genuine sense of religious relationship with Reality. A living God thus became a mind-made concept. It is true, as Etienne Gilson once pointed out, in the history of Western culture, every chapter begins with the Greeks, but it is still not clear where one should look, in the thought of ancient Greece, for the origins of our philosophical notion of God. With Aristotle, the Greeks had gained an indisputably rational theology, but they lost their religion.[3] After the Reformation, Christian scholars failed to give philosophy a positive lead by making theology the keystone of the edifice of human knowledge; and thus philosophy took up the task of natural theology. The epoch-making change became apparent, when Descartes (1596-1650), the so-called "father of modern philosophy" enunciated his *dictum "Cogito ergo sum,"* and avowed his decision "to seek no other knowledge than that which" he "was able to find 'within' " himself.[4] He "devised a new method which proceeds from methodical doubt, while his own existence becomes the starting point of his *meditations*." Henceforth, moderns "live and move and have (their) being" not in God (cf. Acts 17:28) but in a world of self-assertion. Descartes established his own reason as the supreme judge of what is true or false. Thus man, the individual, was now on his way to supreme sovereignty.[5] This trend of thought was conducive to the impact of Zen. But the greatest weakness in Descartes' chain of reasoning was that he confused "an idea" with the actual existence of "the object of the idea." One might have all sorts of gods, but one's idea hardly guarantees their actual existence.[6]

From Descartes on, Western philosophy became more antagonistic to the Christian faith in its epistemology. Since the rise and development of the empirico-scientific world and life view that made its appearance in the so-called Enlightenment movement, and later was clarified, strengthened, and extended under the influence of David Hume, Immanuel Kant, Charles Darwin, August Comte, and John Dewey, the mind of the West has been dominated by a thoroughgoing naturalism.[7] This naturalism made a complete break with the notion of God and the idea of a divine revelation. Especially since the last century, it embraced the scientific theory of evolution. "In a thousand and one ways, the Western world has been taught that nature is the ultimate reality. The whole movement from Descartes to Dewey, involved a shift to a homocentric or geocentric view and away from a supernaturalistic principle of explanation."[8]

In "The Decline of the West," Spengler pointed out: "With the setting-in of the Later period, philosophy becomes urban and worldly, frees itself from subservience to religion and even dares to make that religion itself the object of epistemological criticism. The urban spirit turns to look at itself in order to establish the proposition that there is no higher judgment seat of knowing beyond itself."[9]

In fact, modern philosophy is even more outspoken than science in its antagonism to the Christian faith. Contemporary philosophers who have exercised great influence over the world of thought, since the dawn of this century, such as Bertrand Russell, Benedetto Croce, John Dewey, etc., are emphatically atheistic.[10] Dewey alleged that the greatest hindrance to the progress of modern man was his belief in the supernatural. A contemporary professor of philosophy recently remarked that Martin Heidegger even regards the atheism of Nietzsche and Karl Marx as a salutary attempt to purge us of idols. Another convinced atheist is a French existentialist, Jean Paul Sartre, a student of Heidegger. He is perhaps the most vigorous atheistic philosopher of our day. His thought is intentionally and brutally opposed to God. In 1951, the *New York Times* had a remarkable article on the hundred greatest books of the preceding century. Careful study of these authors, however, would reveal that not more than eight of them could be called Christian and more than half were deliberately and vigorously antagonistic to Christian principles.[11]

On the other hand, owing to the failure of humanistic culture, the growing tension of the present age, and the unbelief within the church that we have discussed in other chapters, the thinking of the Western world has moved toward the mood of the East. Prior to the 1930's, Kierkegaard was generally considered as the "Mad Dane"; however, in the past thirty years, Kierkegaardian thinking has increasingly dominated liberal thought. It is a change which simply followed the general intellectual and cultural climate. Kierkegaard is now accepted because the cultural climate has caught up with him; it has found its old optimism intellectually and practically untenable and has passed into a relativism and general pessimism.[12]

Generally speaking, the new mood of Western thinking is spoken of as a departure from the naive optimism and shallow rationalism of the preceding centuries. The innovators take a stance against the Enlightenment with its conception of human reason and technical progress. The shift of sentiment has of necessity involved a criticism of Western humanistic culture and some of its most hallowed traditions, as represented by Spengler's *Decline of the West*. This is a sign of the insufficiency of human knowledge as well as its anxious concern to seek a truth which lies beyond the human plane. However, man, as a hater of God does not want to hear about God, but rather seeks to suppress the pressure of God's revelation in nature that is about him, to suppress the pressure of conscience within him, and to suppress the revelation of grace that speaks in the Bible. So, unfortunately, the mood of thinking is manifested in the form of existentialism. It tries to answer the problems of our day and to unveil the mystery of life. It attracts the modern man by appealing to his attitude toward life. (It is a philosophy of the meaninglessness of life which is the kernel of Zen teaching of Voidness.)[13] The failure of Western culture and the profound upheavals and catastrophies of the twentieth century have caused the masses to lose faith in former values and ideals as well as in historic Christianity. Thus they are ready to listen to false prophets. Hence Existentialism, a philosophy that has been extolled as the "highest form of wisdom," but offers man a religion without God—a religion in apostasy, found a fertile soil in which to grow.[14]

However, further analysis shows that Existentialism remains in the slough of humanism. Humanism has always been committed to a philosophical faith in the autonomous freedom of human personality. The rationalistic conceptions of humanism trust solely in exclusive redemptive power of reason. Although all existentialists are passionate in their opposition to this doctrine, they are equally vehement in their own insistence on the autonomy of human freedom. No matter how much the various representatives of existentialism may differ among themselves, they all agree that man is absolutely autonomous, and, in fact, fall into the same pitfall of humanism which they claim to oppose.[15]

So here we see a very interesting picture that non-Christian philosophers are nothing more than the "children who pay their fare to take another ride on the 'merry-go-round'."[16] From time immemorial, humanistic and mystical tendencies had contended for primacy in the heart and mind of man. As Dr. Gordon Clark has pointed out, the history of philosophy began with naturalism and now ends with naturalism. The pre-Socratic naturalism dissolved into Sophism, from which metaphysics arose; and metaphysics lost itself in a mystic trance. Thus, under the influence of an alien source, Western Europe appealed to a divine revelation. However, since the Enlightenment movement, the West has turned again to unaided human reason. Hegel was made the champion of reason: "The real is the rational and the rational is the real." But soon after even the fixed truths of naturalistic science were radically repudiated. Thus the latter movement of rationalism has now again dissolved into sophism. It is evident that the whole trend of the history of philosophy so far as it was estranged from the Word of God and antagonistic to the Christian faith has fully demonstrated the skeptical futility of human wisdom.[17]

II. THE MORBID REACTION AGAINST EASY RATIONALISM

As discussed in the preceding section, Existentialism is a comparatively recent development in Western thought; it is a realistic reaction against shallow optimism and easy rationalism. It has become a provocative factor in the modern word; its devotees claim that they have brought philosophy down to earth for the first time in the West. On the other hand, it has been denounced as the onset of a tide of despair and irrationalism, also as a justification for the individual libertinism and a disastrous surrender to nihilism. The term Existentialism is vague and almost indefinable; besides, within its camp, there are marked divisions and even contradictory interpretations; nevertheless, in very general terms, it may be described as an attempt to reach the inmost core of human existence in a concrete individual fashion. It is essentially a turning inward, a probing of the layers of the self.[18]

Although Existentialism is a new mood of Western mentality, no philosophical system is entirely new and Existentialism is no exception as it has its root in the past history of philosophy. While its remote origins could be traced back to Greece and the Delphic maxim, which was inscribed on the wall of the temple of Apollo: "Know thyself,"[19] its main roots stem from modern Humanism. It will suffice here to consider briefly two thinkers who have been generally regarded as the fathers of modern existentialism.

1. Sören Aabye Kierkegaard (1813-1835) was the first to use the term "existence" in this new sense and therefore has been regarded as the "father of Existential-

ism." He is a man of paradox. His thinking is irrationistic and opposed to anything that is systematic. He points out that, apart from philosophic or scientific systems, there is another kind of systematization, i.e., that deadening wall which is built up around man by daily routine. He designates this the "universe of the immediate neighborhood." Enveloped in this, man becomes ego-centric and loses his freedom. The syncope of freedom leads to anguish. In the eye of Kierkegaard the completely self-centered individual, shut up with himself, is the true demoniac. He consequently realizes that subjectiveness is really the most complete objectiveness. Yet, paradoxically, he holds that in order to maintain our inwardness, we must abandon pure inwardness. He always fought with stubbornness that idea which had dominated European thought since the Renaissance. His spiritual man is perpetually detaching himself from himself, from his passion, and from the paralyzing effect of his own perfection. Thus, we are told, one can achieve the experience of transcending human experience by the act of transcending himself.[20]

Although Kierkegaard claimed to be a Christian and placed faith in direct opposition to knowledge and regarded the intellect as the root cause of all bondage, he also sought to incorporate the encounter with nothingness into the experience of God. Nevertheless, in his system, there is already a secularization of Christian concepts, since for him, human experience is understood apart from the revelation in Christ.

Kierkegaard believes human existence is a free spontaneous inner act, it is man's free realization of himself. In and through such voluntary acts, man is his own "father." His life lies in his own hands. In freedom, he disposes of his own future and his future being; in free self-actualization, he is the free cause of his "becoming." And it is this becoming that is genuine history. Real history is the history of transition from potentiality to actuality resulting from a voluntary decision. Therefore, the first "law" of human existence is: Be what you become! Do not be what you are![21]

Human freedom, as the director of self-realization, gives human passion its impetus, making it into an infinite passion. It arouses an existential dialectical movement through which self-denial (denial of one's self as finite) is simultaneously self-election (choice of one's self as infinite). Self-disclosure is concurrently self-affirmation and existential spontaneity is self-transcendence, in which man climbs above himself. Man's passion may be described as his anxious concern to attain his own infinity, his absolute self and his eternal salvation.[22]

Kierkegaard is an extreme individualist. He is critical and skeptical of human fellowship and society. For him, what goes beyond the individual is finite, temporal, external and relative. A person who lives existentially is alone; he is hidden in the mystery of his hiddenness. Within this region, one can devote his entire attention to the "infinite, eternal, absolute self." His whole attitude and conviction are anti-social. For him, individual subjectivity alone is truth. To exist is to be with oneself alone with God. True Christianity is not of the masses, but of the individual existential man who is a man of freedom, not bound of any law.[23]

He distinguishes existential outlook into three stadia, i.e., (1) the aesthetic, (2) the ethical and (3) the religious. Authentic human existence is neither aesthetic nor ethical, but religious.

The first is the attitude of spontaneous indirectness typified by the non-Christian romanticists which can be exposed as a flight from the self-conscious existential and normative attitude. Such a person is a rationalist and a positivist in his thought and in his deeds, he seeks his own satisfaction. The aesthetical in a man is that by which he is immediately what he is. The aesthetic stage is characterized by a passion for enjoyment. A man, bent upon nothing but happiness, gradually becomes aware that each moment of happiness vanishes like snowflakes on water, and unsatiable boredom sets in.

The second is an official existence, it does not arrive at a spontaneous free relationship to one's own individuality; it does not engage in an absolute striving to attain one's own highest individual infinite salvation. It has lost the immediateness of life. The ethical is that whereby a man becomes what he becomes. The ethical sphere is that of requirement and this requirement is so infinite that the individual always goes bankrupt. For the demands of duty are infinite, yet he is finite, the disproportion between what he is and what he ought to do is experienced as despair.

The true existential outlook is to be found solely in the third or religious stadium which can be reached only by an "existential leap" (sudden Enlightenment, in the term of Zen). There is no gradual transition. It is the sublimation of both attitudes into a higher sort of plane. It is a conscious relationship to one's self in one's own finitude and infinity, while retaining the immediacy and spontaneity of existential passion. The religious stage must go beyond the rules and laws of the ethical and the civil. It must be "ex lex," outside the law.[24] Kierkegaard's hatred of system is shared by most existential thinkers. He used his dialectical power in one continual protest against the established church, the state, institutions, and system, against routine, against natural man, against things and objectivity, against the historical and temporal view of man, against the universal, against the intellect itself; in short, against everything which he felt to be a bondage.[25] And thus Existentialism breaks the myriad chains of causation and leads to deliverance, as Zen teaches.

2. Friedrich Nietzsche (1844-1900) "Nobody has influenced modern Existentialism as much as Nietzsche." [26] He is a self-avowed enemy of Christianity, a militant atheist. He sought to set himself uncompromisingly against God and the bourgeois culture which he thought was the product of the decadent influence of Christianity. He advo-

cated that "the practice of the church is hostile to life; the concept of 'God' until now was the greatest objection to existence. We deny God, we deny the responsibility in God; only thereby do we redeem the world."[27] "Christianity has sided with all that is weak and base, with all failures; it has made an ideal of whatever contradicts the instinct of the strong life to preserve itself. The Christian and the anarchist: both decadents, both incapable of having any effect other than disintegrating, poisoning, withering, blood sucking: both the instinct of mortal hatred against everything that stands in greatness, that has duration. The Christian church has left nothing untouched by its corruption; it has turned every value into an unvalue, every truth into a lie; every integrity into a vileness of the soul." He calls Christianity "the one great curse, the one great innermost corruption... the one immortal blemish of mankind."[28]

Nietzche was a divided personality. In him there were two sides, often at war with each other. His aim was to transcend both, to turn the polarity into unity and to attain a higher humanity—the superman. His life was one of tragedy; after 1879, he withdrew from society and worked in secluded surroundings. He was always tormented by terrible headaches and finally was seized by an incurable mental disease.[29]

He is a radical irrationalist. He disqualifies both reason and systematic knowledge. For him, true philosophy is action, ("Just walk on," according to Zen) reason is not unassailable and self-sufficient, and science is not sovereign in its objectivity. He sought to transcend his own ego and pushed ahead to what he took to be the essence of humanism, the living man, who is himself self-sufficient, who makes the law himself, who himself is sovereign.[30]

His philosophy can be divided into three periods. In the first period, he was under the influence of Schopenhauer's pessimistic philosophy of the will. In the second period, he sought the highest end of life in science which knows no limit and higher authority. Its task is to liberate the real man and to make him the master of his own fate. In the third period, his scientific outlook was violently replaced by the Dionysian passion, and he proclaimed the supremacy of the will to power of the superman as the meaning of life. The ideal of power is beyond norms of good and evil. What is good gratifies and increases the lust for power. What is evil proceeds from weakness and diminishes power and might. The superman will create a new culture and new morality. The current morality of the herd is the Christian slave morality. The new morality is that of the superman who has the duty to develop the vital energy of man and defend the will to power against anything which resembles humility, sympathy, or any other Christian virtue, and has the right to trample underfoot anything that gets in his way.[31] It is interesting to note that while in the West this philosophy was later developed into a militant form of Nazism, in the East "Zen was seized by the Japanese military class and became a warrior creed. It called for action for rigorous self-discipline, for contempt of life, and thus Zen was able to reach the culminating point of its development under the influence of Shintoism,"[32] which was abused by militarists as an incentive of their aggressive war.

Nietzche is not only the prophet of nihilism, but he wishes also to be a priest of nihilism. He viewed all those masks of what people in our day call progress as the very things which are the works of decadence. To him, morality is merely a necessary lie. Its motives are not love, but fear and hope. Christianity consists of sheer fictions. God, the soul, free will, sin, punishment, grace, repentence, temptation, the Kingdom of God, eternal life—all are purely imaginary. The most dangerous of the fabrications of Christianity is pity. He sees in this greatest of vices simply a weakness of will. To Nietzsche, the highest values are void,[33] nothing holds, no law, no norm, and everything is meaningless.

But if existence should be completely meaningless, if it yearns for the void of nothingness, then before void, all

CRISIS IN PHILOSOPHY

law would vanish, and the examination of existence would be impossible. Thus a nihilistic philosophy becomes a self-contradictory idea! Although he meant by his remark in *The Will to Power* that Nihilism is not enough, that there must be a counter-movement away from nothingness, he seeks an escape from the meaninglessness of annihilation and hopes for a "new dawn." He did try to search the other shore of the ocean of nothingness and to develop an active nihilism to rise above decadence and passive nihilism, shows simply that he rebelled against nihilism but not that he escaped from it. He realized this full well. He knew that he was fundamentally a nihilist. For within the realm of his own limited experience there was only a solitude and silence, and nihilism and nothingness ruled that realm. He annihilated everything including himself. He could find no means to bridge the gap which would not be illusion and pretense.

For Nietzsche, God was dead, and man was an animal whose animal instincts could give him a direction or goal. So like a frantic prisoner, he shook the bars of his cell, trying to escape from nihilism, or rather trying to preserve nihilism and find a justification for it. He expected thus to achieve victory over decadence and passive nihilism.

Nietzsche's philosophy is the worship of power, the valueless activism, always restless, driven by the fear of meaninglessness and finally pouring itself out in annihilation and self-annihilation. Consequently, his soul was never at peace. His joy was not real. He never escaped his problem. He could develop nothing new, for he sought a way out in the very place to which he knew the self-sovereignty of man would lead him: nihilism. But, there is no way out in nihilism.[34]

Although Nietzsche was a militant atheist while Kierkegaard claims to be a believing Christian, nevertheless there is an inner connection between their conceptions which enabled them to be forerunners of subsequent existentialism. In the first place, they are both irrationalists, rejecting the supremacy of reason. The mysteries of life cannot be fathomed or explained by rational thought. Secondly, they are both anthropocentric. Extremely interested in man, they seek real being in human existence with or without any relation to the transcendent being of the deity. Thirdly, they are both radically subjective and anti-social. They strive to attain a philosophical foundation of the idea of man as an absolute autonomous being whose existence is characterized by absolute freedom. Human existence is not subject to any ordinance or laws which came from outside of man. Existence is a law unto itself, the creator of its own norms.[35]

The purpose of the present chapter is only to present the background of the advent of existentialism, so we stop here without dealing with modern existentialists such as Karl Jaspers (1883-), Martin Heidegger (1889-), Gabriel Marcel (1889-), Louis Lavelle (1883-), Jean Paul Sartre (1905-), and Arnoldes Ewont Loen (1896-). etc. But, from this new mood of Western mentality and its morbid reaction against shallow rationalism, it is interesting to note that we find out there are many points of correspondence with Zen which we will discuss in the following chapters.

---

[1] Cf. Cailliet, *op. cit.*, pp. 5, 18, 19, 23.
[2] Cf. *ibid.*, p. 131-135.
[3] Cf. Etienne Gilson, *God and Philosophy*, pp. 1, 34.
[4] Cf. Descartes, *Discours de la methode*, Premiere Partie IV 9, II 21, 22.
[5] Cf. Cailliet, *op. cit.*, p. 163, same with Zen, it purposes to discipline the Mind to make its own Master. Cf. Suzuki, *Introduction to Zen Buddhism*, p. 40.
[6] Cf. Warren C. Young, *Christian Approach to Philosophy* chapter II.
[7] Cf. Samuel G. Craig, *Christianity Rightly So Called*, pp. 5, 12; and Emile Brunner, *Revelation and Reason*, p. 5.
[8] Cf. Carl H. Henry, *op. cit.*, pp. 23, 24.
[9] Cf. Oswald Spengler, *The Decline of the West*, Vol. I, p. 365.
[10] Cf. Dr. I. M. Bochenski, *Contemporary European Philosophy;* Prof. Wilbur M. Smith, "The Bible and Our Faith," *Christianity Today*, Aug. 28, 1961.
[11] Cf. *ibid.*

[12] Cf. Francis A. Schaeffer, "The Tragic Loss of Our Age, *Christianity Today*, May 22, 1961.

[13] In the famous gatha of Hui-Neng, we read "originally there was nothing that has real existence" (Pen-lai-wu-i-wuh). Cf. Part One, Chapter II, Section I, 2, 6 of this volume.

[14] Cf. Spier, *op. cit.*, pp. XVII-XIX; and Prof. R. D. Knudson, "Current Mood of Our Century," *Christianity Today*, Oct. 13, 1961; Emil Brunner, *Revelation and Reason*, p. 7; and Van Til, *The Defense of the Faith*, p. 165.

[15] Cf. S. U. Zuidema, *Karakter Van de Modern Existentiephilosophie*, p. 1.

[16] Gordon H. Clark, *Thales to Dewey—A History of Philosophy*, p. 534.

[17] Cf. Clark, *ibid.*, pp. 469, 533, 534.

[18] Cf. K. Guru Dutt, *op. cit.*, pp. 1, 2.

[19] It is interesting to note that according to the teaching of Hui-Neng, Zen is "the seeing into one's own nature." The secret of Zen is "ming-Hsin chien-Hsing" which might be interpreted as an Eastern Delphic maxim "Know thyself." Thus there are not without points of correspondences between Zen and Existentialism which we will discuss fully in the following chapters.

[20] Cf. Dutt, *ibid.*, pp. 12-18.

[21] Zuidema, *Kierkegaard*, p. 15; Cf. also Kierkegaard's: (1) *Either/Or;* (2) *Fear and Trembling*; (3) *Concluding Unscientific Postscript;* (4) *Sickness unto Death;* (5) *Training in Christianity;* (6) *The Journals;* (7) *Attack upon "Christendom,"* etc.

[22] Zuidema, *ibid.*, p. 16; Cf; also Kierkegaard: (1) *Either/Or;* (2) *Fear and Trembling;* (3); *Philosophical Fragments;* (4) *Sickness unto Death,* etc.

[23] Zuidema, *ibid.*, p. 18; Spier, *op. cit.*, p. 8; cf. also Kierkegaard's (1) *Postscript;* (2) *The Present Age,* etc.

[24] Cf. Zuidema, *op. cit.*, pp. 25-33; Spier, *op. cit.*, p. 9; Carl Michalson: (Ed.) The Witness of Kierkegaard, pp. 50, 57, 118, 119; cf. also Kierkegaard's: (1) *Stages on Life's Way;* (2) *Either/Or;* (3) *Postscript,* etc.

[25] Cf. Dutt, *Extentailism and Indian Thought*, p. 13.

[26] Paul Tillich, *"Courage to Be,"* p. 143.

[27] Cf. *"Twilight of the Idols"*—in *"The Portable Nietzsche,"* pp. 487, 501.

[28] Cf. *The Antichrist, ibid.*, pp. 570-655.

[29] It is interesting to note that "Adolf Hilter, while adopting Nietzsche's philosophy, was also seized by a serious mental disease which was a "top secret" during World War II. Cf. Van Riessen, *Nietzsche*, pp. 11-14.

[30] Cf. Van Riessen, *ibid.*, p. 10.

[31] Cf. Spier, *op. cit.*, pp. 11, 12; cf. Nietzsche's; (1) *Beyond Good and Evil;* (2) *The Geneology of Morals;* (3) *Ecce Homo,* (4) *The Birth of Tragedy,* etc.

[32] Cf. Chikao Fujisawa, *Zen and Shinto,* p. 69. It is interesting to note that in the West. Hitler was an existential thinker. Cf. A Kierkegaard Anthology (Ed. by Robert Bretall) Introduction XXI.

[33] This is the kernel of Zen teaching. Cf. Part One, Chap. II, Section I, 2, 6 of this volume.

[34] Cf. Van Riessen, *ibid.*, pp. 26, 37, 39-45, 51.

[35] Cf. Spier, *op. cit.*, p. 10, 110-119.

CHAPTER THREE

CRISIS IN RELIGION
—RELIGIOUS BACKGROUND OF ZEN'S IMPACT—

I. THE SCHEME OF SELF-NEGATION

Religiously speaking, the impact of Zen on the West, to a great measure, is the result of Western negativism rather than Eastern initiative. Since the eighteenth century, cultural and religious dissatisfaction has gone through various periods. Revolt against the rationalistic character of Western culture, the allegedly dogmatic exclusiveness of Christianity, cultural and religious snobbery, and a chase after the exotic, were some of the main aspects of this conspicuous self-negation in the West.[1] In other words, the impact of Zen on the West is rather the scheme of Western scholars; its root cause lies within rather than without.

For instance, in a collection of data about China, Gottfried Wilhelm Leibniz, a world famous German mathematician and philospher, said that although the West surpassed China in mathematics, astronomy, and logic, the Chinese surpassed the West in the ordering of life and in state of morals. When the sacred books of the East were published in Europe, European philosophers burst into exclamations of admiration. Leibniz thought that it seemed almost necessary to send Chinese missionaries to Europe in order to teach the value and practice of natural theology.[2] Schopenhauer said: "How thoroughly do the Upanishads breathe the holy spirit of the Vedas. And oh! how the mind is coached clean here of all its early ingrafted Jewish superstition! It is the most profitable and most elevating reading that is possible in the world. It has been the consolation of my life and will be the consolation of my death." Again he said: "Let no one think that Christianity is favorable to optimism, for in the Gospel, world and evil are used as most synonymous. The innermost kernel of Christianity is identical with that of Brahmanism and Buddhism.[3] Especially did Schopenhauer, through his writings, become a great factor in creating interest in Buddhism by the deep appreciation he evinced for it. It is of particular significance that he frequently suggested the superiority of Buddhism over Christianity. He noted many similarities between the two, both being able to produce saintliness of the first order, no matter whether it is theist or atheist. The most pertinent thing is that he is the leading pioneer of an opinion which up to the present time has increasingly conquered a great number of people in the West, to the effect that Buddhism has a deeper and higher wisdom by its freedom from unphilosophical encumbrance and that Buddhism is superior to Christianity.[4]

Modern Western scholars, such as Toynbee, hold the idea that "the present religions of India and the form of Buddhism that is practiced today in the Far East may constitute new elements to be grafted into Christianity in days to come."[5] Toynbee advocates that Christians must winnow the non-essential chaff (mostly theology) from the wheat of their religion, must abandon the 'chosen people' claim to the uniqueness of their Saviour and their revelation.[6] During his visit to Japan in 1957, he pronounced that "the future in Asia belongs to Buddhism rather than to Christianity."[7]

In fact, long before Toynbee, tremendous efforts had been made by many Western scholars to pervert the truth and manufacture alleged facts so as to make Christainity dependent on Buddhism. One of the earliest attempts to "prove" the Buddhistic origins of primitive Christianity is Nicolas A. Notovick's work on *La Vie inconnue de Jesus*

Christ (Paris, 1894) which on the basis of a professedly Indian document asserted that Jesus had been initiated into his career by sixteen years' stay with Brahmans and Buddhist monks. He concludes that Jesus might "have gone to Tibet", claiming to have found traces of the presence of Jesus in Tibet. Tibetan texts refer to the existence of "Saint Isso" and maintain that he was crucified between two evil-doers.[8] It is interesting to note that the Essenes were in 1867 presented by a German scholar, Hilgenfeld, as Buddhists. Hilgenfeld, by interpreting Jesus as an Essene in this indirect way made Christianity dependent on Buddhism. Scholars from different countries combined in this same endeavor are not few.[9]

Another scholar who might be mentioned here is Hermann Keyserling. His work has exercised and still exercises wide influence in the West.[10] He judges that Mahayana Buddhism far excells Christianity in philosophical respect. In regard to doctrine, Buddhism is nearest to the seekers for a new religion in the West because of its undogmatic character.

Still another who might be added is H. S. Olcott in America, one of the most conspicuous theosophists in relation to Buddhism in the West and even in the East. In 1881, he published a Buddhist Catechism which numbers many editions in various languages. He applauded the esoteric doctrine of Buddhism as a system teaching the highest goodness without confessing a god; the continuity of existence without accepting the existence of a soul; happiness without a belief in a heaven; a way of salvation without a Saviour; salvation by one's own endeavor, without rites, prayers, etc.[11]

A more slanted position is represented by Robert Linssen of Brussels. In his work entitled *Living Zen* we read "A close study of the history of Brahmanism and Christianity reveals a striking identity in the process of progressive degeneration of these religions. The fundamental element responsible for this degeneration lies in a certain quality of inertia inherent in the human mind. This inertia leads men to seek the easy way and comfortable solutions which save them from effort and initiative."[12] In his view, Christianity is a degenerate form of religion compared with Buddhism.

And worst of all, we are told by an author of *Christianity before Christ*, that there were "sixteen crucified Saviours of the world," that Christ is not unique, that there were "three hundred and forty-six striking analogies between Christ and Krishna," that "Christianity derived from heathen and oriental systems," and there were "two hundred errors both in the teachings and practical life" of Jesus Christ.[13] And this book was soon reprinted only after a few months of its publication.

In reference to the growing influence of Buddhism, it was reported that before the Billy Graham Crusade in New York, the Unitarian Minister of a church in Manhattan preached a sermon on "the Living Truth" of Buddhism before his congregation of five hundred in commemorating the Spring Festival of Buddha and urged his congregation "to turn to the teachings of Buddhism before Billy Graham hits New York with his over-simplified formula of salvation." Again, this church in 1962 celebrated the 70th anniversary of Buddhism in the U.S. and the "essential unity of all man's Religions" and asked a Buddhist priest to chant: "we reverently pay homage to the Eternal Buddha. . ."[14]

II. THE WAVE OF SYNCRETISM

Another feature which fertilizes the soil for the impact of Zen in the West is the pernicious influence of the syncretism of modernist theology. The Layman's Foreign Missionary Inquiry Committee, headed by Dr. W. E. Hocking, published in 1932 a book under the title *Rethinking Missions*, which arrived theologically at a conclusion consistent with the humanistic syncretism of the hour. First and foremost they asserted: Christianity is not unique, nor the only possible avenue and approach to God. Their plea was for a common search for truth together, recognizing the good and bad in each religion including Christianity. Insofar as they asserted the direct continuity between all religions, based on a supposed common religious essence, Christianity was reduced to an ethnic phenomenon in common with non-Christian religions and no room was made for the work of the Holy Spirit. Moreover, standards of spiritual values, normative principles, social order, all are divested of any absolute character or significance.[15]

A similar feature is manifested by another book, an ecumenical symposium on *The Theology of the Christian Mission* edited by Gerald H. Anderson. As a dominant trend, the symposium essayists follow the same path of William Hocking and see Christianity as the fulfillment rather than the contradiction of heathen religion. They emphasize "the good in all religions." They regard all religions as paths to the same Reality and believe that devotees of the non-Christian religions are prepared thereby for the Gospel. This thesis is supported zealously by the following scholars:[16]

1. A. C. Bouquet contends that one Divine Truth permeates all religion. Therefore it is not impossible to speak of "Christian Buddhists, Christian Moslems, Christian Vedantists and Christian Confucianists."[17]

2. Ernest Benz proposes a reconstruction of the history of religions that relates other religions affirmatively to Christianity, rather than as heretical or as demonic independent movements. Religions differ from each other only in degree, not in kind.[18]

3. L. Harold DeWolf stresses the continuity of Biblical with non-Biblical religion. "Various scholars believe that they can find evidences in the ancient Old Testament religion of contributions from Egyptians, Midianites, Canaanites and Babylonians." "The Christian teachings of the New Testament include contributions from other religions in addition to. . . Judiasm," such as Hellenistic philosophy, mystery religions, and Persian influence.[19]

4. Floyd H. Ross writes "The Christian mission today involves bearing witness to a profound search for living truth which can never be confined within any language,

theological or non-theological, Christian or non- Christian." "God is known in relative ways only." The early Christians "may have been over zealous" in affirming "there is no other name given under heaven" for the salvation of man!²⁰

5. Paul Tillich affirms that the Church is "latently present" in paganism, humanism, and Judaism. Christian mission aims, we are told, to transform this latency into existential reality. He boldly sets aside the finality of Jesus of Nazareth. The goal of history is "never actualized in history." The center of history or the "moment in which the meaning of history becomes fully manifest is "the New Being in Jesus *as* the Christ." This center is not A.D. 1-30, but is existential: "Many people, even today, are living *before* the event Jesus as the Christ." He misses the significance of special historical revelation objectively climaxed in Jesus Christ, and dilutes the essence of redemptive religion to a speculative idealism in whch the scandal of the cross is gone.²¹

Paul Tillich's theology is most deceptive as it repudiates orthodoxy in the name of science, follows the secular philosophers by affirming their view that the Incarnation of God in Christ is a scandal, and rejoices with Nietzsche that "God is dead." Rejecting the existence of God, he retains God in a symbolic sense but in fact reduces Him into a meaningless abstraction! He contends that God cannot be spoken of as existing or not existing, for this would imply the limiting the unlimitable. He defines religion subjectively as the exercise of a human faculty in contrast to an objective definition in terms of man's response to God. On this basis, an atheist, according to Tillich, may properly be said to be religious, so long as there is something which he values absolutely. Thus, the communist party, Buddha, Nirvana, ultimate good, Tao—are all god. He also argues that to identify revelation with the Bible is a serious mistake of theology. God's word is not limited to the Bible. Thus the authority of the Bible is denied.²²

Paul Tillich lights matches in darkness and might well attract people probing in dawnless night, but he fails to open wide the windows of his mind to let in the true Sun of Righteousness! He reduced God and Christ to sheer symbols. His "system has affinities with the ancient Docetic heresy which was roundly condemned by the church."[23] "Tillich may be a great thinker but human thought does not manufacture God."[24] "Tillich, Niebuhr, Bultmann and company promulgate their infidelity as 'theologians' and 'clergymen.' Tillich's religious vaporing— a kind of twentieth century Gnosticism—would rob Christianity of its Christ, its Bible, its God, its salvation and its sense."[25]

Another feature of syncretism was manifested by a thesis of Dr. Herbert C. Jackson, Director of Missionary Research Library. He feels that in order "to make the Christian faith truly valid universally as well as to make it relevant to the needs and thought of men today, an ecumenical theology must be created. And this will require no less than a radical mutation in theology!" He contends that "to urge that we 'stand fast' regardless of any flood of untruth that might sweep over the world in the forthcoming era of non-Christian religions—such restriction of Christian faith not only is not valid, but is a positive detriment to and violation of what God is seeking to do in our day." "Christianity, if it hopes to 'stand' with the resurgent non-Christian religions, must ecumenicize its theology by drawing from the whole world and creating something entirely new." "The Eastern structuring of juxtaposition-identification also leads, inescapably, to a consciousness of the primacy of harmony in the outcome of mental processes, in all human relations, and in the relationship of men to the ultimate realities, and Ultimate Reality, of the universe." This produces a sincere seeking after the "whole truth," with a total absence of the belligerent and divisive "defense of truth" which characterize Occidental understanding of truth as propositionally stated. He thinks the Oriental approach presents a far more "Biblical spirit" than does the theological warfare that "has marred and still mars Occidental Christianity." For this reason, Dr. Jackson strongly advocates that a "radical mutation is necessary," and, in order to have a period of so-called "creative theological advance," even "the appearance of another age of the Heretics is inevitable!"[26]

III. THE MOOD OF SECULARISM

The inevitable outcome and the most disastrous aspect of the self-negation of Western scholars and the syncretism of modernist theologians have been manifested in the failure of missions and the secularization in the Church. The pulpit has lost power where the rationalizing movement has transformed the supernatural Christianity into a system of morality mixed up with secular topics. Preaching has become rationalistic. The core of the Gospel is not to be found in many sermons. Strange to say, it is even impossible to discern whether the preacher of the Church of Christ is a real Christian or a follower of pagan religions.[27] For instance, a noted minister of a church in New York City preaches that: "the exploration of the evolutionary theory as expounded by Charles Darwin may produce the new concept of an evolutionary God to be conceived as 'Universal-Being-Becoming.' . . . According to him, the evolutionary idea of God restores to man a fully responsible role in which his daily choices are of ultimate significance. He is no longer God's puppet, but a part of the God-process. This new religious conception is largely in correspondence with what the Shintoists call the spiritual coalescence of Kami and Man."[28]

Frequently, modernist missionary leaders have believed that through education, social uplift, and the worldwide application of the golden rule of Christ, the whole world would be Christianized. Underlying the social gospel concept and modern educational approach, is the wholehearted acceptance of the theory of evolution, the assurance of the inevitability of progress, and the idea of the inherent goodness of man. Supernaturalism, the true diety of Jesus Christ, and the inerrancy of Scriptures, have consistently been subjected to attack and ridicule. Man is given the dignity and the hope that he can become a perfect man in his own power and by his own efforts.

In effect, God has become no longer necessary, or at best His nature and work are interpreted to fit their new scheme, rather than testing the new scheme to see whether it is in agreement with the revelation of God. Thus in order to retain new theology, revelation has had to be eliminated. The homocentric theology of the psychologist has found sin to be a maladjustment that could be treated like a medical doctor treats an organic illness.

As early as 1910 most of the theological seminaries had been captured by modernists. At the International Missionary Conference in Jerusalem in 1928, the weight of the meetings swung over in favor of the social Gospel, the ethnic conception of religion, in which Christianity was denominated as differing in degree rather than in kind from other religions.[29]

Since the modernists have robbed the church of its Gospel, there is no wonder why she lost her power to witness. Mahatma Gandhi once wrote about his experience after attending a Wesleyan Church in South African every Sunday at a moment of his greatest religious restlessness: "The church did not make a favorable impression to me ....The sermon sounds to me uninspiring. The congregation did not strike me. They are not an assembly of devout souls, appeared to be rather world-minded people, going to church for recreation or conformity to custom. I could not go along like that and soon gave up attending the service."[30]

It is true, "Christianity is losing its influence on modern man. And this is the deepest religious source of all misery. Old truths which for centuries were never doubted are now set aside. God, virtue, and immortality are no longer believed in by the masses."[31] Modern "theologians" such as Paul Tillich and Rudolf Bultmann, no longer hold fast the Bible truths. They define religion as the form of culture, repudiate orthodoxy in the name of science, replace salvation with the concept of the "New Being," and deny divine truth of its permanent and absolute significance. The term original sin is redefined to mean the limitation of human existence; resurrection is at most a regenerate life here and now, but not a future life in an incorruptible body in a new heaven or eternal age; redemption does not come through the objective work of a personal Lord but through the human decision, and it is not a future victory, but a present adjustment. The historical Jesus is not in the traditional sense the personal Lord born by the Virgin Mary and raised from the tomb the third day. God is a meaningless abstraction and Christ is merely a symbolic term.[32]

The blight of secularism in the church is rampant. In an Easter editorial in *Life* magazine, we read: "There are the standard responses to 'secularism,' the attitude that permeates so much of American life (even in church).... The whole trend of modern thought has been to make God and religion intellectually respectable again. Why is not God already real to Americans who are among the most church-going people in the world? Probably because of the blight of secularism in the churches which have become just another valued branch of American democratic culture instead of its center. What used to be the minister's study is now his office and as a busy agent of social Gospel, he is less a spokesman of God."[33] As one scholar has pointed out, the existing religious vacuum issues not only in irreligion, but also in the creation of a host of "pseudo" or "parody" religions, idolatries and mythologies. There are constantly growing "pseudo" churches with a more or less strong Christian residue. They are marked by new elements of emphasis on healing, on peace of mind, on happiness, on prosperity, on success, on plenty, etc., attracting thereby a host of people, the more so because they develop an enormous advertising program. The stress is on longing for healing, peace of mind, security in regard to the good life here and now.[34] Such religious climate also explains why some people became easy prey of Zen Buddhism.

The spiritual condition in Europe is also far from healthy. It must suffice here to note one or two things about the religious state of Great Britain in general terms.

The chief enemy of the Church in Britain today is spiritual indifference. Most people view the church with a benevolent eye as a venerable and sometimes useful institution, to be patronized on such occasions as baptism, weddings, and funerals, but otherwise not to be taken too seriously. The average man-in-the-street does not think much about religious issues. The "church" is not a vital factor in his life. Undoubtedly this attitude of indifference is due to the contemporary scientific mood. The intellectual climate of the age is not conducive to deep religious thought. Another factor to be reckoned with is the welfare state, together with the present wave of material prosperity. Their bodies are well fed; their health is looked after. They are amply provided with cultural and intellectual interests. There is no obvious sense that something vital is missing, that life lacks purpose and power. In consequence, the relevance of the Gospel became all the more remote.[35]

A report about religious and spiritual conditions in Britain stated that "nearly 99 per cent of London's teenagers and more than 90 per cent of all British people do not regularly attend any place of worship. In many areas there is virtually no effective evangelical witness. It is not uncommon to see places of worship shut or used for other purposes. One can enter churches with a seating capacity of one thousand and find a dozen in attendance."[36] The situation is not without hope, particularly from the evangelical view;[37] but a review of the present situation will surely help to heighten our vigilance and to understand how the way is paved for the pseudo-religion of Zen Buddhism.

A recent mood of secularism is manifested in the works of Paul Van Buren and Harvey Cox. In his book, *The Secular Meaning of the Gospel; Based on an Analysis of its Language,* Van Buren points out that "the scientific revolution with its resulting technology and industrial developments, has given us another empirical way of thinking and of seeing the world. That which cannot be conceived in terms of men and the world explored by natural science is simply without interest, because it is not real. We are told that the whole tenor or thought of our world today makes the biblical and classical formulations of the Gospel unintelligible."[38] "Our English speaking culture has an empirical tradition and the world today is increasingly being formed by technology and whole industrial process."[39]

Van Buren put the cart before the horse when he says: "Although the Gospel calls for repentence, it also proclaims liberation,"[40] and he ignores that fact of the bondage of sin and that without true repentance there is no liberation, and that no one can be set free without knowing the Truth (John 8:32). He perverts the biblical truth by saying: "In all the letters to his various readers, Paul never urged them to go out to convert the unbelievers."[41] Denying that Christianity is the divine revelation from heaven, he reduces Christianity to the secular level of human learning and contends: "In almost every field of human learning, the metaphysical and cosmological aspect has disappeared and the subject matter has been limited to the human, the historical, the empirical." Thus, he concludes that "theology cannot escape this tendency. . . .And such a 'reduction' of content need no more be regretted in theology than in astronomy, chemistry, and painting."[42]

Harvey Cox is even more radical. While Van Buren contends that "our principal difficulty today, is not bad religion but bad language"; Cox thinks Van Buren is wrong—the problem is not bad language" but "bad religion."[43] He suggests that "we shall have to stop talking about "God" for a while, take a moratorium on speech until the new name emerges. Maybe the name that does emerge will not be the three-letter word God, but this should not dismay us—the word God is not sacred."[44] He even charges that Rudolf Bultmann is not really radical enough for "he fails to reach the man of today because he translates the Bible from mythical into yesterday's metaphysics rather than into today's post metaphysical lexicon."[45] Cox subtly defends himself by differentiating secularization and secularism, so as to cover his sense of guilt; then he boldly distorts the Bible truth by saying that "the Genesis account of Creation is really a form of atheistic propaganda."[46] In the story of Exodus, we are told that what occured was the "desacralization of politics" as in the creation story what is described is "the disenchantment of nature." The Exodus "symbolized the deliverance of man out of sacral-political order and into history and social change, . . .into a world where political leadership would be based on power gained by the capacity to accomplish social objectives."[47] At Sinai, "the deconsecration of values" takes place. Therefore, Cox proclaims that "A God who emasculates man's creativity and hamstrings his responsibility for his fellowman must be dethroned."[48] Here Cox becomes the judge and God is under his judgment and is condemned! Harvey Cox, to be sure, is iconoclastic, but he is iconoclastic in the interest of a humanitarian ideal. He denies the relevancy and grace of God, because he thinks that belief in God interferes with man's freedom and social progress and is completely destitute of the great truth that God is "the fountain of living waters."

Modern man is fascinated with all kinds of fads and seductive doctrines; but as a mater of fact Cox has nothing new to offer. He simply projects August Comte's old view, attempting to reduce Christianity into a mere humanistic system—a religion of humanity. The problem which Cox brought is not new either, it is as old as that of the Tower of Babel. Sociologically speaking, there might be some difference between tribal society, town culture, and the technopolis; but theologically speaking, human nature has never been changed. As historian Toynbee pointed out: "Western man, at the present level of his intellectual powers and technological aptitudes, has not sloughed off Adam's heirloom of original sin."[49] If all men bow to the "Technopolitan" culture, and overemphasize or exalt human "responsibility" (only to fellowman not to God) and "reason" (unaided by divine revelation) in terms or under the pretense of "deliverance of man from religion and metaphysical controls," of "deconsecration of values" and of "theology of social change," then mankind will surely repeat the same tragedy of the Tower of Babel.

We do not deny the fact that the situation of the world has been changed. But it is more important to discern whether it has been changed for better or for worse. And it is entirely wrong to emphasize that which changes. That which changes cannot be "norma normans." Our hope is not on "those things that are shaken (cf. Heb. 12:26-28), but only on which itself is free from the cycle of changeability. Moreover, as history evinces, Christianity, instead of emasculating man's creativity, is "the mother of the best elements of modern culture."[50] The Western culture is indebted to Augustine who was raised by God at the time when the dying empire of the West was passing on to the Barbarians. It was Augustine who shifted the center of gravity and set western culture on its God-given course. It was Augustine's vision that gave meaning and orientation to the new social order. The *City of God* laid the foundation of Christian sociology and Western civilization.[51] But now Cox tries to shift our foundation from "rock" to "sand" (Matt. 7:24-27)—i.e., *The Secular City*. Cox is blind to the fact that the "secular city" is soulless as Oswald Spengler in his noted book warned modern man;[52] and it is rootless, though affluent, and only a "cut flower" as Trueblood depicts it.[53] Now the sickness and disease of modern culture is becoming more apparent, therefore, our hope is not in the "Secular City" but in the Kingdom of God.

These modern theologians are natural men who receive not the things of the Spirit of God and only look at the things which are visible and temporal, not things which are eternal. They acknowledge only that the historical process of mankind is toward secularization—the increasing control of man over the universe, while the dominion of God is seemingly diminishing.[54] They are blind to the truth that "He must increase" and never "decrease" (John 3:30). C. S. Lewis once wrote: "Although religion is still only a part, . . .in all of us, God still holds only a part. The bite so far taken out of Normandy shows small on the map of Europe. The resistance is strong. There is a line of demarcation between God's part in us and the enemy's region. But it is, we hope, a fighting line not a frontier fixed by agreement."[55] "The Kingdom need not necessarily be visible in order to be real. During the last World War, when several European nations had been overrun by invaders, they maintained governments in exile. Their leaders resided outside the country but still commanded the allegiance of their people, even though the people were in territory that was under the enemy's dominion. Similarly the Kingdom of God is composed of those who cherish Christ as invisible Lord of their lives, even though they may reside in the territory controlled by "the god of this world." The invisible kingdom will appear in its true nature when its King returns to inaugurate His rule and assert His royal rights."[56] Though we do not now see Him, we believe in Him and rejoice with joy unspeakable and full of glory (Cf. I Peter 1:8). His Kingdom is "like a grain of mustard seed which is indeed the least of all seeds, but when it is grown it is greatest among herbs" (Matt. 13:31, 32). "So seek ye first the kingdom of God and his righteousness, and all these things shall be added unto you" (Matt. 6:33).

Tragically, mankind has failed to grasp this solemn truth and forsaken the fountain of living waters, (Jer. 2:13). So "the history of human progress," as an eminent sociologist diagnosed, "is a history of incurable stupidity."[57] Some critics allege that though Harvey Cox's theology is poor, his sociology is sound. However, just as a corrupt tree cannot bring forth good fruit his sociology is also poor. He is like a person living in trance induced by post-hypnotic suggestion of liberal theology. He only sees things on the surface, but not from the root; he only sees a secular-city, but not the kingdom of God. So he has neither true information nor an adequate solution. For the cure of human disease is regeneration not secularization.

---

[1] Cf. Hendrik Kraemer, *World Cultures and World Religions*, pp. 230, 231.

[2] Cf. J. H. Bavinck, *Impact of Christianity on the Non-Christian World*, Chapter V.

[3] Cf. *Die Welt als Wille und Vorstellung*, Vol., I, III; Hartmann holds the same view that "Christianity is a system of pessimism." Cf. his, *Selbstzerstzung des Christentum*.

[4] Cf. Kraemer, op. cit., pp. 235, 236.

[5] Arnold Toynbee, *Civilization on Trial*, p. 240.

[6] Cf. Toynbee, *An Historian Approach to Religion*, 1956.

[7] Cf. "Christian Study Center on Chinese Religion," *Quarterly*, No. II, May 1957, Hong Kong.

[8] Cf. Robert Linssen, *Living Zen*, p. 208.

[9] Cf. Kraemer, op. cit., p. 239. Writing of the better known ones include: Rudolf Seydel's *Das Evangelium Jesus in seinem Verhaltniss zu Buddhasage und Buddha-Lehre*, 1882, and *Die Burrha-legende und das Leben Jesus nach den Evangelien*, 1884; A. J. Edmunds' *Buddhist and Christian Gospels* now first compared, 1902, G. A. Van den Bergh van Eysinga's *Indische Einflusse und evangelische Erzählungen*, 1909; Richard Garbe's *Indian und das Christentum*, 1914, etc.

[10] Cf. *Das Reisetagebuch eines Philosophen*, — The Travel Diary of a Philosopher, (Tr. by J. H. Reese) 2 Vols. N. Y. Harcourt, 1926.

[11] Cf. Kraemer, op. cit., p. 245.

[12] Robert Linssen, *Living Zen*, p. 208.

[13] Cf. Kersey Graves: *The World's Sixteen Crucified Saviours*, or *Christianity Before Christ*, Boston, Colby and Rich, 1878.

[14] *Time* magazine, October 26, 1962.

[15] Cf. *Rethinking Missions*.

[16] Cf. *Christianity Today*: "A New Crisis in Missions," April 24, 1961.

[17] Cf. G. H. Anderson, (ed.) *The Theology of the Christian Mission*, "Revelation and the Divine Logos."

[18] Cf. Anderson ibid, "Ideas for a Theology of the History of Religions."

[19] Cf. *ibid.*, "The Interpretation of Christianity and the Non-Christian Religions."

[20] Cf. *ibid.* "The Christian Revelation in Larger Dimension."

[21] Cf. *ibid*, "Missions and History"; also "A New Crisis in Missions," *Christianity Today*, April 24, 1961.

[22] Cf. "Lost Dimension in Religions," *Saturday Evening Post*, June 14, 1958; "The Lost Dimension of Death," *Christianity Today*, July 21, 1958; "Theology for Protestants," *Time*, March 16, 1959.

[23] Rev. James G. Manz's letter to *Time*. March 30, 1959.

[24] Rev. B. L. Frey's letter to *Time*, March 30, 1959.

[25] Rev. George Scotchmer's letter to *Time*, April 13, 1959.

CRISIS IN RELIGION 95

[26] Cf. "A Forthcoming Role of the Non-Christian Religions Systems as Contributing to Christian Theology," *Missionary Research Library*, March 15, 1961.

[27] Cf. Thomas H. Pattison, *History of Christian Preaching*, pp. 247-249.

[28] Dr. Chikao Fujisawa, *Zen and Shinto*, p. 91.

[29] Cf. H. Lindsell, *A Christian Philosophy of Missions*, chapter I.

[30] Cf. *Young India*, October 14, 1926; also S. K. George, *Gandhi's Challenge to Christianity*, N. Y., Norton, 1939.

[31] J. M. Spier, *Christianity and Existentialism*, p. 16.

[32] Cf. note 20; and Robert Paul Roth, "Christianity and Existentialism," *Christianity Today*, March 27, 1961.

[33] *Life* Magazine, March 30, 1959.

[34] Cf. Charles S. Braden, *A Study of Modern American Cults and Minority Religious Movement*, 1953; and Kraemer, *op. cit.*, pp. 323, 324.

[35] Cf. Frank Colquhoun, "Great Britain: the Spiritual Situation Today," *Christianity Today*, July 31, 1961.

[36] Cf. Gilbert W. Kirby, "Religious Life in Great Britain Today," *Christianity Today*, April 10, 1961.

[37] Cf. Dr. K. S. Latourette's article, *Christianity Today*, March 2, 1962.

[38] Van Buren: *The Secular Meaning of the Gospel*, p. 6.

[39] *Ibid.*, p. 17.

[40] *Ibid.*, p. 178.

[41] *Ibid.*, p. 190.

[42] *Ibid.*, p. 198.

[43] Harvey Cox: *The Secular City*, p. 260.

[44] *Ibid.*, p. 266.

[45] *Ibid.*, p. 252.

[46] *Ibid.*, p. 23.

[47] *Ibid.*, p. 26.

[48] *Ibid.*, p. 72.

[49] Cf. Arnold Toynbee: *Civilization on Trial*, pp. 151, 261.

[50] Cf. Philip Schaff: *History of Christian Church*, Vol. II, pp. 267, 625, 626.

[51] Cf. Emile Cailliet: *Christian Approach to Culture*, p. 142.

[52] Cf. Spengler: *The Decline of the West*, I. p. 364, 424.

[53] Cf. Elton Trueblood: *The Predicament of Modern Man*. pp. 59, 60.

[54] Larry Shiner: *The Secularization of History*.

[55] C. S. Lewis: *Letters to Malcolm, Chiefly on Prayers*. p. 47 ff.

[56] Merrill C. Tenney: "The Glorious Destiny of the Believer," *Christianity Today*, Dec. 23, 1966.

[57] P. A. Sorokin: (1) *The Crisis of Our Age*. pp. 318-326; (2) *Man and Society in Calamity*. pp. 318, 319.

Chapter Four

CRISIS IN THEOLOGY
—THEOLOGICAL BACKGROUND OF ZEN'S IMPACT—

I. PANTHEISTIC THEOLOGY
—THE ONENESS OF GOD AND MAN—
("THE ART OF GODMANSHIP")

In recent years, it has been considered as "a large theological event," by the unwary that "Godmanhood is to be discovered here and now inwardly, not in the letter of the Bible."[1] It is alleged that "the eternal home will never be found as long as you are seeking it, for the simple reason that you are the center, you have no further need to see it."[2] "The true parousia comes at the moment of crisis in consciousness."[3] However, such thought is not altogether original, but rather derivative. Evidently, the West has been haunted by the spirit of Zen and inspired by liberal theology since Schleiermacher. A review of the present day theories shows that their roots are in the past. It is Schleiermacher's invisible hand that is laid upon the whole enterprise of making the Gospel "meaningful" as it is desired in our day.[4] In his work, *Person of Christ*, Dorner says: "The characteristic features of all recent Christologies is the endeavor to point out the essential unity of the divine and human," founded on the principle of the oneness of God and man. Dr. Allman further points out that the doctrine of the oneness of God and man as the fundamental idea of Schleiermacher's theology is not entirely new. It was inculcated by the German Mystics of the Middle age.[5] Here we see the reason why oriental mysticism found its fertile ground to grow in the West and why the modern theologians are apt to accept the spirit of Zen.

In modern systems, there is such a blending of pantheistic principles with theistic doctrine. Theologians of this class deny that God and man are essentially different; man may become God. It follows, in the first place, from this doctrine, that the incarnation of God is from eternity; and, in the second place, that the process is continuous, complete in no one instance, but only in the whole.[6] Strauss says: "The idea of the oneness of the divine and human natures is never exhibited in all its fullness in a single examplar," but "is always realized in a variety and multiplicity of examplars, which complement each other, its richness being diffused by the constant change of individuals, one succeeding or supplementing another....Mankind, the human race, is God-man."[7] Blasche says: "We understand by God's becoming man, not the revelation of Himself in one or more of the most perfect of men, but the manifestation of Himself in the race of men (*in der ganzen Menschheit*)."[8]

Schleiermacher, the father of liberal theology, having succumbed to the attacks which rationalistic criticism had made against faith in the Bible, thus determined to construct a Christology and a whole system of Christian theology from "within," to weave it out of the materials furnished by his own religious "consciousness," rather than upon the objective teachings of the Word of God. His system is not only speculative but essentially pantheistic. He denied any proper dualism between God and the world and between God and man. He did not admit the existence of a personal extra-mundane God. He swung to and fro between the idealism of Kant and Fichte and the pantheism of Spinoza and Schelling.[9] His system also ignores the doctrine of the Trinity. Christ had no pre-existence beyond that which is common to all man. This system makes

Christ a mere man. The difference between Christ and other men is simply one of degree. The incarnation of God is not a unique manifestation in the flesh, in the person of Christ. On the contrary, it is the introduction of the life of God into humanity rendering it divine.[10] Schleiermacher assumes that Christ took up the divine into his human nature, and assumes that human nature is a constant; so that we can generalize from one instance to all, from Christ to humanity. Incarnation must be reckoned an innate possibility in human nature. Incarnation, while marking a decisive stage in world-development, is seen also to happen in order to advance an evolutionary pattern: "He alone is destined gradually to quicken the whole human race into higher life."[11] Moreover, the plan of salvation, according to his doctrine is entirely different from that revealed in the Bible. There is nothing supernatural and no place for the work of the Holy Spirit. Man's redemption consists in the triumph of the good principle, as Christ awakens the dormant good that is *already* in man's nature. This system speaks of Christianity as a life, as developing itself organically and naturally, not by supernatural assistance, but by an "inward" life-power, as in other cases of organic development. It assumes to rise to the conception of the whole world as an organism, in which God is one of the factors; the world and God differing not in substance of life, but simply in functions. It concedes to "speculation" that the fundamental truth of philosophy and of Christianity is the oneness of God and man. Man is God living in a certain form or state of development. It is a system of "phrases" which endeavors to heal the wounds of orthodoxy by empty words.[12] It is also the spirit of heathenism that man "shall be as gods" (Gen. 3:5) by self-improvement or self-deification or, in the term of Zen, self-enlightenment, "satori."

II. THE THEOLOGY OF IMMANENCE

—SONS OF SCHLEIERMACHER—

"Neo-orthodoxy seemed to be a movement dedicated to turning man away from the humanism and this worldliness of liberalism"; but "to wish to alter the course of the ship of theology was not necessarily to intend to have it sail in the opposition" (Such as Niebuhr, who after half a lifetime of attacking liberalism, confesses to being "a liberal at heart.") "To wish to steer a middle course turns out to be the determination to cling to a 'theology of immanence.' Consciously or unconsciously, neo-liberals rally under the banner of Schleiermacher. Strangely enough, few of Schleiermacher's modern sons are ready to acknowledge him as their spiritual father. Among neo-liberals, Tillich is the one who has most to say about his debt to Schleiermacher.[13] He admits that Schleiermacher's "feeling of absolute dependence" is similar to his own "ultimate concern."[14] "It is apparent that modern philosophical theology generally is developed under the shadow of Schleiermacher making God consciousness its common starting point. The perspective is one of 'immanence,' for though the definitions of God advanced may contain the word 'transcendent,' they actually refer to a deity immanent within experience and transcendent as the ground of experience."[15]

According to Schleiermacher, every movement of the life of Christ was "a new incarnation and incarnatedness of God; because always and everywhere all that is human in Him springs out that divine."[16] So incarnation was presented as the flowering of the eternal in the temporal, whenever immanent divinity became actualized in a human subject."[17] Thus when Tillich protests that Jesus Christ is not a proper name, and that instead we ought to use the expression "Jesus as the Christ," he is following where Schleiermacher led.[18] "Neo-liberalism shows itself standing under Schleiermacher's banner. At the center of its understandings of redemption is not the forgiveness of sin, but the actualizing of human potential."[19] Thus our faith is not in Jesus Christ the Saviour, just as the Zen teaches that one should look to no Person or God for help, for all the exterior ways only lead to perdition. The practice of Zen or the way of deliverance is to see into one's inner being, an intuitive realization of the self nature, for everyone is a potential Buddha.

This position is further developed by John A. T. Robinson in his work *Honest to God*. He suggests that we should press through to the God of the depths, the ground of our being, for God is not a Being but the depth of our being. He attacks the supernatural framework of orthodox Christianity in terms of "myth" and "barriers" so as to meet the level of "scientific man" and "modern reason." He subtly argues in the terms of the "greater depth of divinity," "the true defense of Christian truth" and self-transcendence, that there is no such God "up there" or "out there,"[20] that "the mental picture of such a God may be more of a stumbling block than an aid to belief in the Gospel." [21] Such teaching is not only antagonistic to the Bible, but also is highly suggestive of Zen. He further charges that our "basic commitment to Christ" may have been "buttressed by many lesser commitments—to a particular projection of God, a particular myth of the Incarnation, a particular code of morals, a particular pattern of religion"; and further alleges that "we must beware of clinging to the buttresses instead of to Christ," for "they are barriers rather than the supports."[22] In this way, the transcendence of a living and personal God, the deity and the glorious mystery of the Person of Christ, the validity and the relevance of God's holy commandments, the need of moral laws, and the supernatural and divine origin of Christianity and its cardinal truths are undermined. And while on the one hand he claims to be "Honest to God," at the same time he confesses his "sympathies are on the humanist's side."[23] Thus his position is practically untenable, for actually he is inconsistent himself.

Furthermore, it is clear that, while he starts his book with an attractive heading—"Reluctant Revolution"—so as to arouse the curiosity of naive readers, his position contains nothing really new. In fact anyone familiar with Zen will quickly discover the resemblance of his thought pattern to Zen. To mention a few instances: Zen teaches "seeing into one's own nature." Zenists hold that the truth of Zen opens itself within. One does not enter Nirvana, for entrance to a place one has never left is impossible. Zen has no use of God. They look to no God for help, for there is no God "up there" or "out there"; neither is there supernatural intervention or refuge. If one says he has attained something, that is the surest proof of his deviation. So all the exterior ways are to them rather "stumbling blocks," "barriers" or ways of perdition! In the sayings of Hang-Po, we read; "Your attachment to objects will all be those of devil-Karma. Even if you do things with a view to Pure Land, these too produce a Karma which is called the Buddha-hindrance." Again, in the sayings of Lin-chi, we read: "Smash whatever you come across... you will be in real emancipation." Now, we read from Robinson: "Beware of clinging to the buttresses, for they are barriers rather than supports: stumbling blocks rather than aides to belief." Should Robinson learn more of Zen, I wonder whether he would follow Zen by saying: When you have mentioned "Our Father in heaven, Wash your mouth!"[24]

III. THE "DEATH-OF-GOD" MOVEMENT

—CULT OF ICONOCLASM—

Robinson's position and his proposal to find a new image of God has been described by the new radical theologians as "soft radicalism." The new radicals represent a spirit of "iconoclasm" and "immanence" which are homogeneous with Zen. They are convinced that any God is unbelieveable if he has to be placed in a transcendent realm. God has come down out of heaven, or up out of Tillich's mysterious depth dimension, to appear in the world of "here and now." We are told that the best theologians of the past have been iconoclastic critics of "religious isolationism," "of Christian ethnolatry." We are told that Augustine was a true iconoclast, the Reformers were true iconoclasts. Therefore, we are urged to revive this attitude in the interest of the "Gospel of the freedom of man through Jesus."[25] After interpreting Augustine and the Reformers so as to support their arguments and to suit their purposes, these radical theologians immediately contradict themselves by alleging that the God of the Augustine-Reformation tradition is "irrelevant." We no longer have any power "to affirm any of the traditional images of God."[26] We are told that "now man is his own redeemer. The clear meaning of the present anthropocentrism is this: the impossibility of God is a practical fact, it is an everyday reality, available to the experience of all existing beings. If anything characterizes the modern temper, it is a radical immanentism." "To kill God is to become God oneself.[26a] This is the meaning of the transition from radical monotheism to radical immanentism which has taken place in Western culture.[27] "The Christian life is not a looking outward to the world and its claim, it is first 'a look within'[28] in order to become Jesus." Again, it says: we shall understand the death of God as an historical event; God has died in our time, in our history, in our existence." "The proclamation of the death of God. . . .is dialectical; a no-saying to God... makes possible a yes-saying to human existence. Absolute transcendence is transformed into absolute immanence; being here and now draws into itself all these powers which were once bestowed upon the beyond." "Now God is dead. The transcendence of Being has been transformed into the radical immanence of 'eternal recurrence.' "[29]

Fascinated with Zen teaching, Altizer could even follow Buddhist thought patterns by saying that: "If a Zenist were to persist in his denial and to assert that Nirvana is Samsara and Samsara is Nirvana, or that there is no difference whatsoever between the sacred and the profane....Then it appears that Christian and eschatological *'coincidentia oppositorum'* in this sense is finally a coming together or dialectical union of an original sacred and the radical profane. By a kenotic negation of its primordial reality, the sacred became incarnate in the profane. Consequently a consistently Christian dialectical understanding of the sacred must finally look forward to the resurrection of the profane in the transfigured and thus finally sacred form."[30] Following the Buddhist teaching on "detachment," he says: "Modern man has lost his homeland in faith. Genuinely contemporary man—he who lives in this moment of history—can never know the real meaning of religion unless he has at least momentarily experienced an alienation or 'detachment' from himself, from the world and from reality. So at last, Altizer completely surrenders to Buddhism and acknowledges that "Buddhism is the religion that is most profoundly challenging Christianity." We are told that "contemplation is the highest of man's activity. For therein he can become God and therein can he become immortal." "Genuine Christianity is the ultimate form of rebellion, the absolute form of self negation." "Nietzsche is the greatest prophet of the modern world because he had the courage and the vision to call man to an absolutely autonomous mode of existence. It was Nietzsche who most clearly saw that the mode of existence of the authentically modern man demanded the death of God." "Nirvana and Kingdom of God, mystical absorption and religio-ethical obedience are parallel or homologous and not contrary to each other." "Just as the Buddhist comes to know Samsara as Nirvana, the Christian must come to know the nothing as the hither of God."[31]

In *The Gospel of Christian Atheism,* Altizer says: "Redemption can only be fully actualized after the transcendent and numinous God has undergone a cosmic and historical epiphany as Satan." "Neither the Incarnation nor the Crucifixion can be understood as isolated and once and for all events; rather they must be conceived as primary expressions of a forward-moving and eschatological process of redemption, a process embodying a progressive movement of spirit into flesh." "The death of God does not propel man into empty darkness, it liberates him from every alien and opposing other and makes possible his transition into what Blake hailed as the Great Humanity Divine or final coming together of God and man." "Once the Christian has been liberated from all 'attachment' to a celestial and transcendent Lord and has died in Christ to the primordial reality of God, then he can say triumphantly 'God is dead.'" "Once God has died in Christ to His transcendent epiphany, that epiphany must inevitably recede into an abstract and alien form, eventually becoming the full embodiment of every alien other and thence appearing to consciousness as the ultimate source of all repression. . . . Faith can name this movement as the metamorphosis of God into Satan, as God empties himself of his original power and glory, and progressively becomes manifested as an alien but oppressive nothingness." "The Christian, who knows the Christ who is the embodiment of the self-negation of God, can know the Satan or the Anti-Christ who is present to us as the actualization or the historical realization of the 'death-of-God.'" "Therefore the Christian is finally called to accept the Anti-Christ or the totality of the dead body of God as a final kenotic manifestation of Christ."[32]

As Zen is claimed to be a way of liberation, the "death-of-God" theologians might be denominated as the propagators of this cult of "inconoclasm." For instance, as Altizer writes: "only by accepting and even willing the 'death-of-God' in our experience can we be delivered from a transcendent beyond. . . .To recognize the Christ who has become manifest and real as a result of a total movement from transcendence to immanence, we must be freed from every 'attachment' to transcendence." "If we can truly know that God is dead and can fully actualize the death-of-God in our experience, then we can be liberated from the threat of condemnation and be freed from every terror of a transcendent beyond." "The Christian must either choose God who is actually manifest and real in the established form of faith or he must confess the death-of-God, and give himself to a quest for a whole new form of faith. If he follows the latter course, he will sacrifice an established Christian meaning and morality, abandoning all those moral laws which the Christian church has sanctioned .... Knowing that his sin is forgiven, such a Christian can cast aside the crutches of guilt and resentment, only then can he rise and walk."[33] But the tragic fact is that, as history demonstrates, when they cast aside the "crutches" of religion, they stumble along with their own poor legs!

IV. "CHRISTIAN ATHEISM"

-THE STRATEGY OF "THE OLD SERPENT"-

The "God-is-dead" movement may have its day as a theological fad; but its doctrines and arguments are altogether deceptive. Its leaders are trees that in season bear no fruit, dead twice over and pulled up by the roots" (Jude 12). In the first place, their views on God and Christianity are totally wrong. Christianity is different from any kind of egoistic religion. Man could be emancipated from the dominion of church authority or its rites and rules, but never from the sovereign and providential rule of God for only His truth can make man free (John 8:12). Religion does not exist for the sake of man but for the glory of God. We often hear the radical theologians say that modern man "has come of age" and so he should throw away the crutches of religion. But such statements stem from their own misconception of religion. As Dr. Abraham Kuyper pointed out, the true "religion ought to be not egoistical, and for man, but ideal, for the sake of God." "Whatever may be the various stages in the progress of the egoistic religion, it never overcomes its subjective character, remaining always a religion for the sake of man." "As soon as the more civilized classes enjoy tranquility and comfort, and by the progress of science feel more and more delivered from the pressure of the cosmos, they throw the 'crutches' of religion, and with a sneer at everything holy, go stumbling forward on their own poor legs. This is the fatal end of egoistic religion;—it becomes superfluous and disappears as soon as the egoistic interests are satisfied. This was the course of religion among all non-Christian nations, and the same phenomenon is repeating itself in our own century among nominal Christians of the higher, more prosperous and more cultured classes of society." Although "religion has also its human and subjective side;... religion produces also a blessing for man; but it does not exist for the sake of man." "The starting-point of every motive in religion is God and *not man*. ....God alone is here, the goal, the point of departure, and the point of arrival, the fountain from which the waters flow, and at the same time, the ocean into which they finally return. To be irreligious is to forsake the highest aim of our existence, and on the other hand to covet no other existence than for the sake of God, to long for nothing but for the will of God and to be wholly absorbed in the glory of the name of the Lord, such is the pith and the kernel of all true religion."[34]

In the second place, their views on Christ are entirely fallacious. The so-called "Christian atheism" is a self-contradictory term. Their scheme to get rid of God while retaining Jesus is a sheer futility. It is not only anti-scriptural and anti-Christian, but also anti-intellectual. "It is impossible to hold on to the historical Jesus without God, because Jesus without God is not Jesus. Peter's confession is: "thou art the Christ, the Son of the living God.' Jesus and the living God go together. There is no such thing as a Jesus Gospel. The Gospel is the news of the redemptive working of God in and through Jesus Christ. As the Apostle Paul puts it; 'God was in Christ, reconciling the world unto Himself' (II Cor. 5:19). Jesus Himself said: "I and the Father are one' (John 10:30)."[35] Karl Barth, in a scathing denunciation of these death-of-God theologians, has well said: "they have thrown out the baby with the bath water. In trying to make Christianity possible for skeptics, they have succeeded only in making it meaningless."

But, above all, we should never be frightened by these so-called "new" doctrines, for in fact they have nothing new to offer and they are not new at all. They are repeating the mad cry of Voltaire and the odious shiboleth of the French Revolution and that animus curse of Friedrich Nietzsche. They are "not modern, but rather very antique; not posterior, but anterior to Protestantism, reaching back to Stoa and to Epicurus."[36] They are so reactionary that they are using the old old strategy of that old serpent in the Garden of Eden. "The underlying principle of all Satan's tactics is deception. He is a crafty and clever camouflager. He invades the theological seminary and even the pulpit. Many times he even invades the church under the cover of an orthodox vocabulary, emptying sacred terms of their Biblical sense."[37] He must use the beautiful label "Christian" in order to sell the "Atheism," so even the very elect shall be deceived! The false prophets are using the enticing words of man's wisdom that seem like the epitome of scholarship and culture, so that a host of high-minded men are led into their captivity!

We are not surprised to see the advance of these radical theologies and seductive teachings of the so-called "Christian Atheism," as God has already revealed unto us that for "the day of the Lord cannot come before the final rebellion against God."[38] In the last days, as Jesus taught His disciples: "many shall come in my name, saying, I am Christ: and shall deceive many."[39] Now the radical theologians take counsel together with "modern" theology, (which is in fact the old strategy of the "old serpent") against the Lord and against His Anointed to reject the established form of faith in deceptive terms of "freedom of man" and "creative negation."[40] But the tragic consequence is this: their negations only negate themselves: when they try to be liberated from God, they do not really become free, but rather plunge all the more deeply into the snare of Satan. For when they break the bands of God and of His anointed asunder, they in fact only bring their own destruction. They are forsaking the fountain of living waters and cutting off their lifeline. As C. S. Lewis well said: "Each new power won by man is a power over man as well. Each advance leaves him weaker as well as stronger. Man's final conquest has proven to be abolition of man."[41] To say "God-is-dead" is logically and theologically untenable, for it is a self-contradictory proposition. It is tantamont to saying fire is cold or ice is hot. Moreover, it is practically impossible to be independent from God. For in Him we live and move and have our being; for we are His offspring. We need His sovereign rule and His providential care. To be liberated from God or to kill God is just like cutting a tree from its root or a kite from its string, for that will only cause their immediate death or fall. This is why modern civilization has become a "cut flower" civilization,[42] as Dr. Trueblood puts it, and is in a process of disintegration.

As Martin Luther rightly said: "when Germany buries its last minister, then it will be burying herself!" Now the radical theologians are endeavoring to kill and bury God so as to liberate and exhalt man, but they are tragically unaware that they are burying themselves. God is not dead. All the books and writings of these radical liberal theologians only identify themselves as unbelievers, who are not born again and have never seen God nor met Him. They have no relation with God whatsoever. They are "natural men" who "receive not the things of the Spirit of God"; they are spiritually blind, who bitterly complain when they cannot see the "Kingdom of God" and the "sun of righteousness"; they are "dead in trespasses and sins" and therefore walk "according to the prince of the power of the air, the spirit that now works in the children of disobedience." They are "false prophets... who secretly bring in destructive heresies, even denying the Lord who bought them and bring upon themselves swift destruction." "They speak great swelling words of vanity... while they promise them liberty, but they themselves are slaves of corruption; and for them the nether gloom of darkness has been reserved forever."[43] The tragic end of the life of their "greatest prophet" Friedrich Nietzsche[44] who taught them this damnable heresy and demanded the "death-of-God" was surely their precedent ensample. They simply condemn themselves, for "he that believes not is already condemned." "He that believes not the Son shall not see life; but the wrath of God abides on him."[45] Modern man! Be not deceived, God is not mocked; though He is love, He is also a consuming fire![46] "Be wise now therefore,... Serve the Lord with fear, and rejoice with trembling. Kiss the Son, lest He be angry and ye perish from the way, when His wrath is kindled but a little. Blessed are all they that put trust in Him."[47]

---

[1] Alan Watts: *Beyond Theology—The Art of Godmanship.* p 115.
[2] *Ibid.*, P. 162.
[3] *Ibid.*, pp. 164, 165.
[4] Kenneth Hamilton: *Revolt Against Heaven*, p. 181-2.
[5] Dr. Allman: *Essay in the Studien und Kritiken* (1846).
[6] Charles Hodge: *Systematic Theology*, II. p. 429.
[7] Strauss: *Das Leben Jesus*, II pp. 766-7; and *Dogmatik* II, p. 214.
[8] Quoted by Strauss, *Dogmatik*, II. p. 214.
[9] Charles Hodge: *op. cit.*, II. p. 444; Baur: Lehre Von der Dreirinigkeit, Vol. III, p. 842.
[10] Hodge: *ibid.*, II pp. 445-7
[11] Schleiermacher: *The Christian Faith*, p. 63 § 63:1; Kenneth Hamilton: *Revolt Against Heaven*, pp. 79, 81.
[12] Hodge, *op. cit.*, II. pp. 450-454.
[13] Kenneth Hamilton: *Revolt Against Heaven*, pp. 95-97.
[14] Paul Tillich: *Systematic Theology*, pp. 112; Nels Ferre reports that in conversation, Tillich said that Schleiermacher was his spiritual father, see his *Searchlights on Contemporary Theology*, pp. 90n.
[15] Kenneth Hamilton: *op. cit.*, p. 100.
[16] Schleiermacher: *The Christian Faith*, p. 397.
[17] Kenneth Hamilton: *op. cit.*, p. 102.
[18] Tillich: *op. cit.*, II p. 97ff; and cf. Schleiermacher: *op. cit.*, p. 391ff.
[19] K. Hamilton: *op. cit.*, p. 109.
[20] John A. T. Robinson: *Honest To God*, pp. 7, 11, 55, 56, 140, 141.
[21] *Ibid.*, p. 16.
[22] *Ibid.*, pp. 140, 141.
[23] *Ibid.*, p. 8.
[24] Cf. Part I Chap. I Section III, IV; Chap. II, Section I and II of this volume.

CRISIS IN THEOLOGY 111

[25] Gabriel Vahanian, *Wait Without Idols*, p. 27.
[26] Wm. Hamilton, *The New Essence of Christianity*, pp. 55, 58.
[26a] It is interesting to note, this was exactly the teaching of Linchi, i.e., "Smash the Buddha, you will be in real emancipation." Cf. Part One, Chap. One, IV-3, of this volume.
[27] Gabriel Vahanian, *"The Death of God, The Culture of Our Post-Christian Era,* pp. 187-190, 230.
[28] This is also the basic teaching of Zen. Besides, Wm. Hamilton is ignorant of the basic truth of the new birth, for an unregenerated sinner is dead in trespasses and sins; he cannot live for Christ nor "shall see life, but the wrath of God abideth on him" (John 3:36) Cf. Wm. Hamilton & Altizer, *Radical Theology and the Death of God.* pp. 49, 50.
[29] *Ibid.*, Altizer; *Theology and Death of God*, pp. 95, 98, 102.
[30] *Ibid.*, Altizer: *Sacred and Profane*, pp. 143, 155. Here Altizer entirely perverts the Biblical truth, for although Jesus Christ "was made in the likeness of man"; although "both he that sanctifies and they who are sanctified are all of one"; although he "was in all points tempted like as we are, yet(he was) without sin" (Phil. 2:7; Heb. 2:11; 4:15).
[31] Altizer: *Oriental Mysticism and Biblical Eschatology* pp. 9, 11, 43, 107, 153, 178, 199.
[32] Altizer: *The Gospel of Christian Atheism;* pp. 97, 104, 107, 111-113, 120, 122.
[33] *Ibid*, pp. 136, 145, 147.
[34] Abraham Kuyper: *Lectures on Calvinism—The Six Stone Foundation Lectures*, pp. 44-46.
[35] Billy Graham: "Is God Then Dead!," *Decision*, May, 1966.
[36] Abraham Kuyper: *Calvinism*, p. 187.
[37] Billy Graham, *op. cit.*
[38] II Thess. 2:1-3. N. E. B.
[39] Matt. 24:15; cf. II Thess. 2:10, 11; I Timothy 4:1.
[40] Altizer: "Creative Negation in Theology," *The Christian Century*, July 7, 1965.
[41] C. S. Lewis: *The Abolition of Man*, pp. 37, 41.
[42] D. E. Trueblood: *The Predicament of Modern Man*, pp. 59, 60.
[43] Cf. I. Cor. 2:14; John 3:3; Eph. 2:1, 2; II Peter 2:1, 17, 18, 19.
[44] Cf. Part Two, Chap. Two, II. 2. of this volume.
[45] Cf. John 3:18, 19, 36.
[46] Gal. 6:7; I John 4:8; Heb. 12:29.
[47] Ps. 2:10-12.

PART THREE

THE TWINS OF ZEN-EXISTENTIALISM

(EAST AND WEST MEET)

—DOOM OF AUTO-SOTERISM—

Chapter One

A TREND IN MODERN THOUGHT

I. THE POINTS OF CORRESPONDENCE

Why is Zen so fascinating to the mind of modern man and existentialism exercising so great an influence today? The basic reason is evident; this is a century of crisis perhaps unprecedented in history. Existentialism is a philosophy of the meaninglessness of life, of the nihility and mortality of human existence which is devoid of any prospect or future; in a word, it is a philosophy of crisis. It attracts modern man by appealing to his attitude toward life which is often characterized by doubt, despair, futility and nihilism.[1] Moreover, the catastrophes of the twentieth century have caused the people in the West to lose faith in their own culture and religion. For this reason, Zen Buddhism—a cult of revolt against reason and authority with its teachings on original nature or genuine selfhood, on non-duality and on voidness or nothingness, etc., finds points of contact in the minds of the West and therefore finds also a land of fertile soil for its growth.

Zen Buddhism and Existentialism have many similarities in their nature and teachings. The discerning student will have no difficulty in discovering their points of correspondence. However, this does not mean that Zen is Existentialism. For in the first place, no two patterns of thought can absolutely be identified, and Zen especially may not be identified with any particular brand of "ism" or with any system of philosophy. Zen is "infinitely more than that." In the second place, these two systems have different backgrounds and they adopt different terminologies. In the third place, they are both difficult to grasp or define. Existentialism is extremely obscure and vague in its constructions and manners of expression and its various representatives are even contradictory in their positions. So is Zen, which is considered to be "extremely elusive" and as a "bottomless abyss." It is beyond perception, description and definition.[2] So far as it is difficult to define or grasp them, any attempt to compare or identify Zen with Existentialism cannot be said "to be quite to the point," as Dr. Suzuki has asserted. But, even for this very reason, these two systems are very much the same, so far as they are both elusive and vague and involve diverse and even contradictory views. Zen is known as a "wordless sect,"[3] and Existentialism as a hermetic philosophy has constructed a language of its own. To the existentialist, even obscurity is itself an instrument of existential clarification because it illuminates the profound and unfathomable obscurity of being. The word is regarded as an inadequate instrument; but, on the other hand, language becomes evocative because it is inadequate, and suggestive because it is insufficient.[4]

According to Suzuki, however, "Zen diverges from Existentialism in this: There are various brands of existentialism but they seem to agree that the sea of possibilities opening ahead is frightening. They mean freedom and unlimited freedom means unbearable responsibility. To these thoughts, Zen is a stranger, because for Zen the finite is infinite, time is eternity, man is not separated from God. Furthermore, Zen does not find anything frightening in infinite possibilities, unlimited freedom, never-ending responsibilities. Zen moves along with infinite possibilities; Zen enjoys unlimited freedom, because Zen is freedom itself; however unending and unbearable responsibility may be, Zen bears it as if not bearing it at all. In Christian terminology, this means that my responsibility is shifted to God's shoulder, that 'not my will, but thy will be done,'

and this is Zen's attitude toward world responsibilities. ...
Kierkegaard was somewhat neurotic and morbid when he
dilated on fear: He was obsessed with the feeling because
he had an abnormal sense of his separation from God which
prevented a full understanding of the meaning of the freedom which issues from the experience of tathata. The
existentialist generally interprets freedom on the plane of
relativity where there is no freedom in its highest sense.
Freedom can be predicated only of tathata and its experience. The existentialist looks into the abyss of tathata
and trembles, and is seized with inexpressible fear. Zen
would tell him: why not plunge right into the abyss and
see what is there?"[5]

Suzuki is wrong at least in two points. First, he only
made comparison with some brands of existentialism but
did not grasp its entirety. Second, he failed to distinguish
between unauthentic existence and authentic existence. In
other words, he did not grasp the kernel of existentialism.
So in his same essay, Dr. Suzuki concedes that "there is
something in the theory of Zen that may pass into a form
of existentialism."[6] Thus, although we do not attempt to
identify Zen with existentialism, as a movement, we may
at least say that Zen is the most radical and ruthless form
of existentialism.

II. THE WITNESS OF HEIDEGGER

To support this view, we may use the witness of
Martin Heidegger, an eminent German existentialist, who
once said to his friend when he was found reading one of
Suzuki's books: "If I understand this man correctly, this
is what I have been trying to say in all my writings."
Certainly we do not deny that "Heidegger's philosophy in
its tone and temper and sources is Western to its core, and
there is much in him that is not Zen, but also very much
more in Zen that is not in Heidegger; and yet the points of
correspondence between the two, despite their disparate
sources, are startling enough... At least, he has come
pretty close to Zen."[7] As Stefan Schimanski reported after

he visited Heidegger in June 1946 and in October 1947, "Heidegger lived on top of a mountain, with a valley deep down below, with nothing but space and wilderness all around in a small skiing hut. His living conditions were primitive; his books were few; and his only relationship to the world was a stack of writing paper. He wanted nothing but to be left in peace to cover those white sheets with his writings. The atmosphere of silence all around provided a faithful setting for Heidegger's philosophy. In him, it was spirit of overwhelming solitude."[8] In this description we see a picture of Heidegger quite similar to that of a Zen monk.

According to Heidegger, Being remains as an immeasurable treasure buried in this devitalized world which is subordinated to the prosaic technological order. The homelessness and self-alienation of modern man, left to the mercy of all-denying nihilism, cannot be overcome otherwise than by his recuperating "genuine-selfhood" now rooted in what Heidegger defines as metaphysical nothingness susceptible of effacing the antinomy between the subjective and objective.[9] Heidegger makes an important distinction between unauthentic and authentic existence. The former is preoccupied with the externals of humanity and is the general attitude of the large masses of people who do not act freely and independently, and are resolved or absorbed in the world, and therefore have fallen from their "genuine selfhood." So to exist is to exceed oneself. Authentic existence is self-determination, self-projection, and self-transcendence. But unauthentic existence places its responsibility, freedom, and self-transcendence upon the shoulders of *Das Mann* of culture. And thus this fallen existence ends in slavery.

The cardinal question in the philosophy of Heidegger is: "How can man pass over from unauthentic existence to the mood of being of authentic existence?" His answer is that man is saved from unauthentic existence by *Angst* (anguish). It rises suddenly out of the depths of our existence and surprises us without any apparent reason. So 'Angst' is a powerful means of revelation which can bring about a great change in human existence, and reveals the world and existential existence to us. When *Angst* enters our life, the delusion of unauthentic existence is broken through. Our conscience is awakened by this *Angst*. It calls us out of the apostacy of unauthentic existence and causes us to return to authentic existence. The authentic man is conscious of the vanity of existence and freely accepts death which is the greatest potentiality of existence. He says that death does not come at the end of life, it is present in every act of life, in the every act of my living. Living authentically is living constantly in its presence. Death threatens only the empirical existence, but has no grip over transcendental existence. In true wisdom, we accept the fact we are not at home in the world and accept our existence in absolute solitude. The authentic man understands the "call of conscience" which calls him to accept nothingness and the meaninglessness of life.[10]

Heidegger thinks that man should "run forward (vorlaufen)" to his death, thoroughly acknowledge it as our own, come to terms with it and cultivate it. For it is death that gives life its wholeness, its completeness. As I now anticipate death I become free from it and life becomes authentic, real. Man need not be overcome by his death haunted existence but by accepting it he can become its master. Thus it is possible for man to be authentic. For Heidegger, the way to move into the sphere of authenticity is by the "call of conscience"; for Zen it is the full realization of Mind, the opening of the mental eye in order to look into the very reason of existence.[11]

In "What is Metaphysics?", an inaugural lecture given by Heidegger when he was appointed to the chair of philosophy as the successor to Edmund Husserl, there are also points of correspondence with Zen. He claims that the only thing that remains and overwhelms us while what-is slips away, is "Nothing." The essence of nothing as original nihilation lies in this: that it alone brings Da-sein face to face with what-is as such. Only on the basis of the original manifestness of nothing can our human Da-sein advance towards and enter into what-is. Projecting into Nothing, Da-sein is already beyond what-is-in-totality. This "being-beyond" what-is we call transcendence. Without the original manifest character of Nothing there is no selfhood or freedom. Nothing not merely provides the conceptional opposite of what-is but is also an original part of essence (Wesen). It is in the Being (Sein) of what-is that the nihilation of Nothing (Das Nichten des Nichts) occurs. The more we turn to what-is in our dealings, the less we allow it to slip away, and the more we turn aside from Nothing. But all the more certainly do we thrust ourselves into the open superficialities of existence. The permeation of Da-sein by nihilating modes of behavior points to the perpetual, ever-dissimulated manifestness of Nothing which only anguish reveals in all its originality. Anguish is there, but sleeping. All Da-sein quivers with its breathing: the pulsation is slightest in beings that are timorous and is imperceptible in the "yea, yea!" and "nay, nay" of busy people; it is readiest in the reserved and surest of all in the courageous. The original anguish can be awakened in Da-sein at any time. It need not be awakened by an unusual occurrence. (This corresponds to a popular saying of Zen: "In carrying water and chopping wood, therein lies the wonderful Tao.") It is always on the brink, yet only seldom does it take the "leap." The anguish felt by the courageous cannot be contrasted with the joy or even the comfortable enjoyment of a peaceful life. It stands on the hither side of all such contrasts—in secret union with the serenity and gentleness of creative longing. Nothing now ceases to the vague opposite of what-is; it reveals itself as integral to the Being of what-is. Pure Being and pure Nothing are thus one and the same. Only because Nothing is revealed in the very basis of our Da-sein, is it possible for the utter strangeness of what-is to dawn on us. "Nothing," conceived as the pure "Other" than what-is, is "the veil of Being." To Zen "form is Void, Void is form," the ultimate of all things is emptiness. "Since all is void, originally there was Nothing" (Pen-lai-Wu-i-Wuh), this is the inmost essence of Zen teaching!

III. THE SHIFT OF MENTALITY

As we discussed in the preceding chapters, owing to the tragic failure of humanistic culture, the growing tension of the present age and the sweeping apostasy of modern man, our century has been witness to a profound shift of mood of mentality. The masses become disillusioned not only with former values and ideals, but even with Christian truth, and were therefore ready to listen to false prophets. The mentality of the Western world has moved toward the mood of the East. The philosophy of existentialism most clearly expresses this shift. The Existentialist movement represents a reaction in the trend of European thought. This is essentially a protest of human nature against the idea of objective order which dominated Western philosophy especially since the time of the Renaissance. It is a turning inward.[12]

Zen purposes to discipline the mind itself, to make it its own master. It is defined as the "unity of man and universe," as the "rhythm of the mind with the changing forms," and as "a state of Oneness."[13] It strongly advocates such doctrines as non-discrimination, non-differentiation and non-duality. They believe the tension of all opposites rises from the dichotomy of the mind. In order to be released from all pairs of opposites, one must transcend beyond Dharma and Adharma. As the Upanishads say: The "Other" is always the cause of fear; to comprehend the "Other" in the self ("other" is but the objectification of the self) is the ultimate wisdom of the highest joy. One scholar interpreted this statement as the true Existentialism which is expressed in the Mahavakya: Tat Tvam Asi, which means "that thou art" or "the other is yourself." "The Eternal is in oneself," "Thou art the Eternal."[14]

This urge towards "inwardness" marks all existential thought. It was Kierkegaard who envisaged most clearly that the very idea of order in the objective world, which had dominated European philosophy, was the source of the slavery of man. Kierkegaard strove to reverse the order and procedure for philosophy and thought, and thus shift the European speculative balance. In India, however, this turning inward has been the mainspring of all philosophy down through the ages. This process of turning was called Dhyana, (Ch'an-na in Chinese; or Zen in Japanese).[15]

In his forceful way, Kierkegaard stresses the opposition between the spiritual self and the limitations imposed upon it, whether externally in the name of institutions like the church and the state, or internally through the sway of philosophical systems or through the deadly routine of "dailiness." Thus he draws out the distinction between the "authentic" and "unauthentic" attitude of the existent.

Heidegger proceeds to extend the scope of the experience of self in space as well as in time. Man is not circumscribed by his immediate present, but he feels the call of the future with all its tragic urgency. The self is essentially a "project" which perpetually keeps its distance from the crude existence (Seiende) in which man may be thought of as an object. This is the region of the unauthentic life which may be compared with the Buddhist concept of Samsara, the tendency to be absorbed in the world of "dailiness." Heidegger calls it the world of the impersonal they-self, where knowledge is only a semblance of it (Abhasā), a standardized reflection (Avidya). According to Gabriel Marcel, this world is completely dominated by "function" which in Buddhist terms is Karma, in which man has lost his feeling for the mystery of being, the world brought under the fictitious category of the "purely natural" so dear to empiricists. It is also the world of the "Other" which haunts the imagination of Jean Paul Sartre like a nightmare, contact with which repels him violently and gives him nausea,[16] the ontological horror experienced as the result of contact with what is variously dubbed "the past," "other people" and "the world." This idea of unclean attachment strongly reminds one of the Indian concept of lepa or kasāya. Authentic existence is freedom from such attachment.[17] This is what Zen called Satori (Enlightenment).

Another feature that demands our attention is what we may call the initial pessimism, the stress on anguish, forlornness, and despair. Kierkegaard thought in terms of anguish; and pointed out that man, enveloped in a "deadening wall" which is built around him by daily routine, becomes egocentric and looses his freedom; and the syncope of freedom leads to anguish. Heidegger resorted to anguish as a means of revelation which arises suddenly and can save man from unauthentic existence to authentic existence. And today Sartre is saying also: "Man is anguish." Indian thought abounds in so many parallels that whether in the Vedanta or in Buddhism or elsewhere, at every step we come across expressions of the misery of human existence and the awareness of this is the condition precedent to any spiritual realization.[18] For instance, according to the teaching of the First Noble Truth, i.e., "Dukkha," to live and to cling to life gives birth to discrimination and hence sorrow. In other words, unauthentic existence is reduced to suffering, because it is miserably subjected to an endless succession of sufferings occasioned by impermanence, transiency, and uncertainty inherent in all things. Thus human existence unavoidably involves birth, sickness, sorrow, grief, decay, precariousness, dotage and death.[19] Only by virtue of knowing this so-called noble truth, as they believe, one shall be able to arrive at the ultimate goal of his spiritual journey. This doctrine has its point of correspondence with Heidegger as he says: "Whoever despairs finds eternal man."

As all the existentialists, Martin Heidegger strongly remonstrates against the erroneous orientation of modern Western philosophy, since it incorrigibly tends to misconstrue one of the beings (das Seiende) as Being (das Sein) or Truth itself. He went so far even to claim that all the schools of Western philosophy beginning with Socrates and ending with Hegel should be brought to erasure, inasmuch as they were too preoccupied with the unilateral assertion of their narrow standpoints to be able to locate precisely where Being lurks.[20] According to the inmost essence of Zen teaching, the ultimate nature of all things is emptiness, because there is after all no form which one can say one has laid hands on. This unattainability of all things is Reality itself. The Unconsciousness is the ultimate Reality, the true form. "Since all is void, originally there was nothing" (Pen-Lai-Wu-i-Wuh).[21] According to Lao Tze, the everlasting Tao cannot be defined; the everlasting Name cannot be named. The origin of the Universe is the Unnameable—the Void. Therefore, the mystery can only be grasped through unconsciousness.[22] What strikes us in this connection is that Martin Heidegger insists on the synonymity of Being and Nothingness as productive of a mulitude of things. His metaphysical concept of Naught is none other than the renewal, in the Occident, of Tao, upon which all things depend for Existence.[23]

---

[1] Cf. Spier, *op. cit.*, p. xvii.
[2] Cf. Part One, chapter I, Sect. II, 2 of this volume.
[3] Cf. Part One, chapter I, Sect. IV, 1 of this volume.
[4] Cf. Norferto Bobbio: *The Philosophy of Decadentism—A Study in Existentialism*, pp. 15-20.
[5] Suzuki, *Zen Buddhism, Selected Writings*, pp. 265, 266.
[6] *Ibid.*, p. 260; and cf. Dr. Van Meter Ames, America, Existentialism and Zen, *Philosophy East and West* I, No. 1, April, 1951.
[7] Suzuki, *op. cit.*, Barrett's Introduction, pp. XI, XII.
[8] Martin Heidegger, *Existence and Being*— Schimanski's Foreward, pp. IX, X.
[9] Cf. Dr. Chikao Fujisawa, *op. cit.*, pp. 86, 87 64.
[10] Cf. Spier, *op. cit.*, pp. 28-36.
[11] Cf. Rodman Williams: *Contemporary Existentialism and Christian Faith*, pp. 81, 166, 174; also Part One Chapter One, II, 2, and Chapter Two I, of this volume.
[12] Cf. Martin Heidegger, *Existence and Being*, with an introduction and analysis by Werner Brock, pp. 325-360; Rodman Williams: *ibid.*, p. 111; Part One, Chap. Two, I, 6, 7 of this volume.
[13] Cf. Alan Watts, *Spirit of Zen*, p. 121.
[14] Cf. Dutt *op. cit.*, pp. 57, 62; also Radhakrishnan: *"East and West,"* p. 20,; also his *"Eastern Religions and Western Thought"* pp. 20-33, 97-102.

[15] *Ibid.*, pp. 65, 66.
[16] Cf. *La Nausée*, p. 25.
[17] Cf. Dutt, *op. cit.*, pp. 67, 70, 71.
[18] *Ibid.*, pp. 4, 80.
[19] Cf. Dr. Fujisawa, *op. cit.*, p. 73.
[20] Cf. *ibid.*, pp. 86, 87.
[21] Cf. Part One, chapter II, Sect. I, 6 of this volume.
[22] Cf. Tao-Te-Ching, chaper I.
[23] Cf. Dr. Fujisawa, *op. cit.*, p. 79; Tao-Te-Ching, chap. 40, 42.

CHAPTER TWO

THE FUTILITY OF PSEUDO RELIGION*

I. THE APPEALING FEATURES OF ZEN

But after all, what can Zen really offer to this troubled world? In order to be fair in my criticism, I should first of all concede that Zen is not without some appealing features. That is why people become easy prey to its plausible teachings.

1. It Opposes Rationalism and Humanism — First, according to Zen adherents, "Mere scholasticism or mere sacerdotalism... will never create a living faith. The intellect is useful in its place, but when it tries to cover the whole field of religion, it dries up the source of life... Zen transcends logic and overrides the tyranny and misrepresentation of ideas."[1] "Logical consistency is not final, there is a certain transcendental statement that cannot be attained by mere intellectual cleverness."[2] "While the majority of the people living in the West do not consciously feel as if they were living through a crisis of western culture,... there is an agreement at least among a number of critical observers, as to the existence and the nature of the crisis... Man has followed rationalism to the point where rationalism has transformed itself into utter irrationality. Since Descartes, man has increasingly split thought from effect."[3]

They point out again that "The present time is the age of humanism in which the human being is the scale of all things. Here his task is to liberate himself from various fetters or bondages. It is a modern characteristic, especially in the West, that man is the master of life... The humanism of the enlightenment in the eighteenth century liberated him from political and economic bondage to the ruling class... [But] humanism can't liberate man completely or satisfactorily."[4] In depicting the plight and predicament of modern man, Zenists seemingly have some penetrating insights. But since this movement is only a turning inward, it still remains ensnared in the very pit of humanism which they claim to oppose.

2. It teaches self-denial and "great death." According to its doctrines on Wu-chu (non-abiding) and Wu-nieng (no thought) "our individual consciousness, merged into the unconscious, must become like the body of a dead man." "Let your mind be like vacuity of space, like a chip of dead wood and a piece of stone, like cold ashes and burnt out coal." "The unconscious is to let 'Thy will be done,' and not to assert my own. All the doings and happenings, including thoughts and feelings, which I have or which come to me, are of the divine will as long as there are on my part no clingings, no hankerings, and my mind is wholly disconnected with things of the past, present and future."[5]

The great death is the ego dying to itself in its radical negativity. But they contend that: "In no sense is it a relative nihilistic destruction or expiration into a hollow void or nothingness; this abrupt uprooting and reversal is, rather, the break up and dissipation of the contradiction, of the abyss, of the *aporia*. The annulment and negation of ultimate negativity, is itself positive. The negative dissolution is at the same time a positive resolution. The ego negated as ego in the central contradiction of its ego-consciousness, attains through its negation, its resolution and fulfillment, positively and affirmatively. In dying to itself as ego, it is born and awakens to itself as self."[6]

In other words, the teaching of "great death" is rather to awaken the "inner life of man." Indeed, the characteristic of modern civilization, as the French philosopher Bernanos puts it, is "a universal conspiracy against the inner life of man." Or, in Kierkegaard's term, there is a deadening wall built up around modern man by daily routine, which is the "universe of the immediate neighborhood." Enveloped in this, man looses his freedom — a "persona" of his own, and becomes other-directed and subject to "conditioning techniques," mediocrity and conformity, and becomes easy prey of secular mass culture and totalitarianism. Moreover, the loss of freedom leads to anxiety. A completely self-centered individual, shut up within himself, is the truly demoniac. So paradoxically, as Kierkegaard holds, in order to maintain inwardness, one must first abandon pure inwardness. This is an existential dialectical movement through which self-denial is simultaneously self-election—choice of one's self as infinite and absolute and thus, we are told, attains eternal salvation.

However, the teachings of Zen on "great death" is inadequate. Although they claim that it has a positive and affirmative resolution of fulfilment, it is entirely different from the Biblical teachings, e.g. "Now if we be dead with Christ, we believe that we shall also live with Him..." (cf. Rom. 6:3-14); "I am crucified with Christ; nevertheness I live, yet not I, but Christ liveth in me" (Gal. 2:20). Only through such an identification with the crucified and risen Christ can man be really delivered from sin and self-centeredness and become "a new creature" (II Cor. 5:17) and "have life, and ....have it more abundantly" (John 10:10).

3. It casts some dim light on the way of life. Some Zen scholars often quote or employ Biblical phrases to illustrate their position or to express their aspiration about the way of life, although they frequently wrest the texts and pervert the truth; e.g., "It is at once the Life, the Truth and the Way."[7] "The Truth shall make you free."[8] "As if walking in 'the Garden of Eden'."[9] "He that loseth his life shall find it."[10] "Let thy will be done." "Take no thought for the morrow..."[11] "Before Abraham was, I am."[12] "Except a man be born again, he cannot see the

Kingdom of God." "Neither circumcision availeth anything nor uncircumcision, but a new creature." "Forget those things which are behind." "The Spirit of God dwelleth in us." "For us the body is one."[13]

These might well prove that "there exists in the human mind, and indeed by natural instinct, some sense of Deity. This we hold to be beyond dispute, since God Himself, to prevent any man from pretending ignorance, has endowed all men with some idea of a Godhead, the memory of which He constantly renews and occasionally enlarges that all to a man, being aware that there is God, that He is their Maker, may be condemned by their own conscience when they neither worship Him nor consecrate their lives to His service."[14] But on the other hand, the modern Zen writers have deliberately borrowed Biblical terminologies to express what they cannot communicate otherwise. In so doing, they are at least unconsciously admitting that the Christian truths are far more adequate than the messages of Zen, even though they so often distort these truths to meet their own ends.

Thus, while Zen is seemingly commendable in some features, with its plausible teachings, it is nevertheless objectionable by reason of its serious inadequacy and sheer futility. As John Calvin well said, "Bright as is the manifestation which God gives of Himself and His immortal kingdom in the mirror of His works, so great is our stupidity, so dull are we in regard to these bright manifestations that we derive no benefit from them."[15] Even though there is some truth in Zen, it is from general revelation which does not convey to man any absolutely reliable knowledge of God, nor acquaint man with the only way of salvation.[16] In this regard, we need further discussion.

II. THE SERIOUS INADEQUACY OF ZEN

1. It supersedes the doctrine of a real Creator. In the first place, Zen is a very peculiar and subtle form of Atheism. It denies the infinity and transcendence of a living personal God by identifying Him with nature. All visible

objects thus become but feeling modifications of self-existence, unconscious and impersonal essence, which may be called God, Nature, the Absolute, Oneness, Suchness, or Tathata, etc. It robs God of His sovereignty by denuding Him of His power of self-determination in relation to the world. God is reduced to the hidden ground. Since Zen does not affirm the existence of God, it is not only absolutely destitute of the special revelation of God in His word, but it is also alien to the God of revelation.

As they contend that they do not deny the existence of God, Zen is more plausible in its pretension, more fascinating to the imagination and less revolting to the reason than those colder and coarser theories which ascribe the origin of the world to the mere mechanical laws of matter and motion. Besides, as it adopts the very language of theism and even employs Bible verses, it may even generate a certain mystic piety. Moreover, their statements are embellished with the charms of seductive eloquence and become the formidable rival of present day Christian Theism. As Suzuki writes, "The highest thing is to be comprehended or intuited even prior to time. It is Godhead who is even before it became God and created the world." "In the beginning there is 'the Word,' but in the beginningless beginning, there is the Godhead who is nameless and no-word."[17] Dr. Suzuki's argument, as subtle and plausible as it appears, only exposes his lack of the knowledge both of the Bible and the original Greek language. "The first important word to consider is the verb 'was' in the first statement. This is in the imperfect tense. It is unfortunate that we do not have a true imperfect tense in English. . . .The Greek verb *een*, 'was,' holds the key to the understanding of John's statement. This is what we call the durative imperfect of the verb *eimi*, 'to be'. . . .It speaks of a time before the beginning of things. In other words, John tells us that this *Logos*, this Word, was in existence before the created world. Therefore, we would be fully justified in translating this first clause, 'Before there was a beginning, the Word had been.' " "If this *Logos*. . .did not exist before there was a finite beginning, then the whole foundation falls. The verb *een,* in the durative imperfect, takes the Word far back of the created world, farther than can be imagined by our finite minds. In it there is the concept of eternity. Eternty is timelessness. Yet God has to use human language to make us understand His thoughts. With God there is neither past, present, future; yet whatever He says to us has to be within the periphery of time. He has to give us a starting point, and that starting point He calls 'the beginning.' But we must remember that God Himself is not limited by the beginning."

The next Greek word that we ought to examine is *archee,* meaning beginning.' "An understanding of its full meaning will help us to determine whether Jesus Christ was merely a creature or the Creator. This is basic to the whole concept of the supernatural nature of Christianity and its consequent uniqueness." "In one Greek lexicon, we are given a total of eighteen meanings for this one Greek word, which in the King James Version, unfortunately, is almost uniformly translated 'beginning.' This has led to much confusion and misunderstanding." "This word is used both absolutely and relatively." "When used absolutely, it refers to 'the beginning, the origin of all things.' " "In the absolute sense, the word *archee,* 'beginning' can be either passive or active. When it is active, we have to take it as meaning 'the cause of all things.' " "In His high-priestly prayer, the Lord Jesus Christ Himself told us that He was before the beginning of the created world (John 17:5). There can be no doubt, therefore, that Jesus Christ was before the beginning of the world," and He was the Creator.[18]

Lacking this basic knowledge of the Bible, Alan Watts even has gone so far as to deny the difference between the Creator and the creature. He alleges that "the something awful that has gone wrong is the production of the original illusion in which the Creator seems to become the creature." "It is the flaming sword that turns in all directions and guards the way to return to Paradise, preventing us from daring to recognize, upon pain of the utmost blasphemy, that we are each the Lord in hiding. Before we can have the courage to attain the recognition, we must follow the difficult way of consciousness and the discipline of the Word to the point where the ego's pride in itself is entirely debunked . . . .Without this particular deflation of the ego, we might imagine ourselves to be one with a God."[19]

2. It engenders a spirit of mysticism. Secondly, it has a strong tendency to engender (although they deny it) a spirit of mysticism by taking refuge in its doctrines of radical intuition, i.e., "No dependence upon words and letters"; "Special transmission of the Mind"; "Seeing into one's own nature"; and in its revolt against reason; and, moreover, its favorable opinions of Meister Eckhart, a German mystic in the fourteenth century. As Suzuki writes, "To quote Meister Eckhart again, 'Simple people conceive that we are to see God as if He stood on that side and we on this. It is not so; God and I are one in the act of my perceiving Him.' In this absolute oneness of things, Zen establishes the foundations of its philosophy."[20] Again, Ogata in his *Zen for the West* says, "I see much common ground in Zen and the mysticism of Meister Eckhart, as he wrote, 'The eye by which I see God is the same eye by which God sees me. My eye and God's are one and the same—one in seeing, one in knowing and one in loving' . . . .When I have shut the doors of my five senses, earnestly desiring God, I find him in my soul as clearly and as joyful as he is in eternity. . . .Meditation, high thinking, and union with God, have drawn me to heaven."[21] Satori is almost entirely lacking in intellectual content and yet filled with intense emotion of conviction and the mystic returns from it with a sense of great illumination. "The source phenomenon is common among Christian mystics who frequently after ecstasy assert that they have had tremendous revelation, yet are unable to state explicitly any of them."[22]

Furthermore, mysticism without divine revelation is dangerous and will lead men to destruction. "All experience shows that without the written Word, men everywhere and in all ages, are ignorant of divine things—without God, without Christ, and without hope in the world. The sun is not more obviously the source of light than the Bible is the source of divine knowledge." "There is a sense in which the Spirit is given to every man. He is present with every human mind, exciting to good and restraining from evil. Without this common grace or general influence of the Spirit, there would be no difference between our world and hell." But, "the fact that the Spirit is present with every human mind and constantly enforces the truth to that mind, is no proof that He makes immediate supernatural revelations to every human being. The fact is, we cannot see without light. It is vain to say that every man has an inward light sufficient to guide him without the sun. Facts are against the theory." Moreover, "there is no criterion by which man can test these inward impulses or revelations and determine which are from the Spirit of God and which are from his own heart or from Satan who often appears and acts as an angel of light." "To tell men, therefore, to look within for an authoritative guide and to trust to their irresistible convictions, is to give them a guide which will lead them to destruction!"[23]

3. It disregards the holiness of God. Thirdly, Zen is a very radical form of iconoclasm. According to Prajna-paramita-hrdaya Sutra, "The void nature of all dharmas is not arising or extinction, not pure or impure, not increasing or decreasing. . . .If one understands that reality is neither pure nor impure, he finds the Buddha in the dung as well as in Heaven." In terms of "Prajna" and "sunyata" and "unconditioned Love" and "highest compassion," Zen admonishes one not only to love God but also to love "devils"; not only to love the Truth but also to love the "heresy"; "a clinging to the 'one true God,' the 'one true religion,' the 'one true principle,' " is condemned as "narrow limitation."[24] Thus Zen compromises the holiness of God in a very serious manner. In the conception of Zen-ists, sin against God does not exist. As they boldly declare that the "immaculate Yogins do not enter Nirvana and the

precept violating monks do not go to hell; to avoid sin and evil by obedience to any moral law is only an idle attempt. Every being must act according to the Nature." "There is no question and no need of rules of morality."[25] Our Lord says of men "By their fruits ye shall know them." The same rule of judgment applies to doctrines. Even they themselves do not deny that "immature disciples would make all-inclusiveness of Zen an excuse for pure libertinism."[26] As Dr. Karl L. Reichelt, an experienced missionary sympathetic to Buddhism observed, "as a general rule, those who have 'broken through' rise well above average, although they do not measure up to the truly Christian standard; but greed for power and honour is on the whole unshaken." "On the other hand, when this attainment of peace and enlightenment is obscured by a tragic process of self-concentration, some of these people develop very odd qualities. The Chinese have coined a humorous name for them and say that they have become "mo-wong, i.e., 'demon-king' which means they have become mentally deranged!"[27] Dr. Reichelt's statements were not only based upon his profound experiences with the Buddhists in the Far East, but can also be supported by the facts which are found in many ludicrous anecdotes and autobiographies of Zen Masters.[28] In the West, the movement of "Beatniks" (although they are very immature in their understanding of Zen), and their philosophy of "anti-organization-man-ism,"[29] is a symptom of its pernicious influences. Since Zen knows not the Kingdom of God, it will inevitably contribute to the moral confusion and degeneration of mankind if unchecked.[30]

The holiness of God is more seriously disparaged by an exponent of Zen in the West. Alan Watts says: "Explicitly (that is on the stage), the light and the dark are enemies, but implicitly (off stage), they are not only friends, not only twins, not only co-conspirators, but constitute a unity." "When the Lord and the Devil came out officially ...they are implacable foes; but may we not suppose that in the green room of heaven, before the show of creation began, there was an 'original agreement' "? "There was God the Father, with God the Son sitting at His right hand. No one ever mentioned who sits at His left hand"; but as Alan Watts presumptuously alleges "of course it was Lucifer Satan who is simply the agent of the Lord's wrath, His left, sinister, and inauspicious hand that does all the necessary dirty work." Since there was only "original agreement," and no "original sin," what has gone wrong is the "original illusion," and there was unity between the light and the darkness, no dichotomy between holiness and profanity.

So he suggests that "What if boys and girls are taught to perform intercourse in class just as they learn dancing? What if it were the rule to change partners each time to facilitate adaptability in sexual adjustment? What if such a program in sexual hygiene were held in a nudist camp, so that all the details of male and female bodies were as familiar as hands and feet?" He concludes: "Naturally, this would be the highway to clean, healthy, honest, open, free, guiltless and perfectly boring sexuality."[31]

It is indeed true, as the Bible says, since "they knew God, they did not honor Him as God" "therefore God gave them up in lusts of their hearts to impurity, to the dishonoring of their bodies among themselves, because they exchanged the truth about God for a lie. For this reason God gave them up to dishonorable passions." So "be not deceived; God is not mocked, for whatsoever a man sows, that shall he also reap. For he that sows to his flesh shall of flesh reap corruption; but he that sows to the Spirit shall of the Spirit reap life everlasting."[32]

4. It denies the need of a Saviour. Fourthly, Zen is a most radical form of auto-soterism. The principle of heathenism, as Herman Bavinck remarks, is negatively the denial of the true God and the gift of His grace; and positively, the notion that salvation can be secured by man's own power and wisdom.[33] In the sayings of Linchi, we read, "Smash whatever you come across. Smash Buddha, smash your parents, and relations. You will be in real

emancipation!"[34] In Zen, "there is no supernatural intervention, ways or refuges. We bear the whole responsibility for our actions and no Sage whosoever he be has the right to encroach on our free will. We are at the same time responsible for our slavery and our freedom; the chains of enslavement have been forged by ourselves, and only we can break them. Only ignorance, laziness, and cowardice can lead us to seek outside aid. One thing seems fundamentally necessary, 'To know ourselves.' If we attain the perfectly clear vision of what we are, we no longer need 'to go elsewhere.' The exterior ways become to us ways of perdition. Just as all men and women of all the people of the earth have said and will say at the moment of their Awakening, so do we say simply, 'I am the way.' "[35] Although they contend that this is not a proof of their pride, this teaching will surely result in self-deification which is the blasphemous characteristic and idolatrous fallacy of heathenism.

III. THE UTTER FAILURE OF ZEN

1. In "seeing into one's own nature." Certain of the philosophers have called man a microcosm, as being a rare specimen of divine power, wisdom and goodness and containing within himself wonders sufficient to occupy our minds. This is not altogether improper. For Paul, after reminding the Athenians that they "might feel after God and find him," immediately adds that "He is not far from everyone of us";[36] every man having within himself undoubted evidence of the heavenly grace by which "he lives and moves and has his being"![37] As Calvin observed: "It was not without reason that the ancient proverb so strongly recommended to men the knowledge of himself. For (if) it is deemed disgraceful to be ignorant of things pertaining to the business of life, much more disgraceful is self ignorance. But our wisdom, insofar as it ought to be deemed true and solid wisdom, consists almost entirely of two parts: the knowledge of God and of ourselves. On the other hand, it is evident that man never attains to a true

self-knowledge until he has previously contemplated the face of God and come down after such contemplation to look into himself. For, such is our innate pride, we always seem to ourselves just and upright, and wise and holy, until we are convinced, by clear evidence, of our injustice, vileness, folly and impurity."[38]

Therefore, self-knowledge is rather twofold: first to the condition in which we were at first created; and second, to our condition such as it began to be immediately after Adam's fall. Relating the first, "when reflecting on what God gave us at our creation and still continues graciously to give, we perceive how great the excellence of our nature would have been had its integrity remained; and, at the same time, remember that we have nothing of our own, but depend entirely on God." Secondly, "When viewing our miserable condition since Adam's fall, all confidence and boasting are overthrown, we blush for shame, and feel truly humble."[39]

Moreover, ever since Adam revolted from the fountain of righteouness, all the parts of the soul were possessed by the sin. For not only did the inferior appetites entice him, but abominable impiety seized upon the very citadel of the mind, and pride penetrated to his inmost heart. Accordingly, Paul enjoins not only that gross appetites be suppressed, but that we be renewed in the Spirit of our mind[40] as he elsewhere tells us to be transformed by the renewing of our mind.[41] The nature of man, in both parts of his soul, i.e., intellect and will, cannot be better ascertained than by attending to the epithets applied to him in Scripture. If he is fully depicted by the words of our Savior "That which is born of the flesh is flesh,"[42] he must be a very miserable creature. Everything which we have from nature is flesh. We have nothing of the Spirit except through regeneration. In no degree more lenient is the condemnation of the heart when it is described as "deceitful above all things, and desperately wicked."[43] In this single passage, as in a bright mirror, we may behold a complete image of our nature. In the writings of the Apostle Paul, in Romans

3:10-18, we see that human beings are not simply vicious by custom (or as some modern Zen scholars put it in terms of so-called "force of habit"),[44] but rather perpetually corrupted by nature, and are therefore all overwhelmed with the inevitable calamity and can be delivered from it only by the mercy of God.[45]

Since the whole human race has been undone in the person of Adam, and the excellence and dignity of our origin being so far from availing us that it rather turns to our great disgrace, it is vain to look for anything good in our nature. As Augustine well said, Why presume so much on the capacity of nature? It is wounded, maimed, vexed, lost. The thing wanted is genuine confession not false defense. "Except a man be born of water and of the Spirit, he cannot enter into the kingdom of God. That which is born of the flesh is flesh, and that which is born of the Spirit is Spirit."[46] Since there was life in Christ from the beginning that the whole world had lost, it is necessary to return to that fountain of life, and by believing in His name, become again the sons of God.[47] Therefore, it is rather necessary to destroy our former nature, instead of "seeing into one's own nature"; and to form in us anew the image of God which was sullied by the transgression of Adam.

2. In the attainment of Enlightenment. In I Corinthians 2:5, Paul well said that: "Your faith should not stand in the wisdom of man, but in the power of God." And further he said in Ephesians 4:17, 18 that: "Ye henceforth walk not as other gentiles walk in the vanity of their mind, having the understanding darkened, being alienated from the life of God through the ignorance that is in them because of the blindness of their heart." Dr. Abraham Kuyper interpreted this passage to the effect that the "vanity of the mind," the "having the understanding darkened" because of the ignorance that is in them, even precedes the "being alienated from life of God," because of the "blindness of their heart." In consequence of sin, there is really no one in a normal bodily and spiritual condition. All sorts of wrong and sickly commotions bestir themselves

in our body and work their effect in our spiritual dispositions. "Sin also works upon our consciousness through endless variety of moral motives. The injurious effect worked by sin also had immediate influences upon our nature. The fatal effect of sin also finds its deeper reason in the fact that the life harmony between us and the object has been disturbed."[48]

Calvin states: "Had Adam stood upright, the course of nature would have conducted us to know God. But in the present ruin of the human race, no one will now perceive God to be either a Father, or the Author of salvation, until Christ interpose to make our peace."[49] "When miserable men do seek after God instead of ascending higher than themselves, as they ought to do, they measure Him by their own carnal stupidity, and fly off to indulge their curiosity in vain speculation."[50] As Dr. Bavinck remarks, "Without special revelation, the religion of man and the philosophy of thinkers do not have a right knowledge of God, and hence no right knowledge of man and the world, and of sin and redemption."[51]

Zen asserts that without 'Satori' (Enlightenment), "Zen is a sealed book."[52] But the problem is that without special revelation, 'Satori' can never be real. This is not our prejudice against Zen, even a psychologist as sympathetic to Zen as Dr. Carl G. Jung shares the same opinion. He says, "We can never decide definitely whether a person is really enlightened, or whether he merely imgines it, we have no criterion of this." "Whether an enlightenment is called 'real' or 'imaginary' is quite immaterial. The man who has enlightenment or alleges that he has it, thinks in any case that he is enlightened. . . .Even if he were to lie, his lie would be a spiritual fact!"[53] And ironically, these words of Jung appeared in the Foreword of *An Introduction to Zen Buddhism* by Dr. Suzuki, often called "the greatest living authority" of Zen Buddhism.

It is true, in the writings of philosophers we meet occasionally with shrewd and apposite remarks on the nature of God though they invariably savor somewhat of giddy imagination. When John says, "The light shineth in darkness, and the darkness comprehended it not," he intimates that the human is indeed irradiated with a beam of divine light, so that it is never left utterly devoid of a small flame, or rather spark; and yet that "this light is so smothered by clouds of darkness that it cannot shine to any good effect." "For the flesh has no capacity for such sublime wisdom as to apprehend God and the things of God, unless illuminated by the Spirit." "Human nature possesses none of the gifts which the elect receive from their heavenly Father through the Spirit of regeneration."[54] For "with Thee is the fountain of life, in Thy light shall we see light."[55] But "the brightness of the Divine countenance which even an apostle declares to be inaccessible,[56] is a kind of labyrinth to us inextricable, if the Word does not serve us as a thread to guide our path";[57] "for the gate of life is closed against all until they have been regenerated."[58]

Although Zen attempts to open a "third eye,"[59] "the mental eye remains shut, until it is opened by the Lord." "He deems the grace of illumination not less necessary to the Mind than the light of the sun to the eye."[60] Due to the fact that "the god of this world hath blinded the minds of them which believe not,"[61] Zen is truly "a sealed book." Only our Lord the Saviour, "the Lion of the tribe of Juda, the Root of David, hath prevailed to open the book and loose the seven seals thereof." 'For [He] was slain, and hast redeemed us to God by [His] blood out of every kindred and tongue, and people and nation."[62] "The natural man receiveth not the things of the Spirit of God."[63] So it is foolish to attempt to convince unbelievers unless accompanied by the special revelation from the Father in heaven.[64] The things of the Spirit of God cannot be known to them except by faith. Justly does Augustine remind us as Calvin quoted that "every man who would have any understanding in such high matters must previously possess piety and mental peace."[65]

One afternoon, while I was writing this chapter, I walked to the beach near my residence and sat down on a bench to read. A drunkard asked me politely, "May I sit beside you?" After a while, taking a bottle of whiskey from his pocket, he asked again, "May I have a drink?" During the time he sat beside me he babbled unceasingly with himself. When I left, he said to me, as if with apology, "Did I bother you?" Judging from his courteous manner, it seems that he was a decent person; but the sad fact remained that he did not "know himself." On my way home, while I was pondering upon this person and pitying him because of his pathetic condition, a thought came to me that the position of this drunkard was the same as that of the Zen masters who are often called in China as "mo-wang" (demon-king). For, while they claim to have attained Satori (Enlightenment) or to have seen their own nature; and while they talk and write with the charms of seductive eloquence, they do not realize that they are shut up in the shadow of death and that they remain in their miserable condition of perdition.[66]

3. In the way of salvation. Can Zen offer the way of salvation? First of all, this question is related with the basic nature of "Satori" (Wu-Enlightenment). As Dr. Carl G. Jung, who is sympathetic to Zen, once observed, I treat Satori as a psychological problem. . . The imagination itself is a psychic occurrence and therefore, whether an 'Enlightenment' is called 'real' or 'imaginery' is quite immaterial. The man who has Enlightenment or alleges that he has it, thinks in any case that he is enlightened. . . The world of consciousness is inevitably a world full of restrictions of walls blocking the way. It is of necessity always one-sided, resulting from the essence of consciousness. . . Hence conciousness is always bound to the narrowest circle. The unconsciousness is an unglimpsable completeness of all subliminal psychic factors, a total exhibition of potential nature. . . A special training and an indefinitely long period of time is necessary to produce that maxim of tension which leads to the final break-through of unconcious contents into the conscious. . . The unconscious is the matrix of all metaphysical assertions of all mythology, all philoso-

phy. . . and all forms of life which are based upon psychological supposition. . . When after many years of the hardest practice and the most strenuous devastation of rational understanding, the Zen student receives an answer from Nature herself, everything that is said of Satori can be understood." [67]

Therefore, Satori always requires a certain amount of subconscious incubation. It is said that a merely chance occurrence—a sight, a sound—may bring it about. Often it is accompanied by intense emotional phenomena such as a trembling, a rash of tears or a cold sweat. A typical example was the experience of Pai-chang Huai-hai (724-814): "his master Matsu abruptly took hold of his nose, and gave it a twist. This made his back wet with cold perspiration. He was said to have 'Satori.' "[68] Another example was that of Yun-men (Ummon). When he was pushed out of the gate by his Master, one of his legs was caught and broken. It is said the intense pain resulting from this awakened him, and he had 'Satori.'[69] This evidently proved that Satori, as Dr. Carl G. Jung asserted, is a "psychological problem."

But a psychology which ignores the religious hierarchy of values is doomed to failure. It is true that a conflict of motives, conscious and unconscious, usually produces the discords in our mind. The aim of psychotherapy is to establish one dominating motive as overlord of the rest, so that the mind is no longer the prey of civil war but keeps the peace under a self-elected king. Zen also purports to discipline the mind and to make it its own master. This is why Zen has a peculiar fascination in the minds of the West, and why the service of the psychiatrist is becoming so much in demand in this world of tensions. But as Christ profoundly said, some new affection of expulsive power from on high must be instilled when the house of life is swept and garnished, lest the former occupant return with seven others worse than himself.[70]

The roots of our problem are not in the mind only, but in the spirit. In this world of chaos and tensions, fear and darkness have ominously increased; new fetters are everywhere enchaining the mind and enslaving the spirit. Our hope is only in One Great Physician, in One Great Psychiatrist. Only His work and power can set us on safe ground, can fully answer the restless strings of our psyche and heal the disorder which results therefrom.[71]

Secondly, according to Linchi (Renzai), Zen is no other than the Mind. Zen is known as 'Hsin-tsung,' the discipline of mind; and Koan exercise is devised to concentrate the mind and to stimulate the will, as stated in previous sections. Thus "Zen demands will power" as Jung asserted.[72] But Zen is altogether ignorant of the serious fact that without the Spirit, the will of man is not free. This is why Augustine does not hesitate to call the "will" a slave. He elsewhere admits that inasmuch as the will of man is subject to lusts which chain and master it, our will can never be free, without the power of the Holy Spirit. He further admits that nature began to want liberty the moment the will was vanquished by the revolt into which it fell. Again, that free will, having been made a captive, can do nothing in the way of righteousness. Again, that no will is free which has not been made so by divine grace. Man at his creation received a great degree of free will, but lost it by sinning![73]

Thirdly, Satori is not regeneration, not conversion. Dr. Karl L. Reichelt asserts, "the attainment of cosmic consciousness (Satori) does not touch the deepest levels of human life. It does not generally reach down to the depths of conscience in its relation to God. Although a cosmic awakening may bring a certain clarity and peace of mind to a man; the life of faith has not been kindled at all, because the object of faith is vague and unhistorical, it is all veiled in the mist of pantheism."[74] Moreover, since Zen is a revolt against any authority and does not affirm the existence of God nor the need of a Saviour, it has no object of faith. Its purposes is to discipline the mind and make it its own master, through seeing into one's own nature. Although Zenists claim "there are certain similarities between 'Satori' and the sudden conversion of Christianity,"[75] in actual fact there is no ground for comparison. This can be shown by their own words, as they say, "conversion is held to come to essentially depraved man from an external God, while Satori is the realization of one's own inmost nature... In Zen, there is no dualism of heaven and earth, natural and supernatural, man and God, material and Spiritual, mortal or immortal; for... Avidya (Ignorance) and Bodhi (Enlightenment) are the same. It is one's own spiritual realization that makes the difference and the mind is its own place, and of itself can make a heaven of hell, a hell of heaven."[76]

Fourthly, as Zen is defined as the "unity of man and the universe," as the "rhythm of the mind with the changing forms," and as "a state of One-ness;"[77] Zenists strongly advocate such doctrines as non-duality, non-discrimination, and non-differentiation. Thus, they even blame God that "the real human tragedy began when nature was to be dominated by man (cf. Gen. 1:28) for when the idea of power, which is domination, comes in, all kinds of struggles arise."[78] However, they have distorted the Biblical truth as they ignore the gravest factor in the history of mankind, i.e., the fall of Adam, by which the ground is cursed and our sorrows are multiplied,[79] and "the whole world lieth in wickedness,"[80] and the "whole creation groaneth and travaileth in pain together until now." [81]

It is true, Adam's spiritual life was originally united and bound to his Maker; it was only his estrangement from Him and his revolt against Him, that perverted the whole order of nature in heaven and earth and deteriorated his race.[82] In the orthodox faith, "it is not admitted that there is anything naturally bad throughout the universe; the depravity and wickedness and sins thence resulting, being not from nature, but from the corruption of nature; nor, at first, did anything whatever exist that did not exhibit some manifestation of the divine wisdom and justice."[83] Zen masters, as other "philosophers, only tell us to live in harmony with nature; but the Bible derives its exhortations from the true source, and only enjoins us to regulate our lives with a view to God its Author to whom it belongs."[84] Since we are all sinners and rebellious, since there is a perpetual and irreconcilable repugnance between righteousness and iniquity, the wrath of God abideth always on us and His hand is raised for our destruction. It is therefore futile to talk about "the unity of man and the universe," or "the rhythm of the mind with the changing forms," or "state of Oneness," or to break through the "iron wall." "It is only by means of the expiation set forth in the death of Christ, that all ground of offense may be removed and all the evil that is in us may be abolished so that we may have the hope of having God completely placable and propitious to us and that we, formerly impure and unclean, by the grace of our Lord the Saviour may appear in His sight just and holy."[85] We are reconciled to God by the death of His Son, our Redeemer, "who hath made both one and hath broken down the middle wall (the "iron wall" in Zen) of partition between us by His precious blood.[86]

Fifthly, salvation is the plan of God before the foundation of the world, not a system of any philosophy or religion. It is the wisdom of God not the wisdom of man. The work of philosophers "under the influence of ambition, may serve to display their genius";[87] but in the end only prove to be vanity. "To be the Redeemer, He must be both God and man; to be a Mediator between God and man, He must have the union of a twofold nature." "Since as God only, He could not suffer; and as man only, could not overcome death; He united the human nature with the divine, that He might subject the weakness of the one to death as an expiation of sin, and by the power of the other, maintaining a struggle with death, might gain us the victory."[88] (For "no man hath ascended up to heaven, but He that came down from heaven, even the Son of man, which is in heaven.") "Our Redeemer should be truly God and man. It was His to swallow up death: Who but Life could do so? It was His to conquer sin: Who could do so save Righteousness itself? It was His to put to flight the powers of the air and the world: Who could do so but the mighty Power superior to both? But who possesses Life, Righteousness and the dominion and government of heaven, but God alone? Therefore, God, in His infinite mercy, having determined to redeem us, became Himself our Redeemer in the power of His only begotten Son. The whole Scripture proclaims that He was clothed with flesh in order to become a Redeemer. That He might renew a fallen world and succour lost man!"[89]

IV. CONCLUSION

From the foregoing discussions, it is evident that Zen attracts people by its specious arguments, but offers no truth. It is the delusion of "blind guides,"[90] but is not the true way. It casts some dim light, but does not give the true light, nor the life, "the life (that) was the light of man."[91] The whole creation groans and travails in pain, searches and probes in darkness. Yet man comprehended not the light which is come into the world and shines in darkness; they loved the darkness rather than the light and thus became easy preys of the false prophets.

Zen is objectionable not only because it is inadequate in its teachings but also futile in its effects. Zen is inadequate, because (1) it denies the infinity and transcendence of a living and personal God by identifying Him with nature. It is in fact a very subtle form of Atheism, disguised by the language of theism, and embellished with seductive eloquence. (2) It engenders a spirit of mysticism by taking refuge in its doctrine of radical intuition by looking into one's own nature. But to look "within" for an authoritative guide without divine revelation will surely fall into the delusion of Satan.[92] The present movement of LSD mysticism in America has led many to suicide and caused serious psycho-social deterioration which we have discussed in other parts of this volume. (3) It denies the need of external rules of morality. This will inevitably plunge mankind into pure anarchic relativism. (4) It rejects the grace of God and the need of a Saviour by exalting and deifying man. This will surely lead the world to eternal perdition because "the whole godless world lies in the power of the evil one." Indeed, it is "a way which seems right unto a man, but the end thereof are the ways of death!"[93]

So Zen is futile: (1) In its endeavors to "see one's own nature." But man can never really know himself before he has first the true knowledge of God, the Father of lights. Furthermore, in the present ruin of the human race, it is useless to glorify one's corrupted nature but rather imperative to form in us anew the image of God which was sullied as result of the Fall. (2) In its attainment of so-called "Satori" (Enlightenment). Because of the injurious and fatal effect of Sin, no one is in a normal condition bodily and spiritually. Although Zen attempts to open a so-called "Third-eye," the spiritual eye really remains shut.[94] Without divine revelation, "Satori" (Enlightenment) can never be real or certain.[95] (3) In this world of tensions and chaos, fear and darkness have ominously increased, new fetters are everywhere enchanting the mind and enslaving the soul, man needs an answer for his restless heart and healing for his disorders which results therefrom. However, what Zen could offer is only a sense of false security. Though it claims to give unlimited freedom of thought and imagination, that freedom is like a prison cell without a roof. His thought may be free, but his situation remains the same; he is still deep in the bottom of the cell, and finds no way out.[96] For their "existential leap" is utterly futile and can never lift them to heaven out of that deep prison cell, for the gate of heaven is closed to all until they have been regenerated;[97] for "no one has ascended up to heaven, but He (Jesus Christ) that came down from heaven even the Son of man which is in heaven."[98] So only Jesus Christ is our Saviour. Thus, Zen is futile in its way of salvation.

THE FUTILITY OF PSEUDO RELIGION

In a word, Zen is not only Biblically and theologically untenable, but also psychologically and socially detrimental. As we pointed out in another chapter, Zen is a technique by which to achieve "a mental breakdown." It is "a bankruptcy of thought process'" or "mental catastrophe." Therefore, Zen is identified by some scholars as "mind-murder" and "the emptiness of idle reverie."[99] It is a cult of iconoclasm, a disastrous surrender to Nihilism. Zen has been exaggerated as "the way of liberation," but it is rather a kind of mystical "self-intoxication,"[100] "a childish dependence upon magical omnipotence," a ridiculous substitution of "firecracker-propelled garbage cans for space rockets." In Japan, it was "condemned by other sects as dangerous to culture because of its iconoclastic teachings." While it had been used by Japanese militarists as an incentive for aggressive war,[101] it is entirely "impotent to do something tangible to aid suffering humanity, judging by the cities and slums and rural misery of Asia."[102] Now many Westerners, weary of their conventional religion and philosophy, find some charm in Zen and have become prey to its plausible teachings. If unchecked, the consequences will be surely disastrous to our culture. This is the crisis of modern man which we have discussed in length in part II of this book.

---

* The excerpt of this chapter has first appeared in *The Challenge of the Cults*. A *Christianity Today* symposium, published by Zondervan, 1961, used by permission.

[1] Suzuki, *Slected writings*. pp. 111, 112, 114.

[2] Suzuki, *Introduction to Zen Buddhism*, p. 67.

[3] Fromm, et al. *Zen Buddhism and Psychoanalysis*, p. 78, 79; and Fromm, *Psychoanalysis and Religion*, pp. 6, 7.

[4] Ogata, *Zen for the West*, pp. 16, 17 .

[5] Suzuki, *Selected Writings*. pp. 197, 198, 200.

[6] Demartino, et al., *Zen Buddhism and Psychoanalysis*, p. 167.

[7] Humphreys, *Zen Buddhism*, p. 1.

[8] Fromm, *Psychoanalysis and Religion*, pp. 6, 7.

[9] Suzuki, *Introduction to Zen Buddhism*, p. 45.

[10] Watts, *Spirit of Zen*, p. 60.

[11] Suzuki, *Selected Writings*, p. 200.

[12] *Ibid.*, p. 239.
[13] Cf. Linssen, *Living Zen*, pp. 204-223; also R. H. Blyth: *Buddhism Sermons on Christian Texts*, Tokyo, 1952.
[14] Calvin, *Institutes* I, Chapter III, 1.
[15] *Ibid.*, I, Chap. V, 11.
[16] Cf. L. Berkhof, *Introductory Volume to Systematic Theology*. pp. 128-133.
[17] Suzuki, *Selected Writings*, pp. 245, 270.
[18] Spiros Zodhiates, *Was Christ God?, An Exposition of John 1:1-18 From The Original Greek Text.* pp. 42, 44, 45, 48, 49.
[19] Alan Watts, *Beyond Theology, The Art of Godmanship*, pp. 81, 82.
[20] Suzuki: *op. cit.*, p. 113.
[21] Ogata, *Zen for the West*, pp. 17-19, R. B. Blakney, Meister Eckhart—A modern translation, pp. 206, 252.
[22] Cf. Leuba, "Tendances Religieuses chez les mystiques Chretiens," *Revue Philosophique* LIV 480; cf. Pratt, *The Religious Consciousness*, Chap. XVIII.
[23] Charles Hodge, *Systematic Theology*, I. pp. 101, 102; Cf. also Introduction, section III of this volume.
[24] Cf. Chang, Chen-Chi: *The Practice of Zen*, pp. 130, 147, 148.
[25] Humphreys, *Zen Buddhism*, pp. 178, 179.
[26] Watts, *Spirit of Zen*, p. 61.
[27] Reichelt, *Meditation and Piety in the Far East*, pp. 14, 15. Dr. Reichelt the founder and leader of the Christian Mission to Buddhists, 1922-1952, was a noted non-Buddhist authority on Chinese Buddhism and one of the few gifted interpreters of the East to the West, who knew the mind of East Asia and had the respect of its religious leaders.
[28] Cf. Chang Chen-chi, *The Practice of Zen*, pp. 34, 40, 85-114.
[29] Cf. John Kerouac, *The Dharma Bums*.
[30] Cf. "Christ and the Beat Generation," *Christianity Today*. Vol. IV, No. 11, Feb. 1960, cf. also following chapters of this volume.
[31] Alan Watts: *Beyond Theology: The Art of Godmanship*, pp. 75, 76, 81, 188, 189.
[32] Cf. Romans 1:21, 24-26; Galatians, 6:7,8.
[33] Cf. Bavinck, *Gereformeerde Dogmatick* II, pp. 425, 426.
[34] *The Sayings of Master Linchi*, cf. Ogata, *Zen for the West*, p. 12.
[35] Linssen, *Living Zen*, pp. 73-75.
[36] Acts 17:27.
[37] Calvin, *Institutes* I, Chap. V, 3; Acts 17:28.
[38] *Ibid.*, I, Chap. I, 1, 2.
[39] *Ibid.*, II, Chap. I, 1: Chap. II.
[40] Cf. Ephesians 4:23.
[41] Cf. Romans 12:2.

THE FUTILITY OF PSEUDO RELIGION 149

[42] John 3:6.
[43] Jeremiah 17:9.
[44] Cf. Linssen, *Living Zen*, pp. 103-106.
[45] Cf. Calvin, *Institutes* II, Chap. III, 1, 2.
[46] John 3:5, 6.
[47] John 1:12, cf. Calvin, *ibid.*, II, Chap. VI, 1.
[48] Cf. Kuyper, *Principles of Sacred Theology*, pp. 114-119.
[49] Calvin, *Institutes*, I Chap. II, 2.
[50] *Ibid.*, I, Chap. IV, 1.
[51] Herman Bavinck, *Our Reasonable Faith*, pp. 260-264.
[52] Suzuki, *Selected Writings*, p. 135.
[53] Suzuki, *Introduction to Zen Buddhism*, Foreword, p. 15.
[54] Cf. Calvin, *Institutes* I, Chap. V, 14; VI, 1, XIV, 3; II, Chap. II, 12, 18, 19, 20.
[55] Psalm 36:9.
[56] I Timothy 6:16.
[57] Calvin, *ibid.*, I Chap. VI, 3.
[58] *Ibid.*, II, Chap. I, 6.
[59] Suzuki, *Selected Writings*, p. 3.
[60] Augustine, *De Peccat. Merit, et Remiss*, Lib. II, Chap. V.
[61] II Corinthians, 4:4.
[62] Revelations 5:1-9.
[63] I Corinthians, 2:14.
[64] Cf. Matthew 16:17.
[65] Cf. Calvin I, Chap. VIII, 13.
[66] Cf. Reichelt, *Meditation and Piety in the Far East*, pp. 14, 15; Chang Chen-chi, *The Practice of Zen*, pp. 34, 40, 85-114.
[67] Cf. Carl G. Jung, Foreword in Suzuki's *Introduction to Zen Buddhism*, pp. 15, 21-24.
[68] Cf. Suzuki, *Selected Writings*, p. 92.
[69] Cf. *ibid.*, p. 12.
[70] Cf. Murray, *An Introduction to a Christian Psychotherapy*, p. 12.
[71] Cf. *ibid.*, pp. 148, 270, 271.
[72] Carl Jung's Foreword in Suzuki's *Introduction to Zen Buddhism*, p. 29.
[73] This view was endorsed by Calvin. cf., *Institutes* II, Chap. II, 8.
[74] Reichelt, *Meditation and Piety in the Far East*, pp. 16, 17.
[75] Watts, *Spirit of Zen*, p. 76.
[76] *Ibid.*, pp. 79, 80.
[77] *Ibid.*, pp. 121.
[78] Suzuki, *Selected Writings*, pp. 232-234.
[79] Cf. Genesis 3:16-19.
[80] I John 5:19.
[81] Romans 8:20, 23.
[82] Cf, Calvin *Institutes* II, Chap. I, 5.

[83] Calvin, *Institutes* I, Chap. XIV, 3 and 16.
[84] *Ibid.*, II, chap. VI, 3.
[85] Cf. *ibid.*, II, chap. XVI, 2, 3.
[86] Cf. Romans 5:10, 11; Ephesians 2:13-16.
[87] Calvin, *Institutes* III, Chap. VI, 1.
[88] Calvin, *Institutes* II, Chap. XII, 2, 3, 4.
[89] *Ibid.*
[90] Matt. 23:16. In fact, Zen masters call themselves "the incompetent but blindly courageous leaders of the blind." See Humphreys' book *"Zen Comes West."* p. 17.
[91] John 1:4.
[92] Cf. Dr. Reichelt: *Meditation and Piety in the Far East* pp. 14, 15; and Chang Chen-chi: *The Practice of Zen* pp. 34. 40, 85-114.
[93] Proverbs 14:12; 16:25.
[94] Cf. II Cor. 4:4.
[95] Cf. Suzuki: *Introduction to Zen Buddhism*, p. 15.
[96] Cr. Surgit Singh: *Christology and Personality*, p. 166.
[97] Cf. Calvin *Institutes* II, chap. I, p. 3.
[98] John 3:13.
[99] Griffis: *Religions in Japan*, pp. 255.
[100] Reischauer: *Studies of Buddhism*, p. 118.
[101] Chikao Fujisawa: *Zen and Shinto*, p. 69; also cf. Harrison: *The Fighting Spirit of Japan*.
[102] Becker: *Zen: A Rational Critique*, pp. 14, 16, 17, 57, 81, 92.

CHAPTER THREE

A MOVEMENT TO ETERNAL DESTRUCTION

I. THE DISASTROUS SURRENDER TO NIHILISM

From our previous studies, we could point out that Zen is a very radical form of iconoclasm. In the first place, it is a revolt against reason.[1] We are told, "it is the most irrational and inconceivable thing of the world. Zen was not subject to logcal analysis or intellectual treatment."[2] In the second place, it is a revolt against authority. Zen purposes to discipline the mind to make it its own master by opening the "third eye" to look directly into one's own nature—the very reason of existence. Anything that has the semblance of an external authority is rejected by Zen. Absolute faith is placed in a man's own inner being. Mind is above all forms. For whatever authority there is in Zen, all comes from within. Zen wants to live from within; not to be bound by rules, but to create its own rules.[3] In Zen, the transcendence and holiness of a living God are altogether denied. Thus there is no question and no need of rules and morality.[4]

Such teaching was so pernicious as we pointed out that in China "some of these people develop very odd qualities ...and have become mentally deranged.[5] In the statement of Griffis, a well-known scholar in the religions of Japan, Zen is made to mean "mind-murder and the emptiness of idle reverie."[6] This view was endorsed by Reischauer as he asserted that Zen is "mystical self-intoxication."[7] These views were radically retorted as "superficial" by Suzuki and he subtly argued that "In point of fact, Zen has no 'mind' to murder; therefore there is no 'mind murdering' in Zen. Zen has again no 'self'. . .by which we may become intoxicated. . . .Nothing really exists throughout the triple world; where do you wish to see the mind? The four elements are all empty in their ultimate nature. . . .'Mind-murder,' and 'self-intoxication'? Forsooth! Zen has no time to bother itself with such criticism."[8]

We do not deny the so-called doctrine of "no-mind" of Zen,[9] nevertheless we should not ignore the facts that according to the teaching of Hui-Neng, their most celebrated master, and the founder of the "abrupt school," Zen is "the seeing into one's own nature and the nature is "mind"; and according to Linchi, great master of Zen, "Zen is no other than the mind." Zen is known as "Hsien-Tsung"—Mind Doctrine or the teaching of the Mind. It is the way of full realization of the Mind. Enlightenment is the complete unfolding of the "inner mind."[10] Suzuki also forgot that while he was arguing, he contradicted himself by writing in his same book, only two pages preceding his argument, these words: "Zen purposes to discipline the *mind* itself, to make it its own master, through an insight into its proper nature. This getting into the real nature of one's *own mind* is the fundamental object of Zen Buddhism."[11] If Suzuki insists on saying that Zen has no mind; then it simply proves that their 'mind' must have been murdered.

And, in the West, these "immature disciples make the all inclusiveness of Zen an excuse for pure libertinism."[12] The Beatnik movement and its philosophy of "anti-organization-man-ism" and its "Zen Lunatic way"[13] are surely its evil fruits. They are proud rebels. They consider themselves to be misunderstood geniuses. As *Life* magazine reported, they are "the hairiest, scawniest and most discontented human specimens of all times which have ever been produced." "They have raised their voices against virtually every aspect of the society: man, dad, politics, marriage, the savings bank, organized religion, and higher education. . . .Beats find society too hideous to contemplate and so withdraw from it. . . Most of the Beat's more outrageous attitudes were trumpeted long ago by nihilists. . . The Beat generation has attracted wide attention and is exerting astonishing influence. Beatdom is a product of post-war disillusionment and restlessness. They are reflections of the most curious men of influence the twentieth century has yet produced. They are antisocial to the point of neuroticism. In the United States there are few colleges without a cell of beared Beatniks, and fewer yet where some overtones of Beat philosophy have not crept into the minds of students." [14] *Time* magazine defined Beatniks as "oddballs who celebrate booze, dope, sex, and despair." Dr. Merril C. Tenny observed that "such an attitude is spiritual suicide. To look upon life as utterly meaningless is equivalent to repudiating God and resigning oneself to an everlasting emptiness. Culture, morality and faith alike perish in the blackness of this chaos."[15]

In correspondence with Zen, Existentialism is also a philosophy of reaction, a reaction against rationalism in all its forms. It is an irrational philosophy, based upon a faith in the autonomous sovereign person of man. It not only defies cosmic law, but defies a subject instead. This anti-rationalism permeates its subjectivism, its individualism, and its theory of nihilism.[16]

1. According to Kierkegaard, God is truth, but truth exists only for a believer who inwardly experiences the tension between himself and God. If an actually existing person is an unbeliever, then for him, God does not exist. God exists only in subjectivity. This results in the destruction of Christianity's objective historicity. In his vivid style, Kierkegaard describes two men in prayer. The one entertains a true conception of God, but because he prays in a false spirit, he is in truth praying to an idol. The other is actually in a heathen temple praying to idols, but since he prays with an infinite passion, he is in truth praying to God. For the truth lies in the inward "How," not in the external "What." This results in the destruction

of Christianity's objective historicity. If there is no objective truth, and if the "How" supersedes the "What," then how could truth be distinguished from fancy? Would not a suffering Satan be just as true as a suffering Saviour? Would not an inner infinite decisive appropriation of the devil be as praiseworthy as a decision for God? Would not an idol be as satisfactory as God?[17]

2. For Nietzsche, supermen repudiate conformity to any norm, except the norm "Be yourself"; each realizes his own unique self. The universe is a monster of energy, without beginning or end. This world is Will to Power and nothing else. The character of the world in process of becoming is not susceptible of intellectual formulation. If the world is such an evolutionary irrationalism, what hope is there of saying anything reasonable about it?[18] In fact he said that in the late 19th century nihilism is for the supreme values to be rendered worthless. He predicted nihilism could prevail during the 20th and 21st centuries.

3. According to Heidegger's pseudo-religious view of life, when man accepts his own "thrown-ness" (Gewartenheit), the fact that he is thrown into existence, then man becomes the ground of his own nullity. Human existence in the past, present, and future is saturated and permeated with nullity. The authentic man is conscious of the vanity of existence and accepts nothingness and the meaninglessness of life.[19]

4. Jean Paul Sartre developed a system of nihilistic anthropology. For Sartre, human existence is structurally determined as a failure. Man is a "passion inutile." He characterizes human subjectivity as nullity, nothingness. Man is always what he is not, and he is not what he is. Because of his absolute subjectivism, he does not have room in his thought for an authentic being-together. He says: "The essence of society is conflict and struggle. The freedom of other people is necessarily a threat to my own freedom. Then my neighbor is for me the devil, and life in social relations with others is similar to the fall of sin." His absolute subjectivism goes hand in hand with a com-

plete individualism, and the latter necessarily results in a rejection of all authority in social relationships and in principle ends in anarchism. Human life is made up of continual unrest, and is without hope and future.[20]

Now it is important to note the serious fallacy involved in this system of philosophy. First, "existentialism is a form of metaphysical pornography," as Guido de Ruggiero, the distinguished Italian philosopher and one of the most formidable critics of existentialism, pointed out. It is a thriller of morbid curiosity. Existentialists are like children playing in the mud without knowing that they are getting dirty. There is something in existentialism, which excites the pathological imagination. For the heavy, somnolent categories of philosophy, it substitutes new and imaginative symbols: "anguish," "the leap," "shipwreck," etc., which give to the happenings of our everyday world a turbid romantic sense at once attractive and repellent. Existence is never a predicate, always a subject; thus all differentiation is impossible and everything is flattened and levelled out.[21]

Secondly, the anti-rationalism of Existentialism is a reaction within the humanist outlook, an emphasis which is based upon the human ideal of the freedom of personality, and therefore defies the historical function of human nature. The Christian, however, rejects rationalism on grounds which are basically different in principle. Whoever rejects rationalism but makes another subject the measure of all norms for reality, remains ensnared within subjectivism and thereby robs God of the honor which only properly belongs to Him as the sole law-giver in His world. God posits His law for all creation, the basic religious law and moral laws. And the logical and analytical is also one of these modal cosmic aspects for which God posits His law. Everything which is made has its subject-function in dependence on the laws which proceed from God.[22] So a genuine rationalist must think in accordance with law. God is not only the Creator, but also our sovereign Ruler. This world has received from Him a definite form and stable order. This order is law. Where the support of the law and norm ceases, there reason becomes uncertain and gropes about in obscurity. God is actually the court which promulgates the law, beyond which man cannot discover any certainty: without that the vision of moral reason sinks to nothing, ethics are reduced to expediency because they are no longer supported by the consciousness of the sacred command "Thou shalt." [23] Thus in the final analysis, the anti-rationalism of existential philosophy is a radical subjectivism and consequently falls into the pitfalls of irrationalism. If human subjectivity is the only source of norm and being, then the being of the world must be normless and meaningless in principle; and chaos will be the polar counterpart of this exaltation of human nature.[24]

Thirdly, Existentialism is a form of reduction philosophy. It entirely rejects the light of Divine revelation and thus destroys the meaning of life. For, if the diversity of things and relationships are not seen in the place in which the Creator has placed them in the totality of His cosmos, the richness of the creation can no longer be approached. The existentialist sees all of reality in the false light of a portion of the cosmos and hence the meaning of life is darkened. The only path that is open is that which leads to a disastrous reduction and oversimplification. Moreover, in Existentialism, this reduction has assumed an alarming form since its advocates have withdrawn themselves from the Word of God; they will not hear the divine law, thus there is no room for any norms or ordinances which would dominate or rule human existence. Therefore, Existentialism has no room for the structures of human society nor for the religious root of society in the covenanted unity of mankind, whether in Adam or in Christ. It strives to attain a philosophical foundation of the idea of man as an absolute autonomous being whose existence is considered to be a law into itself, the creator of its own norms. And finally we must recall the fact that the humanist view of the autonomous and absolute freedom of man is undermined by a nihilist theory of man.[25]

Fourthly, it missed the mark and deviated from the path of the truth. About one hundred years ago, Alexander Vinet, the great Swiss thinker, a distinguished preacher, wrote in his *Vital Christianity* that all human thinking which ignores or does not know Christ is the endeavour of man to establish his own law. This is an impossible undertaking, because one's own creation never can be one's absolute authority. Developed to its last consequences, the autonomy of man must end in anarchy and lawlessness, because the only valid and indestructible law can be the Law from above and not from "within." Today this immanentist thinking with its ruthless logic has manfested its latent consequences in the form of Existentialism and in the impact of Zen on the West. It is a desparate endeavor to overcome relativism by self-made absolutism. However, after annihilating God, man, the inveterate god-maker, creates new gods or makes himself god. But, just because his gods are self-made, they are void and false.[26] For man was created in God's image, he is like God, but must always be different from God and always on a creaturely scale. Man can never in any sense outgrow his creaturehood. However, it has always been man's attempts to do without God in every respect. Man sought his ideal of truth, goodness, and beauty somewhere beyond God. He made himself the ultimate court of appeal in the matter of all interpretations. He refused to recognize God's authority and declared his autonomy as over against God.[27] But the tragedy is that we cannot even know ourselves in any true sense, unless we know God, the Father of lights.

Moreover, inasmuch as God created in accordance with His plan, that is, as God created us in accordance with His absolute rationality, so there must be a rational relationship between us and God. Christian epistemology believes in an ultimate rationalism.[28] "The fear of the Lord is the beginning of knowledge" (Prov. 1:7). There is only one order of knowledge. Since what God says is true, all that contradicts the Word of God must be at once excluded as false. The Word of God excludes all contrary errors because the Word of God is true.[29]

Here we notice two forms of knowledge: revealed knowledge and rational knowledge which are poles apart. These two forms of knowledge are as far from each other as heaven is from earth. A good Christian is not only humble, but proud—proud of the fact that he has received a gift of this revealing knowledge which many have been vainly seeking for centuries. Jesus Christ is not the enemy of reason, but only of the irrational arrogance of those who pride themselves on their intellect and of the irrational self-sufficiency of reason. The Augustine motto ("If you will not believe, you shall not understand") far from repudiating reason, suggests that the Christian is the only genuine rationalist. The reformers were not hostile to reason but only to self-sufficient autonomous reason.[30] "Reason is a genuine power in man—put there by God." Reason and faith are not necessarily repulsive to each other. We do not say that faith is the rational self-activity of man but that it is the logical grammatical understanding of that which is said; without this mental rational self-activity the Word of God cannot be understood; without it there is no faithfulness. In faith itself both revelation and reason meet.[32] In this respect, faith is only reason enlightened and rectified by the grace of God.[33] But faith is not something that man can "learn," it is the free gift of God.[34] Man as the creature of God, needs supernatural revelation; and man, because a sinner, needs supernatural redemptive revelation.[35] As Dr. Gordon H. Clark well suggested: "we neither abandon reason, nor use it unaided; but on pain of skepticism acknowledge a verbal, propositional revelation of fixed truth from God. Only by accepting rationally comprehensive information on God's authority can one hope to have a sound philosophy and a true religion."[36]

In short, the whole movement of Zen-Existentialism is a revolt against authority and reason and all religious conventialism. It is a very radical form of iconoclasm and becomes "the most irrational and inconceivable thing in the world," as Zen devotees have themselves recognized.[37] Although it can be conceded that this movement is not without commendable features, such as its attitude against shallow humanism and easy rationalism, its anti-rationalism is a reaction within the same framework of humanism. Thus it defies the historical function of human nature and exalts man himself as his own master. So far as each one makes himself his own master, "there is no need of rules of morality" as they assert.[38] Such philosophy of radical freedom and subjectivism which makes man autonomous from all objective forms and divine law and revelation, will surely lead mankind to an horrible chaotic and nihilistic darkness!

II. THE MAN'S AUTONOMY OVER AGAINST GOD

As pointed out in preceding chapters, Zen is a very peculiar and subtle form of Atheism. It denies the infinity and transcendence of a living personal God by identifying Him with nature. It robs God of His sovereignty by denuding Him of His power of self-determination in relation to the world. Although its adherents sometimes adopt the very language of theism and even resort to Biblical expressions to induce people, they never affirm the existence of God. Indeed, "When they knew God, they glorified him not as God, neither were thankful; but became vain in their imaginations and their foolish heart was darkened" (Rom. 1:21). Professing themselves to be wise, (they claim they have opened their "third eye," and consider themselves to be misunderstood geniuses) they blasphemously contend that "In the beginning there is the Word, but in the beginningless beginning there is the Godhead who is nameless and no-word." "It is Godhead who is, even before it became God and created the world."[39] They view reality as Tathata. A tree is not a tree until it is subsumed under the concept "tree." Tathata is what precedes this conceptualization; it is where we are even before we say it is or it is not; it is when God was still in a state of absolute self-contentment, when He had not yet conceived the idea or will to create, when He had not yet uttered His fiat "Let there be light."[40]

On the other hand, they not only deny the existence of a living personal God, but rather deify themselves by asserting blasphemously that "Before Abraham was I am";[41] and "I am the way."[42] They consider that a greater stumblingblock to the acceptance of Zen is the general belief in God. In the Western mind which for two thousand years has been rammed into the mould of Christian dogma, God is an "assumption" in every sense of the term. When a Western mind in fact breaks free from the dogma, there is a wonderful sense of freedom as if a burden is dropped or a fog clears away![43] We are told that "Zen practice has no use for God. Look to no person or Person or God for help. In the West it is necessary to remove the personal God-concept and all that implies of salvation by faith alone."[44]

While Zen is a subtle form of Atheism, there is also a tremendous cleft between Christianity and Existentialism, whether atheistic or theistic. It is a cleft between true religion and all forms of pseudo-religions, in which the secularized modern man of culture seeks his comfort. However, we must point out the apostate nature of Existentialism and its secularization of the Christian ideas of creation and freedom.

In the first place, man is held to be the creator of his own norms. Human existence is deified. Man is honored and exalted as the absolutely free being. There are no external laws to which he is bound. He can make of his life whatever he wills and is responsible only to himself, not to God.

In the second place, the Biblical motive of creation is secularized by ascribing the power of creation, which belongs to God alone, to human existence, the deified creature. And God's sovereign freedom which does everything according to the good pleasure of His will, is also ascribed to man, in the humanistic ideal of personality. All things proceed from man and exist for man;[45] this is diametrically opposed to the Bible truth we read in Romans 11:36, that "For of him, and through him and to him, are all things: to whom be glory for ever."

Although some existentialists speak of God, it is not the God of the Bible and Father of our Lord Jesus Christ, but only a philosophical god, a meaningless abstraction. This god is created in accordance with the example of human existence, a hidden god, who has not given unto us any revelation of himself. For instance, Karl Jaspers occupies an intermediary position between atheistic nihilism and Christianity. He believes in the "transcendent," a philosophical god. However, his god is not a sovereign God, not the Creator and Ruler of the universe. According to Jaspers, we are absolutely free and completely independent of Him. If the latter were to exercise any influence upon the life of the real existential man, this would be in conflict with man's autonomy.[46]

However, many other existentialists are convinced professors of Atheism which they propagate with all the vigor at their command. For instance, according to Heidegger, man in his authentic existence feels guilty if he is not self-sufficient and completely equal with God. He feels guilty because the words of Satan: "Ye shall be as gods" cannot be fully realized.[47]

Still worse is the position of Jean Paul Sartre, former student of Heidegger. He is the most radical atheist of this generation. His doctrine is built on the antithesis between what is called "en-soi" (the being in itself) and the "pour-soi" (the being for itself). This is the most extreme form of freedom the history of philosophy has ever presented. "Pour-soi" can never be identified with "en-soi." As "pour-soi," a being for himself, man cannot become an "en-soi," a self-sufficient being. Therefore, man must step outside of himself; he must transcend himself and become "en-soi." He is absolutely free. Human freedom has no limits. Freedom has no other limit except its own. The "pour-soi" tries continually to become "en-soi" and yet wants to remain "pour-soi." The ideal of the "pour-soi" is to be a "pour-soi" in "en-soi." This would be God.[48]

But creation is not self-sufficient. Nothing exists by itself and for itself. Everything exists in a coherence with other things. The creation does not contain any resting point in itself, but it points beyond itself towards the Creator. God is the giver of meaning. He alone is self-sufficient. God exists from Himself and for Himself. He alone is Supreme. "I am the First and the Last." Everything finds its destiny and goal in Him.[49] In fact, Sartre denies the Christian belief that God is the free all powerful Creator of all things, and by attributing creative power to man, he predicates to man this very idea of creation.

According to Sartre, man not only creates his own law, by his absolute power, but through his absolute free deeds, man is also the creator of the world. He says that we do not only believe that God does not exist, but we think that the problem is not one of His existence; it is necessary that man regain himself and persuade himself that nothing is able to save him from himself, even if there was a valid proof for the existence of God.[50] Nothing will be changed if God does not exist. We shall find ourselves with the same norms of honesty, progress, and humanism, and we shall have made God an outdated hypothesis which will peacefully die off by itself. He quotes with approval Dostoevsky's writing: "If God did not exist, everything would be possible." This is the charter of Existentialism! Indeed, everything is permissible if God does not exist.[51] The goal of man is to become self-sufficient. He must become his own foundation and rest in himself. Man must constitute himself as God and thus be his own highest good. Man is in his absolute freedom the creator and the foundation of all value in his life. If man is to gain his freedom and autonomy, the idea of God cannot be tolerated. Therefore, says Sartre, "human freedom requires the death of God!"[52]

Through the fall of mankind in Adam, sin has been most ruinous in the heart and mind of man. Apostate man, having drawn his heart from his Creator, is unwilling and unable to seek and set his affection on those "things which are above" (Col. 3:1, 2). Since non-Christian philosophy began by absolutizing and deifying some created aspect, it is implicitly blasphemous, especially since it seeks to honor and deify the sovereign man who always attempts to do everything without God. He wants to live within, puts absolute faith in his inner being, and disciplines his mind to be his own master. He makes himself a false measure of all truths. He believes salvation can be secured by man's own power and wisdom and denies the need of a Saviour and the gift of His grace. He refuses to recognize God's authority and declares his autonomy over against God's. According to the teaching of Zen, if one wants real emancipation, one should "smash whatever you come across!"[53] Such teaching easily coincides with the view of Sartre as mentioned above. But this is a great tragedy, for man is in fact destroying himself by trying to destroy God his Creator and Saviour.

As Dr. Suzuki, blasphemously writes, after quoting a passage from Genesis 6:5-7, "Is God now in earnest engaged in the gigantic task of effacing man from the earth? Apparently he is. If so, inasmuch as man is man, he must have a philosophy to cope with the situation. Can Zen offer this?"[54]

This will illustrate, the rebellious attitude of autonomous man: the manifestation of the "rage" of "the heathen," their imaginations of "vain things," to "break their bands asunder," "to take counsel against the Lord and against his anointed," "to cast away their cords,"[55] for Zen is known as "the way of liberation."[56] But Zen masters utterly ignore the serious fact of God's warning: "He that sitteth in the heavens shall laugh; the Lord shall have them in derision; then shall he speak unto them in his wrath and vex them in his sore displeasure;" and "When his wrath is kindled but a little," they shall surely perish forever!"[57]

"Our God is a consuming fire," though He is love.[58] "For if the message declared by angels was valid and every transgression and disobedience received a just retribution, how shall we escape, if we neglect so great salvation."[59] As Dr. Suzuki himself said: "in as much as man is man . . . ,"[60] but what is man? His days are only an handbreadth. His life is even a vapour that appears for a little time and then vanishes away. "And it is appointed unto men once to die, but after this the judgement."[61] Human philosophy, so far as it is after tradition of man and not after Christ, is nothing but "vain deceit" which only spoils mankind,[62] and can never "cope with the situation" and offer the way of salvation as Zen devotees imagined.

III. THE SWEEPING APOSTASY OF MODERN MAN

Since the world by the wisdom of man knew not God but rather revolts against God, today we are experiencing the constant impact of the ongoing forces of secularization which lead modern man to a mood of sweeping apostasy. Even so-called Christian nations are forsaking and revolting against God. We are told that man has "come of age," and no longer needs God, for "God hinders man's free development." Professing themselves to be wise, new "theologians" put themselves under the norm of their own imaginations and concoct a system from their own speculation, distort the Gospel to suit their own needs and manipulate it for their own purposes. They exalt themselves above the authority of the Scriptures and deify themselves as lords over His divine Word and revelation. The point of departure is total adaptation to a philosophical system in which the only valid reality is the "here and now." This purely immanentistic thought system discards every suggestion or thought of a metaphysical other world, any thought of transcendent reality. The result can be only a thoroughgoing transformation of the Gospel. One can no longer speak of God as some one above and beyond this world who in sovereign majesty and power can step into the world as Creator and Redeemer; and Jesus Christ can be honored only as a man, not as a world's Redeemer who died on the Cross for mankind, not as the risen Lord in whose life rests the basis of eternal hope.[63] These thinkers are giving too prominent a place to man; they are paying much attention to the dicta of modern man but little to the revelation of God. Man, instead of Christ, is thus given the preeminence in all things.[64] They even say that "to be a man is the whole definition of Christian."

Further they completely ignore God's saving activity in Christ. Men are not asked to repent and seek their salvation in what God has done for them in Christ. This in effect is a revival of Pelagianism which was condemned by the church in A.D. 418. John A. T. Robinson even says that: "the secret of our existence" is not a "recall to religion." It is to join those on the Emmaus Road who have no religion left. This statement appears to mean that Christians should no longer "teach all nations; baptizing them. . . .teaching them" whatsoever the Lord has commanded, but rather should surrender to this world and join those who have no religion.[65]

Indeed, the decay of the religious spirit, the loss of habits and attitudes of piety, the coming of secularity, the feeling that a world of universally accepted standards and values has gone and that we are living in a "post-Christian-age"—are some of the elements that have come to perplex all thinking Christians. The world intellectual climate is rapidly moving ever further away from the biblical view of God and man. In the West, a new unprecedented rejection of Christian ideas, attitudes, and conduct is evident in the culture at large. Former bastions of Protestant orthodoxy are succumbing to a deceptive secularism that contradicts the revealed words of Scripture and distorts the meaning of the Gospel.[66] The leading feature of our times is the establishment of a "Secular city" as the way of life for modern man. This is the background against which the "death-of-God theology" has arisen.[67]

These "theologians" teach that modern man has come of age, that he should "cast aside the crutches" so that "he can rise and walk."[68] We are told the freedom of man demands the death of God. But the truth is "when a man surrenders his ties to God, he does not become really free; rather he plunges all the more deeply into the grip of Satanic powers. He loses every moral norm, and creates his own rules for living, which are often his very undoing. Deification of power, of money, of material possessions, of sex, brings him not salvation but rather destruction. He falls prey to lusts, passions, and desire and becomes enmeshed in sins and guilt. Our so-called pluralistic society no longer has any determinative life core or centrality, it is subservient rather to the spirit of this world, the spirit that rules the sons of disobedience (Eph. 2:2).

While the world indeed mobilizes spiritual and moral forces in opposition, it cannot delay or vanquish the doom that has broken upon mankind in all areas of life.[69] Though modern man has made tremendous advances in the fields of science and technology, he has not been successful in other realms of life. He solves one problem only to discover that he has created seven new ones. He thinks he is progressing toward good but he finds he is progressing toward evil. He cracks the mysteries of nature, but learns that the victim of his discoveries is himself. Facing squarely this human dilemma, he becomes pessimistic and sinks into gloomy philosophy of meaninglessness and voidness, or escapes into a nightmare cult of decadence—indulging in eroticism, barbituates, and LSD. And above all, the advance of the New Morality is surely a satanic design to "call evil good, and good evil,"[70] which will lead mankind to moral nihilism and swift destruction.

IV. THE URGENT MESSAGE FOR THIS GENERATION

Indeed, modern man is as a sheep without a shepherd, caught in the throes of anxiety and despair. He wanders aimlessly and becomes easy prey of the false prophets. "The great neurosis of our time in emptiness," as Carl Jung pointed out. Zen and Existentialism are but a sort of philosophy of meaninglessness and voidness, of nihility and frustration, they are abolutely devoid of any positive prospect or future. Their masters are "the incompetent but blindly courageous leaders of the blind" as a Zen master confessed in his own book.[71] Thus the whole movement of Zen-Existentialism if unchecked, will inevitably lead mankind "into the ditch."[72] At this juncture of history and in this generation of tension and despair, Christianity has an urgent message to preach. Jesus says: "I am the Way, the Truth and the life."[73] "I am the Light of the world."[74] This Gospel must be proclaimed in every sphere of life. Zen and Existentialism pretended that they have found an answer to the problems of modern man. We have a solemn task to perform in philosophy and must examine this answer and test it in the spirit of the time and in the light of Christ. We must have courage and wisdom to vindicate the truth and refute the falsity which can never give light but only adds to the darkness of a dawnless night.[75]

In the matter of the salvation of man, a line of division should be drawn between the naturalist and the supernaturalist approach—whether God has planned simply to leave men to save themselves; or whether He has planned Himself to intervene to save His creations. The issue is eminently simple but absolute: Does man save himself or does God save him? The former is the doctrine of universal heathenism and the latter is the message of Christianity.[76] The principle of heathenism, remarks Dr. Herman Bavinck is negatively the denial of the true God and the gift of His grace, and positively the notion that salvation can be secured by man's own power and wisdom. All pseudo-religions are autosoteric. And philosophy has made no advance upon this. Even Kant and Schopenhauer, who with their eye on the inborn sinfulness of man recognize the necessity of a regeneration, but come in the end to an appeal to the will, to the wisdom and power of man.[77] But, unfortunately, as William Temple pointed out: "The disease is in the will. How can the diseased will provide the cure? The seat of problem is our will." He therefore cried out: "We could be good, if we would, but we won't, and we cannot begin to will it. Who shall deliver me from the body of this death. I thank God through Jesus Christ our Lord. If I am to be changed, something must lay hold of me and change me."[78]

Among all the mistakes of non-Christian thinkers, the fatal one is their ignorance or denial of sin, the dominant factor in human lives. Originally, man was under the stimulation and control of God. He knew no pain, anxiety, depression, fear, hatred or anger. His mind was at ease, his soul at peace, because he was in perfect harmony and accord with God. But sin entered into the world like an atom-blast which shook all of creation. Sin exploded in the mind and heart of man and left a huge gulf between God and man. Adam changed masters, and henceforth he was to be dominated and controlled by Satan, and in the darkness he learned the meaning of fear, torment, guilt, remorse and despair. The Bible also tells us that sin is the factor in our lives that causes us to run from God. In the book of Genesis, we learn Cain killed his brother Abel in a fit of jealousy and went out from the presence of the Lord. Biblical history is an account of man out of touch with God. Since Cain, history is a record of murder, jealousy, hatred, violence, idolatry, and immorality. As sociologist Sorokin pointed out, every page of human history bears witness to wars. From 500 B.C. to 20th century, there were 967 international wars and 1623 important civil wars. In the course of human history, several thousand revolutions have been launched, but none of them has ever acheived its purpose either "to establish a paradise on earth" or "to end war." From this viewpoint, the history of human progress is indeed a history of incurable human stupidity.[79]

While sin has done its work in separating man from God, God's ultimate purpose and plan was to bring the mind and heart of man back under His control. "God is not far from every one of us" (Acts 17:27). Only our iniquities have separated us from Him, our sins have hid His face from us (cf. Isaiah 59:1). This gulf must be bridged. So in the fulness of time, His consummate plan of redemption was carried out at Calvary. God has reconciled us to Himself by Jesus Christ (II Cor. 5:18); and "slain the enmity" by the cross (cf. Eph. 2:16); and by the blood of Jesus, we have boldness to enter into the holiest (cf. Heb. 10:19, 20).

Over against this, Satan has devised a network of many avenues of pseudo-escape. Especially is this true for modern men, who professing themselves to be wise, and being darkened in their foolish hearts (cf. Rom. 1:21, 22), yield to the temptation of Satan and receive not the truth that they might be saved, but choose rather to believe a lie. Never has a generation possessed as many counterfeit means and ways of escape as we have in our day. But the Bible warns us: "Wide is the gate, and broad is the way, that leads to destruction" (Matt. 7:13).

Modern man is restless. He experiences anguish and seeks every road of escape. He denies the true God and the need of His saving grace. With the impact of Zen on the West and the enchantment of Existentialism in this century, autosoterism has reached its most subtle and radical form. The emphasis is on the autonomy of man, and some even demand "the death of God"! Among the most popular books being sold today are those designed to restore man's lost confidence in himself. "Have faith in yourself," psychiatrists counsel this egocentric generation. "Belief in yourself," is the message of many a modern pulpit. But a drowning man going down for the third time does not need faith in himself; he needs a lifesaver, a Saviour! A condemned man walking the last short distance to the electric chair does not need faith in himself; he needs forgiveness. A man lost in the tropical jungle does not need faith in himself; he needs to know the way out! We need an awareness of man's total inadequacy to save himself... What the Bible speaks of is "Christ in you, the hope of glory." It is the Lord Jesus living in redeemed, transformed, born-again men, that is the hope of this perverted and depraved world.[80] This is the only message that we can preach with great confidence and vigor, which will save this world from eternal destruction. And it is an urgent task now, for modern man has gone too far down the road of destruction as a result of his arrogance.

---

[1] Cf. Alan Watts, *The Way of Liberation in Zen Buddhism*, pp. 28, 38.
[2] Suzuki, *Selected Writings*, pp. 3-13.
[3] Cf. Suzuki, *Introduction to Zen Buddhism*, pp. 40, 44, 45, 64.
[4] Cf. Humphreys, *Zen Buddhism*, pp. 178, 179.
[5] Reichelt, *Meditation and Piety in the Far East*, pp. 14, 15.
[6] *Religions in Japan*, p. 255.
[7] *Studies of Buddhism*, p. 118.
[8] Suzuki, *Introduction to Zen Buddhism*, pp. 42, 43.
[9] Cf., Suzuki, *The Zen Doctrine of No-Mind*.
[10] Chang, chen-chi, *The Practice of Zen*, p. 25.
[11] Suzuki, *op. cit.*, p. 40.
[12] Alan Watts, *Spirit of Zen*, p. 61.
[13] Cf. John Kerouac, *The Dharma Bums*—The author is known as "The Zen Loving Model."
[14] Cf. "The Only Rebellion Around," *Life*, November 30, 1959; or "Life Among the Beatniks," *Readers' Digest*, April 1960.
[15] Cf. "Christ and the Beat Generation," *Christianity Today*, Vol. IV, no. 11, February 1960.
[16] Cf. Zuidema, *Karakter Von de Modern Existentiephilosophie*, p. 10ff. and Spier, *op. cit.*, pp. 103-105.
[17] Cf. Clark, *op cit.*, pp. 485-491.
[18] Cf. *ibid.*, pp. 492-498; also Part Two, Chap. Two, Sect. II, 2 of this volume.
[19] Cf. Spier, *op. cit.*, pp. 34-36; Martin Heidegger, *Existence and Being*, pp. 36, 37.
[20] Cf. Sartre, *L'Etre et Le Neant;* and Spier, *op. cit.*, pp. 61-72.
[21] Cf. De Ruggiero, *Existentialism—Disintegration of Man's Soul*, pp. 28, 29, 41, 42.
[22] Cf. Spier, *op. cit.*, pp. 125-127.
[23] Cf. Brunner: *Revelation and Reason*, pp. 325-327, 381.
[24] Cf. Spier, *op. cit.*, p. 135; and Zuidema, *Demensche als Historie*, p. 13.
[25] Cf. Spier, *op. cit.*, pp. 101-112, 139.
[26] Cf. H. Kraemer, *The Christian Message in a Non-Christian World*, pp. 10, 11, 16.
[27] Cf. Cornelius Van Til, *The Defense of the Faith*, pp. 29, 31, 48, 52.
[28] Cf. *ibid.*, p. 58.
[29] Cf. E. Gilson, *God and Philosphy*, Preface p. xi.
[30] Cf. Brunner, *Revelation and Reason*, pp. 1, 16; and Cailliet, *op. cit.*, p. 20.

[31] Charles Malik, "A Civilization at Bay," *Christianity Today*, Nov. 24, 1961, p. 6.
[32] Cf. Brunner, op. cit., pp. 413, 418.
[33] Cf., James H. Thornwell, *Collected Writings* III, 302; I.52.
[34] Cf. Brunner, *op. cit.*, p. 420.
[35] Cf. Van Til, *op. cit.*, p. 165.
[36] Gordon H. Clark: *Religion, Reason and Revelation*, p. 87.
[37] Humphreys, *op. cit.*, pp. 2, 3.
[38] *Ibid.*, pp. 178, 79.
[39] Suzuki, *Selected Writings*, p. 245. This argument is a fallacy. See previous chapter, Section II.
[40] *Ibid.*, p. 270.
[41] *Ibid.*, p. 265.
[42] Robert Linssen, *Living Zen*, p. 75.
[43] Cf. Humphreys, *op. cit.*, pp. 206-208.
[44] Cf. Humphreys: *"Zen Comes West"*; A short article of the present author,—Zen, Symptom of Crisis, *Christianity Today*, July 17, 1961.
[45] Cf. Spier, *op. cit.*, pp. 135, 136.
[46] *Ibid.*, pp. 138, 139 and 18; also Part Three, chap. II, § II, 1 of this volume
[47] Cf. Spier, *op. cit.*, p. 34.
[48] Cf. Wilfred Desen, *The Tragic Finale*, pp. 160-166; and Spier, *ibid.*, pp. 64, 69.
[49] Spier, *Christian Philosophy*, p. 20; Romans 11:36.
[50] Cf. Sartre, *L'Extentialism est un Humanisme*, p. 85; and Spier, *Christianity and Existentialism*, p. 138.
[51] Cf. Sartre, *Existentialism* (Benard Frechtman trans.), pp. 26, 27.
[52] Cf. Spier, *Christianity and Existentialism*, pp. 64, 67, 68.
[53] *The Saying of Linchi*; cf. Ogate, *Zen for the West*, p. 12.
[54] Suzuki, *Selected Writings*, p. 275.
[55] Psalm 2:1-3.
[56] Cf. Alan Watts, *The Way of Liberation in Zen Buddhism*.
[57] Psalm 2:4-12.
[58] Hebrews 12:29; I John 4:8.
[59] Hebrews 2:2,3.
[60] Suzuki: *op. cit.*, p. 275.
[61] Hebrews 9:27; Psalm 8:4; 39:4, 5; James 4:14.
[62] Cf. Colosians 2:8.
[63] Walter Kunneth: "Hindrances to Evangelism in the Church," *Christianity Today*, Oct. 28, 1966.
[64] Cf. Colossians 1:18.
[65] Leon Morris: *The Abolition of Religion—A Study in Religionless Christianity*, p. 69-71, 100.
[66] Editorial, *Christianity Today*, Oct. 28, 1966.

[67] Kenneth Hamilton, *op. cit.*, p. 21.
[68] Thomas J. J. Altizer: *The Gospel of Christian Atheism*, p. 147.
[69] Johannes Schneider: "The Authority for Evangelism," *Christianity Today*, Oct. 28, 1966.
[70] Isaiah 5:20.
[71] Humphreys, *Zen Comes West*, p. 17.
[72] Luke 6:39; cf. "Zen, Symptom of Crisis," *Christianity Today;* July 17, 1961.
[73] John 14:6.
[74] John 8:12.
[75] Cf. Spier, *Christianity and Existentialism*. Intro. pp. xvii-xix.
[76] Cf. B. B. Warfield: *The Plan of Salvation*, pp. 16, 33.
[77] H. Bavinck: Gereformeerde Dogmatiek II pp. 425, 426.
[78] Wm. Temple: *"Foundations—A Statement of Christian belief in terms of modern thought."* pp. 237, 256.
[79] Cf. P. A. Sorokin: (1) *The Crisis of Our Age*, Chap. IX; (2) *The Reconstruction of Humanity*, Chap. I.
[80] Cf. *Decision*, January, September, November issues, 1963.

CONCLUSION

I. THE HIGHEST GOAL OF MAN
-THE KEY TO THE MYSTERY OF LIFE-

The spiritual history of mankind has been beset with problems about the creation of the universe, the redemption of man, and the consummation of the world. These problems have been the concern of thinking men in both the East and the West. Great answers have been given by great minds, but one cosmogony after another is raised only to fall. On the ruins of one, another thought structure is built in a vain attempt to probe into the heart of these problems. Man today is wrestling with these same problems with the same valiant but vain energy of mind and spirit.

The irony is that the answer is always there. God himself has given it plainly and fully in his only begotten son Jesus Christ, who is the eternal Word made flesh to dwell among us, full of grace and truth. For "by him were all things created that are in heaven and that are in earth, visible and invisible. . . .And he is before all things, by him all things consist" (Col. 1:15-17). In Jesus "are hidden all the treasures of wisdom and knowledge" (Col. 2:3). In Jesus is the center of all divine revelation in the entire universe. In Jesus is found the answer to man's pressing problems about his nature and destiny. "God was in Christ, reconciling the world unto himself" (II Cor. 5:19). All things proceed from God to be completed by God to move back to God. God is the creator and sustainer of all things, the source of all life, and the Father of all goodness. All living creatures owe their existence from moment to moment solely to God the Creator who is the one eternal and omnipotent Being. The highest goal of man, therefore, is knowing and glorifying God, instead of "seeing into one's own nature" as Zen stresses.

Man is the crown of God's creation and was created in God's own image and likeness. He can never deny nor destroy his divine origin. He is not only a citizen of a physico-natural order of life, but he also belongs to a supernatural order. Man cannot be satisfied with what the corporeal world has to offer. He requires and seeks a goal which is spiritual, immutable, and eternal. Augustine has rightly observed that the heart of man was created for God and that it cannot find rest until it abides in the Father's heart.

All men seek after God, as Augustine declared, but they seek Him in the wrong way and in the wrong place. Consequently man is engaged simultaneously, in seeking and in fleeing from God. This results in his bitter complaint that "there is no God" or as Nietzsche and the modern mavericks have pronounced: "God is dead." Indeed, in his desperate seeking after God and fleeing from Him (to borrow Pascal's phrase) consists the misery and grandeur of man. Man longs for truth but is false by nature. He yearns for rest and throws himself from one diversion to another. He seeks for God and loses himself in his own creaturelines. "Because that when they knew God, they glorified him not as God, neither were thankful; but became vain in their imaginations, and their foolish hearts were darkened. Professing themselves to be wise, they became fools. . .and changed the truth of God into a lie. . ." (Rom. 1:21, 22, 25).

Man is an enigma whose solution is God. God's eternal thoughts are in no wise mere ideas floating far above the everyday course of earthly affairs, but are creative deeds which are interwoven into all of human history, "for in him we live and move and have our being." God's eternal counsels are embodied in the eternal Word, and "has in these last days spoken unto us by his Son whom he hath appointed heir of all things by whom also he made the worlds, who being the brightness of his glory, and the express image of his person, and upholding all things by the Word of his power, when he had by himself purged our sins, he sat down on the right hand of the Majesty on high (Heb. 1:1-3)." The glorious vision that permeates all the Bible is the sovereign lordship of Jesus Christ. After His resurrection, He spoke to His disciples "All power is given unto me in heaven and in earth" (Matt. 28:18). And Stephen, the first martyr of the church, "saw the glory of God and Jesus standing on the right hand of God" (Acts 7:55). He is "far above all principality and power, and might, and dominion and every name that is named, not only in this world, but also in that which is to come" (Eph. 1:21). "That at the name of Jesus every knee should bow, of things in heaven, and things in earth, and things under the earth; and that every tongue should confess that Jesus Christ is Lord, to the glory of God the Father" (Phil. 2:10, 11).

The Bible is the key to the enigma of man, the events of the world and the mystery of life; without it we are but helpless creatures groping and fumbling in the darkness without light and without hope.[1] "The secret things belong unto the Lord our God" (Deut. 29:29). "Only the Lion of the tribe of Juda, the Root of David has prevailed to open the book in the right hand of him that sat on the throne, and to loose the seven seals thereof"; for (He) was slain and hast redeemed us to God by (His) blood out of every kindred, and tongue, and people, and nation; and has made us unto our God kings and priests: and we shall reign on the earth." "Worthy is the Lamb that was slain to receive power, and riches, and wisdom, and strength, and honor, and glory, and blessing" (cf. Rev. 5:1-12).

II. THE VANITY OF THE MIND

Our faith, therefore, is not founded on man's wisdom but in God's power. This does not mean the denial of the value of science and philosophy. But a faith in the powers of science is a residue of a naive 18th century belief in absolute "laws of nature" based on observation and measurement. As a matter of fact, science never proves anything in an absolute sense. It does not even produce evidence on the two vital realities of man's being: his free will and his consciousness.[2] And non-Christian philosophy is immanentistic and anthropocentric by its nature. It begins by absolutizing and deifying a created aspect. By and large, secular philosophers believe that all knowledge is innate in the mind. They attempt to transmute the human mind into a pseudo-maker. Thus they run the risk of becoming a prisoner of their own mind. They no longer see reality and lose their genuine sense of relationship with the living God.[3] Therefore "whether there be knowledge, it shall vanish away. For we know in part, . . . But when that which is perfect is come, then that which is in part shall be done away" (I Cor. 13:8-10). Any man who ignores God's wisdom in His general and special revelation and makes himself "the measure of all things," must become darkened in his heart. For how can a man know the Infinite and Incomprehensible God who cannot be measured by time or eternity, who lives in inapproachable light, and who allows no man to see His face.[4]

When man does seek God, as Calvin points out, man measures Him by his own carnal stupidity and engages in vain speculation.[5] It is true that in certain philosophical writings we are occasionally met with some apposite remarks as to the nature of God, but these views invariably savor somewhat of a giddy imagination. The human being is, indeed, irradiated with a beam of divine light that "shines in darkness, but the darkness comprehended it not." Because the light is smothered with the darkness of clouds it cannot shine to any good purpose. The flesh has no capacity for such sublime wisdom as to apprehend God and God-like things unless illuminated by the spirit of regeneration.⁶

Moreover, owing to the terrible consequences of sin all roots of wrong and sickly commotions bestir themselves in the body and work their effect in their spiritual dispositions. Our human soul is subservient to falsehood and blind to reality. Alongside of this falsehood we are guilty of intentional mistakes in observation and memory as well as thought process. Self-delusion and self-deception are no less important factors in this process. Due to sin no man lives in a normal bodily and spiritual condition. Besides, the imagination also exists in an abnormal condition. When overexcited, it retains imperfect images, subjects our minds to the dominion of these images, and thereby falsifies our self-consciousness. Thus the deliverance of our inner selves is lost in this imagery.

Other influences resulting from the injurious effects worked upon man by sin are immediately perceived in our nature. Sin has not only weakened the energy of thought but has also darkened human understanding.⁷ Sin is opposed to love. Without the sense of God in his heart, man shall never attain to a knowledge of God; and without love for God, that knowledge shall never be rich in content.

Unfortunately the Zen master closes his eyes to the terrible phenomenon of sin. He indulges himself in morbid reactions and intoxicates himself in vain speculations. He struggles to open a "third eye" but the mental eye remains shut until it is opened by the Lord.⁸ He demands will power but is ignorant of the fact that without the Holy Spirit the will of man is not free. He teaches that "Satori" (illumination or enlightenment) is the realization of one's own nature and believes that the mind is the key to life. The Zen master endeavors, therefore, to "master the mind" and advocates that the mind is its own place and of itself can make a heaven of hell and a hell of heaven.⁹ "Such language is indeed an emotional outburst. It is an empty imagination from an empty mind. It is not only a vain deceit but also a tragic futility."¹⁰

III. THE PERVERSION OF THE TRUTH

Now modern theologians, being alienated from the life of God through the ignorance that is in them because of the blindness of their heart, adopt the iconoclastic stance of Zen, revolt against the authority of the Scriptures, completely ignore God's wisdom, and reject His revelation. They contend that modern man has "come of age," the Bible is no longer "meaningful." But before the judgement "this is meaningless" can be accepted, the query "on what terms" must be raised.[11] A symphony is meaningless to the tone-deaf; and a sign with the word "Exit" printed on it is meaningless to those uacquainted with the Roman alphabet or to the blind. Yet to musicians and to those who can read, they are meaningful. Consequently, we are justified in asking modern theologians who are endeavoring to "demythologize" the Bible, to "secularize" the Gospel, to declare a moratorium on talk about "God," or even to kill and bury God so as to make Christianity more "meaningful" to the contemporary "empirical mind," on what terms they judge that the Bible and the teachings of the church are not understandable today?[12] Such attempts to reach the goal of so-called contemporary meaningfulness must reckon with a twofold difficulty: (1) It is difficult to reach an agreement which is understandable to enlightened men today. Different interpreters of the present day cultural situation advance conflicting reports. (2) There is no absolute consensus on the matter of what is meaningful to the modern man, because there is no universal standard of meaningfulness to which reference can be made.[13] Furthermore, the great creeds and confessions of the church are not simply empty words or dead language on paper, but rather the reminders of prolonged struggles in the past to preserve the wholeness of the Kerygma against attempts to make Christianity meaningful at the cost of ignoring or suppressing those parts which did not fit readily into the contemporary world views.[14] In fact, modern theologians indeed contradict themselves. For instance, John A. T. Robinson's position and his proposal to find a new image of God have

CONCLUSION

been described by the new radicals as "soft." Again, while Van Buren contends that our principal difficulty today is "not bad religion but bad language," Harvey Cox thinks Van Buren is wrong.[15]

Thus, the attempt to turn away from divine revelation to a secular philosophy, to find a new foundation for the meaning of the Gospel and to make the "contemporary empirical mind" the criterion of truth, is the vanity of vanities. It is the "exchange of the truth of God for a lie" (Rom. 1:25), of the foundation of rock for the sinking sand (Matt. 7:24-27). But the Bible warns: "Be on your guard, do not let your minds be captured by vain deceit, "according to the traditions of man and the rudiments of the world" (cf. Col. 2:8). To think science is omnipotent and that technopolitan man can know and do all things is a crass misconception. Rather a faith in the powers of science is not modern but a residue of a naive 18th century belief in absolute "laws of nature" as we pointed out above. Besides, science has limitations. Modern technicians cannot discover the mystery of life in a test tube. Those who follow science blindly come to a barrier beyond which they cannot see. So Dr. Vannevar Bush, the father of the modern analogue computer, honorary board chairman of the Massachusetts Institute of Technology advises modern man that he can only "follow science where it leads, but not where it cannot lead. And with a pause, he will admit a faith."[16] Modern theologians who refuse to believe the truth of the Bible in the name of science and technology only demonstrate that they do not understand science properly. A true scientist will acknowledge that it is in Christ, and in Christ alone, that men will find all the treasures of wisdom and knowledge (Col. 2:3).

There is another fact which the modern man should not ignore i.e., "with the Lord, one day is as a thousand years and a thousand years as one day" (II Pet. 3:8). In other words, there is nothing "new" or "modern" in the sight of the Lord, for He is eternal. Since He is "making all things new" (Rev. 21:5), He is ever new. "Jesus

Christ is the same, yesterday, today and forever" (Heb. 13:8). "Forever his word is settled in heaven" (Ps. 119:89). "Heaven and earth shall pass away, but [his] words shall not pass away" (Matt. 24:35). The Gospel is "meaningful" yesterday, today, and forever. Even such a non-theologian as Arnold Toynbee could venture to prophesy that "Jesus Christ will still be important for mankind two or three thousand years hence."[17] Properly speaking, there is no secular meaning of the Gospel. The Gospel was the invasion of God's revelation into history, it was an event of redemption accomplished by God. It cannot be fathomed by human wisdom (cf. Rom. 11:33-36). The futile attempt of the modern theologians is not a new one. In Napoleon's time, there was also a "modern theologian," M. Lepeaux, who on one occasion confided to de Talleyrand-Perigord his disappointment in the ill-success which he had met in his attempt to bring into vogue a new Gospel which he regarded as an improvement on Christianity, and then asked Talleyrand's advice as to what he should do. Talleyrand replied that it was difficult indeed to found a new religion. But after a moment's reflection, he said, "Still, there is one plan which you might at least try. I should recommend that you be crucified and rise again on the third day."[18] This answer shattered his vain imagination! Salvation belongs to Jehovah and eliminates any and all human initiative and activity. As Paul wrote to the Galations, "not that there is another Gospel, but there are some who trouble you and want to pervert the Gospel of Christ" (Gal. 1:7). There is no need for a secular meaning of the Gospel in order to be meaningful. The whole effort of modern theologians to save the Gospel by secularizing it is not only unnecessary, it is a vain deceit that will only pervert the Gospel and bring Christianity to sheer nihility.[19]

IV. THE DIVINE PLAN OF SALVATION

Ever since the first Adam revolted against his God, every member of the human race has been possessed by sin. The human race, according to Calvin, is ruined, "no one will now perceive God to be either a Father, or the Author of Salvation, until Christ interposes to make our peace."[20] The nature of man in both intellect and will, requires regeneration of the Spirit. In Romans 3:10-18, we see that our humanity is not simply vicious by custom or by "force of habit,"[21] but by perpetually corrupted nature. All men are overwhelmed by the inevitable calamity of sin and can be delivered from it only by the mercy of God. Since the whole human race has been undone in the person of the first Adam it is vain to look for anything good in our human nature.[22] Augustine has rightly said that our nature is wounded, maimed and vexed. The thing that is needed is genuine confession not false defense. It is necessary, in fact, to destroy one's old nature instead of "seeing into one's own nature"; and to form in us anew the image of God which was sullied by the transgression of the first Adam and restored by the crucifixion and resurrection of the second Adam, our Lord Jesus Christ.

The idea of redemption or salvation appears in all religions. The fundamental issue is: how can man save himself since his nature has been wounded, maimed, vexed and his soul plunged into a deadly abyss?[23] The answer is obvious. The counsel of God teaches that the work of redemption is His, and has been His from the beginning, and will be His to the end. Nothing comes as a surprise to our God. In his omniscience he has prepared solutions for man's problems before they arise. Before there was a sinner there was a Savior. Before the fall of the first Adam there was a plan of Salvation to be carried out by the second Adam, "the Lamb of God was slain before the foundations of the world." The way of salvation provided in timeless eternity. In the whole work of redemption it is Almighty God who manifests Himself as the seeking and calling One and is the speaking and acting One. The whole work of redemption begins and ends in God. The Father thought our salvation; the Son bought it; and the Holy Spirit wrought it; but man could do nothing in it, yet man rejected it and continues to fight it today. Entirely on His initiative, God comes down to earth to seek man out and to call him back into His fellowship. Man has no part in this act of redemption except to listen and to accept it in childlike faith, for God promised: "as many as received him, to them gave he power to become the sons of God, even to them that believe on his name," "for God so loved the world that he gave his only begotten son, that whosoever believes in him should not perish, but have everlasting life" (John 1:12; 3:16).

Promise and faith are the content of the covenant of grace which discloses the way to heaven and gives access to eternal salvation. The total purpose and great mystery of God's covenant is that His children will grow more and more like God, so that He may have unhindered and uninterrupted fellowship with them. "Behold what manner of love the Father has bestowed upon us that we should be called the sons of God....Now we are the children of God, and it does not yet appear what we shall be, but we know that when he shall appear we shall be like him" (I John 3:1, 2). The ultimate message of the gospel, "is not demand but promise; not duty, but gift."[24] The ultimate basis of salvation for man, "lies in eternity not in time." God's everlasting love from before the foundation of the world is the eternal fountain from which flows the river of salvation with all its manifold blessings from regeneration to glorification. And in God's merciful plan of redemption Christ occupies a place of central importance. There is an eternal federal union between Christ and all those who were destined to become heirs of salvation in the course of time.[25] Man's hope for "eternal life in another world depends on God."[26] Salvation belongs to Jehovah. It is God and God alone who saves. C. S. Spurgeon stressed that if there be one stitch in the celestial garment of salvation which man himself has sewed then mankind is lost.

Therefore, to "master the mind" or "to see into nature" so as to deliver or deify oneself is the sure way to doom for all autosoterism of which Zen is perhaps the most radical form. Unfortunately Zen has made a great impact in the West in the realms of philosophy and theology owing to its seducing doctrines.

V. THE POWER OF THE GOSPEL

"The preaching of the Cross is to them that perish foolishness," But "it is the power of God unto salvation to every one that believes."[27] It was not a mere system of philosophy or ethics, but "a historical event of revolution accomplished by God that eliminates any and all human initiative and activity. This is the unique, once-for-all, unrepeatable fact, valid for all time."[28] This unique fact "is the invasion of God's revelation into history. The fact that Almighty God descended into the earthly realm of His creatures manifests a reality that is totally new and beyond comparison. Therefore, this reality of the God revealed in Jesus Christ cannot be measured in human terms. Human reason, the world's reasonableness must shatter upon it."[29]

The Gospel was the divine dynamite that destroyed the power of sin and darkness and brought abundant spiritual life and a glorious and radiant hope for mankind. With this divine dynamite the early Christians—those "unlearned and ignorant men" were empowered to "turn the world upside down." "In less than one-hundred years, (they) proclaimed the Gospel of Jesus Christ to the world powers of that age—the Roman Empire with its materialistic paganism, illustrious Greece with its philosophy and Jerusalem with its religion."[30] "The city that had crucified Jesus was hostile and hateful to His newly-born church, and it is a miracle that the church survived. Arrayed against it were hypocritical Pharisaism, secularistic Sadduceeism, the intolerant and idolatrous Roman government, and vain, humanistic Hellenism. The Church appeared as a lamb in the midst of wolves. Yet the lamb survived. And not only did it survive; the church of Jesus Christ grew and spread until at last it conquered all its foes and changed the course of history with its redemptive truth.

"The story of the Jerusalem Church during the first century is the history of the Church throughout the centuries. Many thought that the last days of the Church had come, when the Roman Empire fell, or when the fanatical Muslim army reached Europe. Nevertheless, despite these foes, the Church not only has survived, but also has created a Christian civilization. During the eighteenth and nineteenth centuries, the Church has had to face many new enemies in the form of natural science and humanistic philosophy that deny the supernatural and rob Jesus of His deity. Yet in these times great revivals broke out in Europe and America that renewed and revitalized the Church and inspired God's people to take the Gospel to the ends of the earth."[31]

Humanly speaking, the condition at the time of His crucifixion was not an auspicious one for the inauguration of a movement that was to impress upon the whole world the fact that a man who had been driven out of Galilee, crucified at Jerusalem, betrayed by His race, and violently put to death was the Redeemer of mankind, whose kingdom should be everlasting. It was almost absolutely incredible that His disciples could have any hope to accomplish such mighty tasks, while the odds against them were so great. However, under the influence of Pentecost, the power of the Gospel was miraculously demonstrated, the weakness of His disciples was speedily changed into boldness. Compared with what the early Christians had to meet and conquer, the opposition which confronts us now should be considered as very insignificant.[32]

The dominating factor of history is not humanity, but divinity. God is the Lord of history. History centers in the eternal Gospel. The shaping of the future is by no means in our hands. Clearly God is at work in the environment, in the past, and in the future. The important thing is how shall we tap the eternal spring of power, the dynamic of His kingdom.[33]

Christianity has displayed an amazing ability to survive the death of cultures. Cultures rise and fall; Christianity modifies their course. There is a false notion today that this is a "post-Christian era." Those who hold this notion fail to see the power of the Gospel manifested in the history of the Christian Church. They are both blind to history and to the present situation. We don't deny that there are indications of another ebb of Christianity that might occur as it did in the past. But up to the present, taking the entire world into our view, if ebb there be, it is not so profound as any of the major ebbs in the past, i.e. (1) 500-950; (2) 1350-1500; (3) 1750-1815. However, in the past, each ebb has been followed by a fresh advance, and each advance has set a new high mark for the influence of the glorious Gospel of Jesus Christ in the total life of mankind. Since Christianity has demonstrated its power to survive in the past, it is to be expected that the present situation of seeming reverse will again precede a time of revival with increasing power to mold the human race even more than before. This is not wishful thinking. Rather past experience gives ground for this expectation, that elsewhere, perhaps in some quiet unexpected region, Christianity can achieve a fresh extension and in which and from which it can continue its growth.

For instance, in that disheartening period of 500-950, when Christianity appeared to be passing, gains were made in Western Europe which formed the basis for most of the next advance. Yet Western Europe was then the most unpromising area. In 500, Christianity was weaker there than in the Eastern Mediterranean. For centuries, moreover, Western Europe was being overrun by barbarians, most of them pagans. During the decline which accompanied the conquests by the Ottoman Turks and the fading of the Medieval European culture, currents of life were appearing which contributed to the later unprecedented revival. The position of the Church as a self-conscious minority whose strength is increasing most rapidly in the lands in which it has been weakest, argues well for the future and gives us confidence and courage to face the adversaries.

Yet the real reason for the continuation and expansion of the influence of the Gospel is in Jesus Christ Himself. Jesus was and is the Logos, the Word, through whom God touches human life and in Him is life that is the light of man. Always the light shines in the darkness and man loves not the light; yet the darkness never puts it out. The history of the past nineteen centuries has justified this insight. It is this life and this light which constitute the secret of the power of the gospel. It is this life and this light which are the sure hope of the future and of the eternity.[34]

VI. THE HOPE OF THE WORLD

Christianity, unlike other natural ethnic religions, is not a set of philosophical systems or ethical teachings; but is "the way of life," a creative force in the history, as well as a dynamic power of the world. Christian world missions is not the enterprise of man, but a movement of the Spirit of the Creator, Almighty God who alone can create out of nothing and announce Himself as ever making all things new. Owing to the destructive influence of sin, this material and corporeal world is not ready to be wrought into an ideal pattern of life and society. No adequate human resources and wisdom and devotion can overcome the present difficulties and give a fresh orientation. It must be regenerated, reconditioned, and renewed. We must cry out for a supernatural renewing power and redemptive power to save this perishing world.

The Church should be a reservoir of His renewing and creative power. Christianity is within us the Spirit of renewal, of aspiration, of adventure. The highest function of Christianity is prophetic, transformative, and creative. Christianity is an agency of the Lord of history

CONCLUSION 187

and Prince of life and also the embodiment of His active presence and constructive energy and creative power in the achievement of human destiny and the glorious hope of mankind. Moreover, we are under deep obligation to recognize the urgency of our task to preach the Gospel—the only religion which is both idealistically and essentially universal, the only way of salvation, and the only answer and hope of all mankind.[35]

Indeed, as most of the current experts and analysts, philosophers and scientists, historians and statesmen agree, this world is sick. Churchill once said, "Our problems are beyond us;" J. P. Sartre acknowledged "there is no exit from the human dilemma." As Dr. P. A. Sorokin, a world-known sociologist diagnosed, "the history of human progress is a history of incurable stupidity," the poison of this decadent sensate culture must be eliminated. The only way of alleviating the crisis of our age is by reintegrating its religious, moral, scientific and philosophical values. And this reintegration must be effected in such a way that "the new system of values is rooted primarily in the values of moral duties and the Kingdom of God." "Without the Kingdom of God, we are doomed to a weary and torturing pilgrimage from calamity to calamity, from crisis to crisis." He particularly pointed out that this way was marvelously formulated a long time ago by Jesus Christ in Matthew 6:31-36—"Seek ye first the Kingdom of God and his righteousness and all these things shall be added unto you."[36]

Millions of people today are searching for a way out and for a reliable voice of authority. Yet, tragically, the Bible, the Word of God which is the only real authority we have, is a closed book to millions! His Word sheds light on human nature, world problems, and human suffering. And beyond that, it clearly reveals the way to God. Our faith should not depend upon human knowledge and scientific advance, but upon the unmistakable message of the Word of God. It is in the Holy Scriptures that we find the answers to life's ultimate questions and the "exit from the human dilemma." "The Bible is old, yet it is ever new.

It is the most modern book in the world today. There is a false notion today that a book as ancient as the Bible cannot speak to the needs of modern man. Men somehow think that in an age of scientific achievement, when knowledge has increased more in the past twenty-five years than in all preceeding centuries put together, this ancient Book is out-of-date."[37] So now those young mavericks, "death-of-God theologians" including some "bishops" come to distort and destroy the Book, the Truth, in terms of scholarship and man's freedom. Some "Christian" leader even advocates that in order "to make Christian faith. . . relevant to the needs and thoughts of men today, an ecumenical theology must be created," "a radical mutation is necessary" and even "the appearance of another age of the heretics is inevitable!"[38]

"It is true that man's concept of the world has changed. But it is wrong to exalt this changing world view to the place of supreme authority. Even logic opposes this. That which changes cannot be *norma normans*.' Only that which is removed from the cycle of changeability can be supreme authority. God is this supreme authority. God is unchangeable." "It is the greatest of errors to make false views of man the yardstick for Christian proclamation." "The spiritual illness of our feverish world is man's proud self-glorification." "The constantly greater turning away from God is the basic evil of our time. The scourge of our age is autonomy and anthropocentrism."[39]

God's message has not changed. For "(his) word is settled in heaven forever" (Ps. 119:89). "Heaven and earth shall pass away but my words shall not pass away." (Matt. 24:35). "Only Christ has the answer to man's tremendous problems. Today as then, He is the only hope, the true light, 'the way, the truth, and the Life.' " "No one can find God apart from Him. It was this Gospel that produced one of the greatest commotions in history. It made the Greek mythology look ridiculous, reduced to impotence the Hebrew religion and gave a death blow to the paganism whose center was Rome." "Christ's Gospel was the divine dynamite that destroys the power of sin. . . .Its purity and authentic glory can inspire us in this day, when social, moral, and spiritual conditions are so like that of the first century. Actually, with the passing of time, evils increased, the night has become darker, resources are more limited and the end is nearer. His life, His teachings, His death on the Cross, His shed blood are now and as then the only basis of Redemption, the unshakable rock on which the soul rests for salvation." "Human needs have grown immensely. There have never been so many destroyed homes . . . .so much crime and hate, so much international unrest, so many social problems. There is no peace and even less hope. Only the Gospel has the solution for so much evil, the answer for so many questions, for only Lord Jesus Christ, the Desire of all nations can put end to this tragic state of affairs." "The Gospel preached by the Holy Spirit sent from heaven looks toward the day when all human problems will be forever ended. Sin will have been removed from the earth and death will be no more."[40]

History centers on Jesus Christ. This is not only the view of theologians. Historian Arnold Toynbee has also said "Life in this world is not an end in itself and by itself; the central and dominant feature in the souls' spiritual landscape is its relation to God." "For the spiritual side of man's life is of vastly greater importance." "Jesus Christ will still be important for mankind two or three thousand years hence." "History passes over unto theology."[41] Dr. Hendrick Wm. Van Loon, in his popular book *"The Story of The Bible,"* writes these words: ". . . they ask for a solution of their problems and they received no answer. . . the old gods failed them. The dispenser of new truth failed them. The learned doctors connected with the worship of Isis and Niethros and Bacchus failed them. Nothing was left, but despair! And then Jesus was born."[42] In other words, when Roman conquerors failed, when Greek philosophers failed, and when religious leaders failed, then "unto us a child is born, unto us a Son is given; and the government shall be upon his shoulder; and his name shall be called Wonderful, Counsellor, the Mighty God, the everlasting Father, the Prince of Peace" (Is. 9:6). The birth of Jesus is a turning point of human history, from despair to hope, from darkness to light and from death to life. Unfortunately, "he was in the world, and the world knew him not; he came to his own and his own received him not" (John 1:10-11). God so loved the world that He sent His only begotten Son from heaven to be its Savior; but men deliberately rejected Him and chose a way of destruction.

Now the sign of His second coming is becoming more and more evident. In 1860, a French chemist Marcelin Berthelot predicted: "Within a hundred years, . . .man will know what the atom is. It is my belief when science reaches this stage, God will come down to earth with His big ring of keys and will say to humanity, "Gentlemen, it is closing time."[43] And it came to pass as he predicted, after only eighty-five years, at 5:30 A.M. on July 16, 1945, a light brighter than a thousand suns illuminated the desert sands of New Mexico. One scientist who was watching wept! "My God," he exclaimed, "we have created hell." We are indeed at the end of an era, moving rapidly into a new period—a period of eschatological change, which will be tremendous and dreadful, and unprecedented in all the human history. As the Bible says: "Then shall be great tribulation such as has not been from the beginning of the world until now, no, and never will be. Immediately after the tribulation of those days shall the sun be darkened and the moon shall not give her light and the stars shall fall from heaven, and the powers of the heavens shall be shaken. And then shall appear the sign of the Son of man in heaven; and then shall all the tribes of the earth mourn, and they shall see the Son of man coming in the clouds of heaven with power and great glory,[44] "in flaming fire taking vengeance on them that knew not God and that obey not the Gospel of our Jesus Christ."[45] As many signs indicate, this could happen at any time. For mankind has gone really too far in its arrogance toward a tragic end. But this is the consequence of man's own apostasy. In fact "God sent not his Son into the world to condemn the world, but that the world through him might be saved."[46] "The Lord is long suffering to us-ward, not willing that any should perish, but that all should come to repentance."[47]

The Lord still beckons and stretches His arms to all who seek Him. He still says: "I am the Way, the Truth, and the Life, no one comes unto the Father but by me." The Cross is still standing in the midst of our dilemma as our only hope and glory. But come unto Him, all ye (Zen-Buddhists, Existentialists, "Death-of-God" theologians, Beatnicks, Hippies, LSD-addicts), that labor and are heavy laden, and He will give you rest.[48] "As for the times of ignorance, God has over-looked; but now he commands mankind, all men everywhere, to repent because he has fixed the day on which he will have the world judged and justly judged, by a man of his choosing; of this he has given assurance to all by raising him from the dead."[49] The Gospel of Christ ought to be accepted only because it is the Truth, the Way and the Life, because it breaks through all human misconceptions and vain imaginations, because it is the only cure of human sins, the answer of all human problems, and because it confronts mankind with the ultimate reality of God Himself. The ultimate end of the church is the kingdom of God, The church should with confidence proclaim the kingship of the Lord in this world. His Kingdom must come; His will must prevail,[50] for He assures us: 'In the world ye shall have tribulation; but be of good cheer; I have overcome the world."[51] And when "that Wicked shall be revealed," "The Lord shall consume him with the spirit of his mouth and shall destroy him with the brightness of his coming."[52] And "we, according to his promise, look for new heavens and a new earth, wherein dwelleth righteousness."[53] Paul sees all this in a great vision when he says "then comes the end, when he shall deliver up the Kingdom to God, even the Father, when he shall have put down all authority and power. For he must reign till he has put all enemies under his feet. The last e n e m y that s h a l l be destroyed is death."[54] And so John sees, when he writes "I saw a new heaven and a new earth, for the first heaven and the first earth were passed away, and there was no more sea. And I John saw the holy city, new Jerusalem, coming down from God out of heaven...And I heard a great voice out of heaven saying, Behold, the tabernacle of God is with men and he will dwell with them, and they shall be his people, and God himself shall be with them, and be their God. And God shall wipe away all tears from their eyes, and there shall be no more death, neither sorrow, nor crying, neither shall there be any pain, for the former things are passed away. And he that sat upon the throne said Behold, I make all things new..."[55] This is the final consumation of the Kingdom of God, and the only glorious hope of mankind. And for this ultimate purpose, the present author who has been called out of pagan darkness into His marvellous light, presents this volume as a witness to his dear readers so they might also come to know the true God, the true Savior, the true way of liberation,[56] which the world has been vainly probing as a fool "seeking a moon in the water" [57] which is only a reflection, not the Reality.

---

[1] Cf. Erich Sauer: *The Dawn of World Redemption*, pp. 15-16.

[2] Cf. Dr. Vannevar Bush's article in *Fortune* magazine, May, 1965.

[3] Cf. E. Cailliet: *op. cit.*, pp. 131-135; Etienne Gilson: *op. cit.*, pp 1, 34.

[4] Cf. Herman Bavinck: *Our Reasonable Faith*, pp. 17-31.

[5] Cf. John Calvin: *Institutes*, BK. 1, Chap. IV, 1.

[6] Cf. *Ibid.* BK. I Chap. V, 14; VI, 1, 3; XIV, 3; BK. II, Chap. II, 12, 18-20.

[7] Cf. Abraham Kuyper: *Principles of Sacred Theology*, pp. 106-119.

[8] Cf. Augustine: *De Peccat, Merit Et Remiss*, Lib. II, Chap. V.

[9] Cf. Alan Watts: *The Spirit of Zen*, p. 80.

[10] Cf. Gordon Clark: "Revealed Religion," p. 14, *Christianity Today*, December 17, 1965.

[11] Kenneth Hamilton: *Revolt Against Heaven*, pp. 16-18.

[12] *Ibid.*, p. 16.

CONCLUSION

[13] *Ibid.*, p. 16.
[14] *Ibid.*, p. 23, 24.
[15] Harvey Cox: *The Secular City*, pp. 260; cf. Van Buren: *The Secular Meaning of the Gospel*, pp. 6, 17, 84, 103, 104, 105, 133, 178, 190, 198. E. L. Mascall: *the Secularization of Christianity*, pp. 74, 93.
[16] Cf. Vannevar Bush, *op. cit.*
[17] Arnold Toynbee: *Civilization on Trial* p. 219.
[18] Cf. Charles H. Robinson: *"Studies in the Resurrection of Christ."*
[19] Cf. Milton H. Hunnex: "Has the Spirit of Confusion Bewitched the Secular Theologians," *Christianity Today*, Dec. 23, 1966.
[20] Cf. John Calvin: *Institutes*, BK. I Chap. II, 1ff.
[21] Cf. Robert Linssen: *Living Zen*, pp. 103ff.
[22] Cf. John Calvin: *Institutes*, BK. I. Chap. III, 2ff.
[23] Cf. B. B. Warfield: *The Plan of Salvation*, pp. 16, 33.
[24] Cf. Bavinck: *op. cit.*, pp. 269-278.
[25] Cf. H. Kuiper: *By Grace Alone*, pp. 40-42.
[26] Cf. Gordon Clark: *op. cit.*, p. 3.
[27] I Corinthians 1:18; 17, Romans 1:16.
[28] Johannes Schneider: "The Authority for Evangelism," *Christianity Today*, Oct. 28, 1966.
[29] Walter Künneth: "Hindrances to Evangelism in the Church," *Christianity Today*, Oct. 28, 1966.
[30] Fernando Vangioni: "Recovering the Apostolic Dynamic," *Christianity Today*, Nov. 11, 1966.
[31] Hyuang Chik Han: "By My Spirit," *Christianity Today*, Nov. 11 1966.
[32] Cf. James L. Barton: *The Unfinished Task*,—Chap. VI, pp. 103-125.
[33] Cf. Kenneth Scott Latourette: *Christian Outlook*, Preface, pp. 17-19, 199.
[34] Cf. Kenneth Scott Latourette: *The Unquenchable Light*, Chap. IX. pp. 124-135.
[35] Cf. W. O. Carver: *Christian Missions in Today's World*, pp. 84, 85, 111-145.
[36] Cf. Sorokin: (1) *The Crisis of our Ages*; (2) *"Man and Society in Calamity."*
[37] Henrietta C. Mears: *What the Bible is All About*, Billy Graham's Preface.
[38] Herbert C. Jackson, "A Forthcoming Role of the Non-Christian Religious systems as Contributing to Christian Theology," *Missionary Research Library*, March 15, 1961.
[39] Gerhard Bergmann: "Reformation 1517 and 1966," *Christianity Today*, Nov. 11, 1966.
[40] Fernando Vangioni: *Recovering the Apostolic Dynamic*, Christianity Today, Nov. 11, 1966.

[41] Arnold Toynbee: *Civilization on Trial*, pp. 219, 260, 262, Preface v.
[42] Cf. Van Loon: *The Story of the Bible*, Chap. 20.
[43] Walter B. Knight, *Knight's Treasury of Illustrations*.
[44] Matt. 24:29, 30.
[45] II Thess. 1:8.
[46] John 3:17.
[47] I Peter 3:9.
[48] Cf. Matt. 11:28.
[49] Acts 17:31, NEB.
[50] Cf. Matt. 6:10.
[51] John 16:33.
[52] II Thess. 2:8.
[53] II Peter 3:13.
[54] I Cor. 15:24-26.
[55] Rev. 21:1-5.
[56] Cf. Appendix I, Brief Testimony of the Author: The Way to the True Enlightenment.
[57] A Chinese proverb which has been widely used to depict the predicament of a seeker of vanity.

EPILOGUE

— A Positive Answer to the Hippies —

After my missionary tour around the world in the second half of 1968, I came back to America with greater confidence and sense of urgency to defend the validity and relevance of the Christian faith in the midst of a crooked perverse generation,[1] where "people will not endure sound doctrine . . . and wander into myths."[2]

The West, (so-called "Christendom") is now confronted with a new menace—a sort of psychedelic mysticism and is being haunted by the spirit of Zen—a cult of "iconoclasm." There is a tendency toward an anti-puritanical mode of hedonism and a detached existence which has resulted in mental troubles, violence, and other psycho-social deterioration—a philosophy of a subculture, the "Hippiedom."[3]

This is a serious symptom of the spiritual decline of the West. Vexed by the great devastation of World War I, Oswald Spengler wrote a book entitled: "The Decline of the West," which has been widely read by the thinking people of the world. However, it seems to me that this book has not produced a power or any influence to arrest this trend of decline. Instead, following World War II, there has been a "spiritual decline" in the West. After my short article on Zen—"Symptom of Crisis" appeared in *Christianity Today* (July 17, 1961), a reader in Tennessee immediately wrote to me and asked me to help him to persuade his son in college to turn away from Zen and to embrace the Christian faith. I deeply realized that this might be the cry of many other parents; and for this reason, I have had an increasing sense of urgency to continue my writing on this subject.

In view of my English language deficiency, I have already exceeded my competence. However, this book is the result of the trial of my faith with fire[4] for nearly 50 years, it is not merely the product of academic research or subjective speculation. It reflects 50 years of bitter experiences of my spiritual pilgrimage in seeking the way of "Enlightenment" and salvation,—from Zen to Christianity, from darkness to light, from death to life. The sole aim of this book is to destroy the strategy of "the old serpent,"[5] and to expose the futility of pseudo religion (Zen, and the drug induced mysticism), the vanity of mind (the "mind-stretching" movement, "mystical cult of feelings," hallucinogens) and the doom of pseudo escapism and auto-soterism, so that modern man, by looking into my experiences, might wake up and flee from the disastrous surrender to Nihilism and the tragic movement to eternal destruction! Moreover, it also aims to give a positive answer to the vast masses of unwary people who are disillusioned with the conventional religion and the established systems, so that they would not become an easy prey of "every new thing" or be "carried about with every wind of doctrine" and "of devils."[6]

With the rise of existentialism and the impact of Zen on the West, there has emerged a mood of the "New Humanism" with its special emphasis on "personal freedom" and "human autonomy." They embrace a false creed that modern man who has "come of age" can now manage very well without God and, thus, even blasphemously pronounce: "God is dead." Such a stance is in fact not "new" but has its old counterpart in the radical school of Zen, founded more than a thousand years ago, by Lin-chi (d. 867) who advocated that: "If you want to grasp the correct view of Dharma . . . smash whatever you came across . . . Smash the Buddha, Patriarchs and Arhats, if you come across them. Smash your parents and all your relations."[7] And then, we are told, you will really be "emancipated." The emancipation of man demands the abolition of all authority and even the "death of God"!

But, in fact, the dignity of man is related intrinsically to the existence of God. To use Dostoevsky's words in his well known masterpieces—"The Devils" and "Crime and Punishment": "If God does not exist, then I am God." In place of the God-man appears the man-god, the "strong personality" who stands beyond morality, to whom "everything is permitted," and feels he can break laws as he wills. Thus the humanity of man disappears. So Mochulsky says, it was one of Dostoevsky's greatest discoveries that "the nature of man is correlated to the nature of God; if there is no God, there is also no man." Instead, there is a "new demonic being."[8]

In China, a special appelation "mo-wong" (which means the "demon-king") has been ascribed to the Zen-Master, who has absolute faith in his own inner being and therefore wants to live from within, not to be bound by rules or any kind of external authority. Now in the West, we have the Hippies as their counterparts or grandchildren. They are the victims of a particularly destructive philosophy. They believe such deceptive teachings as that the human being has marvelous resources within himself that can be released and made available to him merely by submission to certain kind of stimuli by letting his psychic equilibrium be disoriented by chemical agencies (such as LSD) that give him the sensation of experiencing tremendous things. There is an absolute freedom in the Hippies' way of life and, above all in the very self-destructiveness with which this freedom often expresses itself, there is a selfishness, a hardheartedness, a callousness, an irresponsibility, and an indifference to the feeling of others. Furthermore, there is a complete rejection of or indifference to the political system,[9] and a nihilistic destruction of all existing forms. This is the product of postwar disillusionment and restlessness. They are reflections of the most curious men of influence the 20th century has yet produced. By inveighing against what they called the "establishment" and the social structure, these 20th century anarchists or nihilists wish only to tear society apart. They have raised their voices against virtually every aspect of the society: parents, politics, marriage, the family, the savings bank, organized religion and higher education. They find society too hideous to contemplate, and so they withdraw from it. They are antisocial to the point of being neurotic.[10] Such an attitude is spiritual suicide. To look upon life as utterly meaningless is equivalent to repudiating God and resigning oneself to an everlasting emptiness. Culture, morality and faith alike perish in the blackness of this chaos.[11]

We are in no wise to defend the humanist system and culture. We are not unaware of the danger of the modern sensate culture which is in process of disintegration. We also realize that "we live in a 'cut flower' civilization," which may be radiant, fragrant and lovely, but will soon wither and die, because it has been severed from its root.[12] We further acknowledge that any humanist system that is alienated from the truth of God has no absolute value and is doomed to failure. As Dr. P. A. Sorokin pointed out "the history of human progress is a history of incurable stupidity. In the cause of human history, several thousands of revolutions have been launched with a view to establish a paradise on earth. Practically none of them has ever achieved its purpose.[13] Man by his finitude and his sinful nature can never build an ideal society.[14] "Human societies were preserved from dissolution not so much through the practical and expert manipulation of economic, political and genetic or other factors, but mainly through the transmutation of values and the spiritualization of mentality."[15] Without the Kingdom of God, we are doomed to weary and torturing pilgrimages from calamity to calamity, from crisis to crisis.[16]

However, although we are against the humanist culture, we are intrinsically different from the Hippies.[17] In the first place, we start from a divine viewpoint, while the Hippies are non-theistic and rather "against the Lord and against His anointed."[18] In the second place, the Hippies' views are negative and even destructive. They provide no positive answer and therefore offer no hope. They simply lift up their voices and protest, but no one can save the culture by mere negative attack or denial. Why is human culture sick? Why is modern civilization breaking down? We must explore to the root cause of human disease. The chief cause of the failure of humanist culture lies in its alienation from Christian faith and its negligence in things spiritual. The whole movement of the Hippies, whether in its modern existentialistic form of the West or in an oriental garb of Zen, only represents a reaction in the trend of human thought. It is essentially a negative protest by human nature against the objective order, the established system, and shallow rationalism. In the third place, it is only a movement of turning "inward," but not turning "upward" as motivated by an "affection on things above."[19] Its kernel is the deification of the historical function of human nature, but it still remains ensnared (not emancipated!) in the very pit of traditional humanism. What mankind really needs is total regeneration by the grace of God not self-deification by the efforts of man.

The "New Humanism" with its emphasis on total freedom and its false notion that modern man has "come of age" and can now manage very well without God, differs from the old one, not for the better, but for the worse, so it will inevitably turn out to be more disastrous. It is nothing more than a way of defeating its own purpose, and, as a result, it will lead to its own destruction.[20] For when man rebelled against the Most High God, and cut himself off from His life and love and fellowship, then he cut his life line and left "the fountain of living waters"[21] which is the source of all blessings, and the glory of God departed. Then man no longer walked in the light, but sat in darkness and in the shadow of death. The modern man is now confronted with the menace of a New Dark Age; he is marching towards nihilistic destruction. The whole culture speaks of the loss of the human and the death of hope. In order to escape the demon of despair, modern man seeks in vain to transcend nihilism by a mystical leap of faith rooted in nothing. The "drug induced mysticism" (LSD) is the most eloquent proof that modern man has come to the dead end of finding rational answer to his existence, and has no hope and no way out of his dilemma whatsoever, unless he completely forsakes and repudiates the false creed of human autonomy, ie., the spirit of Zen, a cult of iconoclasm, and comes back to God, looking unto Jesus Christ who is "the Light of the world"[22] the hope of glory,[23] and the only Saviour and emancipater of mankind.[24]

---

[1] Phil. 2:15.
[2] II Tim. 4:3,4.
[3] *Time* magazine, July 7, 1967.
[4] Cf. I Pet. 1:7.
[5] Cf. Gen. 3:1-6.
[6] Cf. Eph. 4:4; I Tim 4:1.
[7] The Sayings of Master Lin-chi; Ogata: *Zen for the West*, p. 12.
[8] Cf. Konstantin Mochulsky's *"Dostoevsky: His Life and Work,"* tr. by Michael A. Minihan, Princeton University Press, 1967; Sherwood E. Wirt: Dostoevsky, *Decision* magazine, Jan. 1969.
[9] George F. Kennan: "The Student Left—Rebels without a Program," *Reader's Digest*, Jan. 1969.
[10] "The Only Rebellion Around," *Life* magazine, Nov. 30, 1959.
[11] Dr. M. C. Tenny: "Christ and the Beat Generation." *Christianity Today*, Vol IV, No. 11, Feb. 1960.
[12] Dr. Elton Trueblood: *The Predicament of Modern Man*, pp. 59, 60.
[13] Cf. Dr. P. A. Sorokin, *The Crisis of Our Age*, pp. 318-326.
[14] Cf. Lit-sen Chang: (1) *Christian Criticism of Humanism;* (2) *The Futility of Humanism*, Hong Kong, The Alliance Press, 1968.

[15] Cf. Sorokin: *op. cit.* and (1) *Social and Cultural Dynamics;* (2) *The Reconstruction of Humanity.*

[16] Cf. Sorokin: *Man and Society in Calamity*, pp. 318-319.

[17] Unfortunately, there is the mistaken view among some of the liberal "clergymen" that "Jesus was a Hippie."

[18] Psalm 2:2.

[19] Col. 3:2.

[20] Cf. Roger L. Shinn: *Man: The New Humansim;* and cf. Harold B. Kuhn: "New Humanisms for Old," *Christianity Today*, Jan. 31, 1969.

[21] Jeremiah 2:13.

[22] John 8:20.

[23] Colosians 1:27.

[24] Cf. Acts 4:12; John 8:32.

APPENDIX I

THE WAY TO THE TRUE ENLIGHTENMENT

-FROM ZEN TO CHRIST-

-Brief Testimony of the Author-

It is a most amazing thing that a former ardent follower of Zen could write this book to bear witness to the Light - the true "Enlightenment," which I have been seeking and probing for almost half a century, though in good earnest, but with the wrong approach.

I was raised in a pagan family. I studied Buddhist literature with my mother from boyhood and was much inspired by her wonderful stories about her vision of Buddha, and later particularly by the unusual experience of her death. While my mother was a believer of the Pure Land sect, my father practiced Zen. My father's raptures in his experience of "Satori" and his daily "beatific vision" over death and life quite convinced me. He even urged me to quit politics for the excellency of the attainment of "Satori." In fact, I was later also quite proud of my own experiences of so-called "Satori." I had a strong sense of airiness, of increasing serenity, of "returning home," a conviction of rightness in all actions, a feeling of exaltation and a joy as if over death and life.[1]

As I am limited by space, I shall confine myself to just mentioning one or two instances. When the whole War Capital was on the verge of ruin during the endless bombing by the Japanese, one of my colleagues asked me with surprise in the dugout, "Why are you still serene as if nothing disturbed you?" "Zen!" I replied with a proud smile. Once I even could foretell with precision how a bomb damaged my neighboring room, but left my room intact. Another instance which might be added, was the unusual experience of the death of my mother. In my boyhood, as I recall, when I left home for boarding school, I used to weep in saying good-bye to my mother; and sometimes wondered whether, in case my mother should die, I could stand such a shock of bereavement. However, when the news of my mother's death reached me in Chung-king, then the War Capital, I did not even shed a tear. For in Zen, Buddha nature or the true-self transcends all duality and is therefore above birth and death. It was said that my mother passed away in peace; and at the time of her death, my little five-year old nephew saw in a vision that she was received up into "heaven" in a sedan-chair followed by a magnificent procession. My father even admonished me in his letter that I should not mourn her death, but rather should rejoice. Since then, Zen became more fascinating to my mind.

After the Second World War, in view of the great devastation and upheaval of my nation and of the world I had a great concern about the future of mankind, and believed that the hope of mankind and peace on earth were to be found in the East rather than in the West, so that I claimed the universal validity and relevance of our religion with strong conviction and vigor. For this purpose, I even resigned from political activities and dedicated myself to this cause by founding a university as an initial step.

When I was elected as the first President of King-nan University with the cooperation of a group of very prominent scholars in Chinese culture and philosophy, I possessed an ambition to promote a revival movement of oriental religions and civilization. In 1949, I was invited by a famous university in India to give a series of lectures on the general theme "The Destiny of Asia," which I accepted with an intention to bring my ambition and dream into realization. But, when my spiritual crisis reached its climax, just before my departure, something happened abruptly and interrupted my program and the door to India was thus shut! Indeed, "He openeth, and no man shutteth; and shutteth, and no man openeth."[2] This was indeed the pivotal point which determined my eternal destiny—and turned me from eternal death to eternal life!

As Paul was converted after direct confrontation with the Lord "in a light from heaven" which "shined round about him," when he was on his way to Damascus, "breathing out threatening and slaughter against the disciples of the Lord."[3] I was led by God to Java as I was on my way to India, aiming to promote a resurgent movement of Buddhism. My family and I left Hong Kong in 1949 after Christmas and arrived at Djakarta in January 1950. And, by His providence, we found a house in Semarang just next to a church which was under construction, and where later I was led by God to attend its dedication service. (We could have had a better house on another road, if we had arrived just one day earlier; but, then I would never have had any relation with that church!) However, I did not go there to worship in spirit and truth, but was invited to participate in that occasion as a social gathering. If it had been an old church, I would never have attended that church either, for I was not motivated by an humble heart to worship, but rather went with a sense of pride of being invited to sit among other social dignitaries and government representatives. But this was the Lord's doing. Surely, the wrath of man shall praise the Lord,[4] and indeed His ways are higher than my ways, and His thoughts than my thoughts.[5] How unsearchable are the riches both of His wisdom and knowledge, His judgement and providence, that I should go to that church and meet the Lord there according to His appointed place and time, in His eternal purpose.

Just this one single step was to change the whole perspective of my life!

During the dedication service, I was not so much impressed by the "enticing words" of the preacher as some rationalists would imagine, but was deeply touched by the mighty power of the Holy Spirit. It was in the time of prayer that I was brought face to face with the Lord Jesus Christ. This was the critical turning point of my life for since that occasion, Jesus has truly come into my heart, and my attitude toward Him and His church has been miraculously c h a n g e d. His Spirit began to work mysteriously in my life, and through His power "mighty to the pulling down of strong holds; casting down imaginations and every high thing that exalts itself against the knowledge of God and bringing into captivity every thought to the obedience of Christ."[6] I just could not stop going to church after that, for there was a power on high drawing me to seek His Kingdom. In fact, I was so thirsty day and night for His divine messages and living water of life, I would even go several hundreds miles away simply to attend an evangelistic meeting. It was so amazing because it was not "with excellency of speech or of wisdom" of the preacher, but rather with "a broken and contrite heart" that I loved to hear the simple gospel message - "Repent" and "believe on the Lord Jesus Christ." As the Holy Spirit convicted me of my sin,[7] "I determined not to know anything save Jesus Christ and him crucified."[8] Several times, after I was first converted, when I saw His cross I wept!

From 1951, I began to read the Bible regularly. As He called me out of darkness into His marvelous light[9], and as I turned to the Lord, the veil which was upon my heart was immediately taken away.[10] It was so amazing that my tears always overflowed on my cheeks when I read the Bible or even a simple gospel leaflet which I formerly laughed to scorn as "foolishness." His words became powerful as lightning, "sharper than any two-edged sword, piercing even to the dividing asunder of soul and spirit, and of joints and marrows, and is a discerner of the thoughts and intents of the heart."[11] Many sophisticated scholars claim that they also read and know the Bible, but here I would ask my reader to notice the strong contrast of my experiences of reading the Bible. The first time, when I was in Shanghai Baptist University, I read the Bible, but with repulsion and hatred; and as a result, I deserted the school, and later supported the anti-Christian movement which was going on at that time, by contributing articles to the newspapers. The second time, when I was co-founder of an Association of Comparative Religions, I read the Bible again in order to show my impartiality to all religions, but with ignorance, because it was a closed book to the natural man. The third time, after my conversion, I read the Bible with a flood of tears as a prodigal son coming home to meet his loving father.[12] This was not just a short-lived emotion, but lasted for many months, and continues to recur from time to time even until now.

This is the strong evidence of the Bible truth that "the preaching of the Cross is to them that perish foolishness but unto us which are saved, it is the power of God."[13] "The natural man receives not the things of the Spirit of God for they are foolishness to him neither can he know them."[14] It further proves that until "the blood of Jesus Christ, His Son cleanses us from all sin,"[15] and until the God of our Lord Jesus Christ, the Father of glory gives unto you the spirit of wisdom and revelation in the knowledge of Him: the eyes of your understanding being enlightened,[16] you can never have genuine "Satori" (Enlightenment) or open your "third eye" as Zen preaches.

Although it is not my intention here to write the whole story of my conversion which would demand a large volume,[17] I do realize it is my solemn responsibility to tell my readers that since I have found the true light and have now an anchor of the soul both sure and steadfast and "a Kingdom which cannot be moved,"[18] I should say now that what Zen offered me was merely a technique of self-intoxication or a sense of false security. As the late Dr. Carl G. Jung, wrote in a Foreword of Dr. Suzuki's "An Introduction to Zen Buddhism": "I treat Satori as a psychological problem....The imagination itself is a psychic occurence. The man who has Enlightenment or alleges that he has it thinks in any case that he is enlightened...even if he were to lie."[19] This kind of sense of security is not only false but also dangerous, because, as Jung pointed out, Satori was a result of "many years of the most strenuous devastation of rational understanding."[20] Such a psychological approach which ignores the religious hierarchy of values is liable to obvious drawbacks and doomed to failure. It does not reach the inner need, for man's problem is not psychological but spiritual. Its line is too short to reach down to the depth of the spirit of man nor does it heal the soul.[21] "What they claim to be as "Satori," is only "self-intoxication." I have discussed this at length in the later part of the book.

Indeed, having been delivered from death to life, and from darkness to light, 1 can say now with Paul, "What things were gain to me, those I counted loss for Christ;"[22] and with Calvin, "In vain for us, therefore, does creation exhibit so many bright lamps lighted up to show forth the glory of its Author. Though they beam upon us from every quarter, they are altogether insufficient of themselves to lead us into the right path."[23] For as we observe in Abraham, the nearer he approaches to behold the glory of the Lord, the readier he is to acknowledge himself but "dust and ashes!"[24] For many years I thought that I was enlightened and boasted myself of righteousness, but at conversion I found myself confronted by a revelation of God which led me to see His majesty and glory and my own sinful nature and utter unworthiness, then said I with Isaiah: "Woe is me! for I am undone, because I am a man of unclean lips and I dwell in the midst of a people of unclean lips, for my eyes have seen the King, the Lord of hosts;"[25] and cried out in repentance with Job; "I have heard of three by the hearing of the ear: but now mine eye seeth thee. Wherefore I abhor myself and repent in dust and ashes."[26] The tragic mistake I made was that I identified Christianity with Western culture and was ignorant of the fact that Christianity had rather an Asian origin and is not a religion merely for the West. With this wrong view in my mind, I was like a defective camera and my perceptive organ began to register the world in a distorted form. When my hope in the West was disillusioned, I thought the way of salvation should be found in the East; but did not realize that "Salvation belongeth unto the Lord."[27] It comes from heaven, not from West, nor from East; it comes from above, not from "within," as the Zen teaches. It is of no profit to look "within," "for in me, that is in my flesh, dwelleth no good thing."[28] It is of no profit to turn to the East, for "there is no new thing under the sun,"[29] "a man can receive nothing, except it be given from heaven."[30] "Except a man be born again, he cannot see the kingdom of God,"[31] nor can he really see his own nature and know his own heart which "is deceitful above all things and desperately wicked,"[32] because of "being alienated from life of God."[33] It is only when we are changed into His image "even as by the Spirit of the Lord," can we behold his glory;[34] and even now, "sit with him in the heavenly places in Jesus Christ";[35] and "when he shall appear", "coming in the clouds of heaven with power and great glory", "We shall be like him, for we shall see him as he is."[36] "Then face to face. . .shall I know, even as also I am known,"[37] and be presented "before the presence of his glory with exceeding joy."[38] This is the true "enlightenment" (Satori), and the true way of salvation.

---

[1] See what was described about himself by Christian Humphreys, President of the Buddhist Society, London, in his book, *Zen Buddhism*, pp. 159-160. Cf. also the Part One, chapter two, II, 5 of this volume.
[2] Rev. 3:7.
[3] Cf. Acts 9:1-22.
[4] Cf. Psalm 76:10.
[5] Cf. Isaiah 55:9.
[6] II Cor. 10:4, 5.
[7] Cf. John 16:8.
[8] I Cor. 2:1, 2.
[9] I Peter 2:9.
[10] Cf. II Cor. 3:16.
[11] Hebrews 4:12.
[12] Cf. Luke chapter 15.

[13] I Cor. 1:18.
[14] I Cor. 2:14.
[15] I John 1:7.
[16] Cf. Eph. 1:17, 18.
[17] Cf. My testimony: *"From Pagan to Christian,"* The *Spire*, Feb. 1961, Park Street Church, Boston, Mass.; and my other articles *South Baptist World Journal*, Jan. 1955; and in *World Vision* magazine, Jan. 1966.
[18] Hebrews 6:19; 12:28.
[19] D. T. Suzuki: *An Introduction to Zen Buddhism*, Foreword, p. 15.
[20] *Ibid.*, pp. 21-29.
[21] Cf. James Orr: *Christian View of God and the World*, pp. 381, 409- 412, and J. A. C. Murray: *An Introduction to a Christian Psychotherapy*, pp. 12, 148, 270-91.
[22] Phil. 3:7, 8.
[23] John Calvin, Institutes I, Chapter V, p. 14.
[24] Genesis 18:27.
[25] Isaiah 6:1-5.
[26] Job 42:5, 6.
[27] Psalm 3:8.
[28] Roman 7:18.
[29] Ecclesiastes 1:9.
[30] John 3:27.
[31] John 3:3.
[32] Jer. 17:9.
[33] Eph. 4:18.
[34] Cf. II Cor. 3:18.
[35] Eph. 4:6.
[36] Matt. 24:30; I John 3:2.
[37] I Cor. 13:12.
[38] Cf. Jude 24, 25.

APPENDIX II

LSD, A NEW RELIGION?

Is There an Alternative to Hallucinogens?

By

Dr. Hudson T. Armerding,

President of Wheaton College

A new cult is seeking acceptance on the college and university campus. Its proponents call it a psychedelic religion, a "mind-stretching" movement using drugs known as hallucinogens. The best-known of these is LSD. By means of these drugs some individuals believe they have had a remarkable spiritual experience and have even established places of worship known as psychedelic chapels. Some users who formerly were skeptics now report they have had a profound religious experience similar to that of the apostles and prophets.

In an article in the *Christian Herald* for October, 1966, Jerome Allison has pointed out that the use of hallucinogens is not new but goes back to the time of Homer. Those described in his writings as the Lotus Eaters apparently were individuals who had eaten plants or herbs which have in them the same substances to be found in these drugs. The same is true in the southwest of our country where the peyote cactus has been eaten by the American Indians to induce a psychedelic reaction.

In view of the growing interest in the use of hallucinogens some may wonder whether, as we involve ourselves in today's world it is legitimate to use these drugs, as urged by Professor Timothy Leary, or whether our Christian faith is adequate apart from the use of these products.

CLINICAL STUDIES CITED

In considering this question, an appraisal should be made of the clinical studies of psychedelic drugs. Some conclusions have already been reached by those who are well-known and respected in the area of medicine and psychiatry. Dr. Dana L. Farnsworth, head of the medical services for Harvard University, writing in the September 14, 1963 issue of *The Journal of the American Medical Association,* said, "Our accumulating day to day experience with patients suffering the consequences of the hallucinogens demonstrates beyond question that these drugs have the power, in some cases with even a single dose, to damage the individual psyche, indeed to cripple it for life." *The New England Journal of Medicine* has warned that LSD is "a dangerous toxic substance" and that "no one can be sure that ingestion of this drug will not harm him immediately or in the long run." Dr. Jame L. Goddard, commissioner of food and drugs in the department of health, education and welfare, says that after twenty years of exploration LSD still has no place in medical practice. In an article in the October, 1966, issue of *College and University Business,* he declared, "There has been a lot of talk and publicity in popular magazines about LSD's supposed powers to expand the mind, to make it function in creative, inventive new ways. This is just not so; such powers have not been scientifically demonstrated. What *is* so is that the records of many hospitals show the admittance of patients who have taken this drug and have literally *lost* their minds."

Dr. Marvin Stern and his associates at the Bellevue Hospital in New York City reported cases of chronic psychosis, longterm hospitalization and possible brain damage as a result of the taking of this particular drug. Dr. Hans-Lukas Teuber, head of the department of psychology at Massachusetts Institute of Technology, was quoted in the May, 1966, issue of *Innisfree,* the MIT journal of inquiry, as saying, "We now have well-documented case histories showing that taking LSD once or a few times, in minute amounts, can lead to a spontaneous reappearance of the psychotic state, at later times, without further ingestion of the drug. Thus, the person using the drug thinks he is putting himself only temporarily into this peculiar state, and then finds that he is suffering what amounts to a chemical lesion in his brain, because the LSD state keeps coming back without further intake of LSD. It is for that reason that we must warn the public against the use of this drug."

Mr. Allison listed the following incidents after interviewing Yale's Dr. Malcolm Bowers, Dr. Gotthard Booth, a New York psychiatrist, and Dr. Stern all of whom had treated patients suffering from the effects of LSD. One girl, secretly dosed as a prank, thought she was going crazy and committed suicide. An Army platoon, secretly dosed as part of a chemical warfare experiment, became completely incompetent. A youth who took some of these drugs had a week-long recurrence of the reaction three weeks later and in despair took his life by driving his car into a suicidal crash. Others under LSD illusions have thrown themselves out of high windows, hurled themselves in front of trains, met death while wandering in high speed traffic. An Amherst student became convinced while under LSD that he was a predatory animal and began to bite people. A New York book editor taking LSD, even under a doctor's supervision, ended up in a panic, convinced that he had met Satan. Another patient thought he had become a plant and admitted, "I felt my spine grow down through the earth and take root. . .I raised my arms and waved them around and really *was* a plant." Another was found crawling around on his hands and knees. He thought he had to walk carefully lest he fall off.

Dr. Timothy Leary, the self-styled high priest of the LSD cult, says that by taking LSD, "you're going to lose your mind." A student, after three days of being under hallucination because of the drug, agreed. He found a doctor who would give him an antidote. Later he said, "I don't care how boring it is. I'd rather be in a sane world. If I had to live with hallucinations I'd commit suicide if necessary to get away from them."

It is admitted that in spite of the evidence to the contrary some sincerely believe that LSD or other hallucinogens can have a beneficial effect if used under carefully controlled clinical conditions. Yet Dr. Ebbe Custis Hoff, dean of the Medical College of Virginia, and a medical doctor and psychiatrist, has said that in his opinion, after analysis of extensive experimentation he was convinced LSD did not produce any discernible beneficial effects in treating patients with emotional or psychological problems. The same opinion is held by Dr. Teuber of MIT who, when asked whether LSD or similar drugs can be used directly in the treatment of psychosis, replied, "So far, the evidence for any usefulness in this respect is unimpressive. In the adult psychotic the drug produces generally an underscoring of the psychotic illness—you make the patient worse rather than better."

UNCHRISTIAN EFFECTS OF LSD

It is also important to consider the effect of these drugs as far as religious experience is concerned. A comparison of such effects with Christian experience discloses definite contrasts. Christians are under obligation to love their neighbors. This means that other persons should be more, rather than less, important than material objects. Yet Aldous Huxley, in describing his experience while under the influence of mescaline, one of the hallucinogens, testified that the legs of a chair or the crease of his flannel trousers were the most important concerns he had during this experience.

Those who have had a real experience with God manifest a humility which stands in vivid contrast to the attitude of contemptuous superiority displayed by the so-called test tube mystics. The outstanding Christians of all ages have used their profound experiences as a basis for constructive contributions to the moral, ethical, and physical well-being of their fellow men. Those influenced by LSD, including such creative personalities as artists and writers, on the other hand tend to decline, both in creativity and discrimination. Dr. Goddard says of them, "They have lost the power to think, to reason and to create, lost all power to use what is so fundamental to a life of achievement." Dr. Teuber agrees, "I see no evidence that people are more creative under the influence of these drugs—rather the reverse."

If the results derived from the use of the hallucinogens, therefore, are not those which should proceed from one living in obedience to biblical imperatives, are there spiritual resources upon which the Christian may draw to enable him to confront the pressures and the paradoxes which characterize much of life today?

SPIRITUAL RESOURCES AVAILABLE

There is a tendency on the part of some to ignore or dismiss as inadequate those resources which God Himself has provided for us. Conceivably this may be due to the opinion that what God has provided does not produce the alleged desired results to be achieved from the use of drugs. Yet it is striking to notice that the prophecy of Joel, quoted by Peter in Acts 2, predicts that in the last days the Lord would pour out His Spirit upon all men. The statement might be paraphrased to read that those upon whom the Spirit would come would have mind-stretching experiences. In those days young men would see visions; old men would dream dreams. This suggests that there is a reality and a perspective to be found in the work of the Holy Spirit far superior to that claimed by the drug takers yet without the unfortunate side-effects which the LSD users experience.

When one is under the control and guidance of the Holy Spirit, he becomes more, rather than less, concerned about others. Instead of becoming indifferent to the society around him, he becomes much more sensitive. An illustration of this contrast may be seen in the Apostle Paul's statement in Ephesians 5:18: "And be not drunk with wine, wherein is excess; but continue to be filled with the Spirit."

It is recognized that there is a difference of opinion about what the filling of the Spirit actually is. For example, many devout, earnest Christians do not believe that of necessity one must speak in tongues in order to have the fulness of the Holy Spirit. On the other hand, it seems tragically true that the great bulk of professing Christians live lives of barrenness and impotence because they are not filled with the Holy Spirit. Hence, whatever our view of the evidence of this fulness, it is manifest that the Holy Spirit is the blessed resource which is available to the Christian. Furthermore, the fulness of the Holy Spirit certainly is evidenced by the fruit of the Spirit which begins with love and culminates in self-control. Such evidence stands in vivid contrast to that which results from the use of LSD.

Another resource available to the believer is the Word of God. Yet increasingly there are comments to the effect that the great propositions of the Word of God do not relate to the concerns and the issues of our day. Evangelicals are criticized it is alleged that when they preach from the Scriptures they are not asking the right questions nor providing the right answers.

The experience of God's people in history as well as today does not support this view. Those who carefully study the Bible and then faithfully do what it commands find that it does relate to contemporary problems. Whether these be anxiety, loneliness, guilt, meaninglessness, or despair, the Scriptures speak to such issues. Furthermore, Christians in cultures in all parts of the world have found that where the gospel has been presented and received these problems can be resolved in the lives of those who have committed themselves in reality to Jesus Christ. Even the dope addicts with whom Dave Wilkerson works and who describe their temptation as the "whispering" inside of them have found release and victory.

SCRIPTURES WHOLLY ADEQUATE

This is not to suggest that there has not been failure in the lives of some Christians. There are degrees of fruitfulness as illustrated by the teaching of our Lord Jesus Christ with respect to the parable of the sower. Yet the fact that there is not a hundred-fold product does not negate the fact that the Word of God can and does have its fruited effect in the world.

Dr. Smiley Blanton, the director of the American Foundation of Religion and Psychiatry in New York City, has described an experience which took place in his office. When a patient noticed a Bible lying on Blanton's desk, he asked, "Do you, a psychiatrist, read the Bible?" "I not only read it," the doctor told him, "I study it. It is the greatest textbook on human behavior ever put together. If people would just absorb its message, a lot of us psychiatrists could close our offices and go fishing." In an address at the World Congress in Berlin in November, 1966, Rev. John Stott of London, England, reported that a friend of his, the head of the largest mental hospital in London, said to him, "If the people in my hospital could only know of the possibility of forgiveness, I could dismiss half of them at once." This forgiveness is what the Word of God discloses to mankind as it reveals the significance of the sacrificial, redemptive ministry of our Lord Jesus Christ.

In the November 25, 1966, issue of *Christianity Today*, a clergyman in one of America's historic denominations personally testified to the benefit of committing Scripture to memory. He found that the promises of God gave to him a remarkable inner tranquility. Sections of Scripture as brief as a single verse were powerful weapons in the ceaseless battle against temptations from the outside and urgings from within. In his memorization of Scripture he found the source for a whole set of fresh, new ideas. Slowly but certainly his mind-set was molded by the Scripture which he memorized and repeated often. From such practice a whole attitude of life began to develop.

The test of the validity of such a testimony is simply to follow the example of the author in learning and meditating upon the Holy Scriptures. The accumulated witness of Christians down the years as well as those who today live in some of the most stressful of situations attests to the validity of the proposition that the Word of God is living and active.

It is incumbent upon Christians not to under-rate the great resources which are available in the Word of God and by the Holy Spirit. The Spirit of God is able to present in His fulness in our lives, and the Word of God is able to give us the assurance, the comfort and direction which have been promised. Let us appropriate these resources for our inner peace and wholeness as children of God by faith in our Savior, Jesus Christ.

Is there an alternative to the hallucinogens? There is. It is biblical, spirit-filled Christianity.

Used by permission of Dr. Amerding

Appendix III

THE ANTI-MIND MOOD OF OUR ERA

A new movement has emerged in contemporary philosophy, paralleling the anti-hero in fiction. It is the vogue of the anti-mind.

Depth psychology in all its forms, including Freudianism, general semantics with its all-out war on Aristotelian logic and kindred language philosophies, the phenomenon known as "hippiedom," Zen Buddhism, and other like movements all converge at the point of debunking the universal values of reason. The appeal of this anti-mind "philosophy" spreads in an era when multiple-media propagandists seek to produce a crowd-culture that would rob the individual of what makes him human: his freedom and responsibility.

The Random House Dictionary of the English Language defines the new word "psychedelic" as of or noting a mental state of great calm, intensely pleasureful perception of the senses, esthetic entrancement, and creative impetus." It also denotes "any of a group of drugs producing this effect." Commenting on those who champion this state, *Time* magazine reported on the difficulty of arguing with people "who, while condemning virtually every aspect of the American scene, from its foreign policy to its moral values, offer no debatable alternatives" ("The Hippies," July 7, 1967). All they offer, Time implied, is the syndrome of the anti-mind philosophy.

However disturbed reasonable citizens may be by this utter nonchalance over any responsibility toward society or any individual redirection toward new goals, it need not surprise us that the hippies wholly disregard other Americans' disapproval or approval. In Zen language they are enlightened; and logic in Zen Buddhism, as in general semantics, is held applicable only to words, never to actual "reality." Verbal reference, involving the logical relations of words-to-thoughts-to-things, has been explained away as the "noises people make" under specific circumstances. In more than one modern semantic view, definitions in any knowledge-field stand at various levels of abstraction from what is being defined. Zen's main tenet, from Bodhidharma in the sixth century to the late Dr. D. T. Suzuki, has been: "All generalizations are false, including this one!" The so-called Zen enlightenment (the experiencing of the oneness of it all) entails the impossibility of telling others what Zen is. Thus the person who fails to attain enlightenment is forever barred from the knowledge of it.

Zen does not hold concepts to be descriptive of the truly real. Christmas Humphreys, a prominent English barrister and Buddhist, wrote: "When thought, infuriated, baffled, and at last aware of its futility, gives up, then suddenly, unmistakably, comes—What? A unique, utterly personal incommunicable experience, in a flash of *that which is beyond description, because it is beyond the plane on which description, which must use the symbols of duality, can function*" (*Encounter*, Dec., 1960; italics added). Conceptualization is said to destroy the enlightened one's "unity." To make the student of Zen wake to the error of his conceptual understanding, said Dr. Suzuki, it may be necessary to strike him and thus to let him realize within himself the meaning of the statement, "One is all and all is one" (*Zen and Japanese Culture*, 1959). By such means alone, at times, may the learner be awakened from his "logical somnambulism."

It is true, of course, that two years later Suzuki wrote in his defense of Zen against an attack by Arthur Koestler: "There will be no name-calling, no kicking, but a 'logical' presentation of Zen philosophy." But, he added, the achievement of satori (defined as "entering fully into life here and now") is helped on by the master's hitting students over the head with bricks, by kicks, slaps, and so on. When he used the term "logical" he put it in quotes, adding as an apology for using the word at all: "The human situation is full of contradictions: When we wish to say that no words are needed, more words are needed to prove it" (*Encounter*, Oct., 1961. He stated, too, that all Zen literature is "a pile of waste paper to be consigned to fire" and proceeded to back the statement by quoting from Arvaghosha, of the second century A. D., Confucius, and Lao-Tzu, all of whose writings have been carefully preserved. Buddha himself was invoked as having said, "I have been talking and talking to you for the last forty-nine years, but in truth I have not spoken a word."

Talking and more talking has gone on over the centuries, of course. And no cult in our era has been so talkative as Zen Buddhism itself. Even in impugning logic, Zen literature is admittedly vast. The highly vocal Dr. Suzuki himself contributed an astronomical number of words to it. In fact, a disciple said admiringly that Suzuki had made English, in which many of his words were written, a second Zen language.

Zen has been praised immoderately as a refreshing nonconceptual philosophy for the rationalism-sodden culture of the West. The late psychiatrist Dr. Carl G. Jung and others have held that it represents a kind of primal simplicity and sanity. But Zen seems, instead, as overly sophisticated as the doctrines of the first sophists, and as unsound. The rational faculty is part of all experience. Hence, whoever distrusts the mind's ability to report truly on reality was certainly made to do so by a false philosophy. He was not born with any such distrust.

Rational criticism naturally has no weight with those who hold metaphysics passé and who immerse themselves as far as possible in the dream of a No-Mind existence. But there is no real choice between eighteenth-century rationalism and the No-Mind mentality at this point. Although both lay claim to "enlightenment," each rests on dangerous half-truth.

The existentialist, to be sure, strives to do justice to the whole person, but with equally inadequate results. Kierkegaard, whom certain Zennists would like to claim, was actually a God-centered intellectual who agreed with Socrates that the paramount duty of every person was to tend his soul. Unfortunately, however, his disjunction of eternity and time so exaggerated the transcendence of God that he was a forerunner of both dialectical and existential theology. In anticipating their denial that divine revelation takes the form of concepts and words, he too merits criticism from the standpoint of the errors of the anti-mind philosophy of our era, however commendable his forthright repudiation of Hegelianism.

The case for the actual ability of language to convey human knowledge without deformation and to serve as an adequate vehicle for divine revelation still stands. This, in fact, is what the Bible teaches and the best the Christian thought affirms. Christianity declares that God has come to man in a speaking and an acting person, Jesus Christ, and that he continues to come to man in the written words of Scripture. "The words that I speak- unto you, they are spirit and they are life." Far from restricting man to a non-real, chimeric existence, language and the rational faculty to receive it are actually the vehicles by which God reveals the real to man. They are vehicles of revelation. Consequently, they are actually among the greatest of God's gifts.

Used by permission of *Christianity Today*, of which Dr. Carl F. H. Henry is the founding editor; it appeared as an editorial in the September 1, 1967, issue.

Appendix IV

WHERE IS MODERN THEOLOGY GOING?
Carl F. H. Henry

Ours is a generation of gyrating theology that seems to have spun off any sure Word of God. Neo-Protestant religious currents are losing force and nearing an end of their special impact, while classic modernism, though politically a volcano, is theologically now but a bag of wind.

What significant developments define the theology of the recent past, and what can we say about them from the evangelical Protestant point of view?

1. Reigning neo-Protestant religious theory has collapsed for the third time in the twentieth century. First, classic modernism broke down; then, neo-orthodoxy; and most recently, existentialism.

Classic modernism was the theology of radical *divine immanence*. Predicated on Hegelian pantheism, it assimilated God to man and nature, and banished miracle and special revelation. Its most influential theologian was Schleiermacher, who eagerly shifted the case for theism from supernatural revelation to religious experience — supposedly as an absolute requirement of the modern mind. But modern thought proved more transitory than the early modernists dreamed.

Neo-orthodoxy was the theology of radical *divine transcendence.* In the context of dialectical theology it reasserted divine initiative, special revelation, and miraculous redemption. Its courageous spokesman was Karl Barth, who later intoned funeral rites for the modernist message in Europe.

Extentialism was the theology of *subjectivity,* heir to the dialectical denial of objective revelation and redemption. Rudolf Bultmann was its champion, insisting that the modern mind demands, not a modernist, not a neo-orthodox, but an existentialist reading of reality. Demythologize the supernatural! Existentialize God's activity! Dehistoricize the kerygma! But Bultmannian scholars soon fell into internal disagreement and were hard pressed by external critics. Like modernism and neo-orthodoxy, existential theology has lost control at the formative frontiers of theology in our day.

2. *The survival span of recent modern alternatives to evangelical Christianity is shrinking.* Anyone who scans the decades of the twentieth century with an eye on the dominant theological traditions will soon note the shortening of intervals between newly emerging neo-Protestant religious theories. It is probably accurate to say that classic modernism reigned over the influential formative centers of theological thought from 1900 to 1930, dialectical theology from 1930 to 1950, and existential theology from 1950 to 1960.

Some theologians speak of a "compression of time periods for the development of theological traditions"— from a thousand years, as in medieval times, to as little as a decade in our own day. Such continuing theological reconstruction, some observers would say, is a necessary result of the knowledge-explosion in our time; others even depict all theological formulations as fallible human theories or tentative religious models subject to constant revision.

But surely such endorsement of theological revisionism is not shared by biblically oriented Christians, who insist on a core of revealed truth by which all human traditions must be judged. One may recall the well-worded sign on a country-church bulletin board: "Our God isn't dead—sorry about yours."

European theology is now an open field; none of the many contenders has control. The revolt of Bultmann's disciples, which began in 1954 with Käsemann's rebellious critique, marked the beginning of a decade of unending theological dissent and division. The growing disagreement among post-Bultmannians over the significance of the historical Jesus was only one aspect of the religious ferment. Among those involved in the widening search for a satisfying alternative were the traditional conservatives, who insisted that divine revelation is both intelligible and historical; salvation-history scholars, who asserted that revelation is historical but that we are left to extrapolate its meaning; revitalized Barthians, who supplemented the early Barth with quasi-objective elements in the mood of the revised *Church Dogmatics;* independent thinkers like Thielicke and Stauffer; and at the frontiers, newer figures such as Pannenberg and Moltmann. But in all this turbulence, it is noteworthy that more radical thinkers like Braun and Mezger, who reduced the reality of God to interhuman relationships and inverted "God is love" into "love is God," offered but one of many alternatives in the pluralistic theological milieu. By contrast, radical secular theology in the United States won wide attention and created a special situation.

3. The death-of-God theology gained prominence in American religious discussion and was openly welcomed within the ecumenical dialogue.

The death-of-God writers gained their importance, not through Gabriel Vahanian's assertion of a modern cultural alienation from the Christian heritage whereby God has died existentially, but especially by their affirmation of the literal death of the Diety. The new radicals misappropriated and distorted the *Letters from Prison,* which Bonhoeffer never intended as a prolegomenon to religious positivism. In their common projection of a secular theology that gave centrality to Jesus in order to displace a supernatural personal God, Altizer insisted on God's ontic death, Van Buren shared his rejection of the realm of divine transcendence, and Hamilton forfeited its significance.

4. Scholars are increasingly aware of the depth of the current religious crisis. . Neo-protestantism today is readily described as a situation of theological chaos.

Some relativists speak approvingly of the "pluralistic character" of the present religious scene, as if open-end diversity were preferable to theological consensus. But many interpreters realize that theology is now in a state of confusion, even anarchy; some characterize our era as a theological shambles. Frederick Herzog describes the situation as one of baffling consternation (*Understanding God*, 1966). He characterizes it by an ancient Greek term revived in the last century to describe the vagaries of primitive religons in the Pacific islands: *aporia* (*a+poros* = "without passage," a state of disstressing doubt about what course to take—where to begin, what to say, where to end.)

5. There is growing realization that the force of the biblical view of God was broken through compressed and fragmented presentations that obscured important aspects of the scriptural revelation.

The present generation was proffered a Twiggy-theology, styled to make one forget that its essential form was little more than a skeleton; a mini-theology that offered high style for the new season but had to run for cover when winter came.

Man's *primal ontological awareness* of religion reality is stressed by some theologians, and in a variety of ways: as precognitive awareness that insistently raises the question of God (Herzog); as precognitive awareness that *is* awareness of God (Tillich); and as precognitive awareness of the mystery of the universe, alongside which God the Mystery assertedly reveals himself only in personal encounter (Hordern).

But others deny any point of contact whatever in man for God's revelation in order to concentrate the case for the reality of God in dialectical confrontation (Barth, Gollwitzer). Still others retain general revelation while repudiating natural theology (Brunner).

Some revive a species of natural theology (Hartshorne, Cobb).

Then there are those who rely on the new quest for the historical Jesus (Robinson, Michaelson).

Linguistic theologians contend that religious language has functional utility but is not conceptually true. (This semantic obfuscation is in part a reaction against the endless and exasperating neo-Protestant redefinition of who and what God is. If the Christian concept of God must be as radically changed as it is in Whiteheadian, Tillichian, and Bultmannian reconstructions, in order to make it meaningful to modern man, would it not be more honest simply to assign to language about God a phychological significance only?)

The theology of the recent past has characteristically attempted take-off on too short runways to get airborne. The vain attempt to support the case for theism by a fragmented theology is especially evident in Barth's concentration on divine-human encounter as the locus of revelation, and in Tillich's concentration on God as the immanent Ultimate. To overcome the immanentist loss of God in man and nature, with its notion that the all-inclusive Absolute is *more* than we are, Barth insisted that God confronts men individually as the sovereign *Other*. But his assertion of personal confrontation involved also a denial of the universal dimension of divine revelation in man, nature, and history. Tillich, on the other hand, emphasized the universal dimension of revelation by anchoring the case for theism in everyman's back yard; he denied a supernatural personal God, presumably to protect the universal access to divine revelation through the Ground of all being.

So each formula goes to its own radical extreme to compensate for the compromises of another, while none incorporates in itself the comprehensiveness of the biblical revelation of God. In view of this reduction of the content of theology to isolated and distorted fragments of the scriptural view, the successive alternatives in recent neo-Protestant thought gain the unhappy character of reactions to reactions to reactions. In this connection it is noteworthy to recall how death-of-God theologians like Altizer and Van Buren depend on the theology of individual confrontation for their comprehension of the Christian religion (Van Buren completed his Ph.D. under Barth, and Altizer misunderstands historic Christianity in the neo-orthodox sense of radically transcendent individual confrontation).

6. *A vast number of highly tentative religious writings reject traditional formulations, reflect the modern spirit, refuse to concede that they are anti-Christian, restate the biblical view in novel forms, and insist that the new statements express what the biblical writers really intended to say.* These speculative reconstructions stretch all the way from panentheistic Christification (Teilhard de Chardin) to God-is-dead speculation (Altizer).

Three patterns of speculative religious thought are now emerging as alternatives to historic Christian theism. All of them represent a critical withdrawal from biblical controls. All reject the reality of the supernatural or of a personal God distinct from the universal. All disown miraculous divine revelation and redemption. These three patterns are:

a. Theories of sociological salvation. Here politico-economic structures are emphasized as the key to human felicity. Alongside the familiar Marxist version (dialectical materialism), so-called Christian versions have been projected in the context of a secular theology by Gogarten in Germany, Van Leeuwen in Holland, Ronald Gregor Smith in England, and Harvey Cox and Paul van Buren in the United States.

b. Theories of cosmological salvation. These espouse a religious ontology wherein mankind gains redemption by cooperating with divine cosmic forces. Anticipations of such views were projected by Bergson in France and

Berdyaev in Russia. Current examples are Teilhard de Chardin's parentheism, Whitehead's pan-psychism, and Tillich's being-itself in which all men participate.

c. *Attempted syntheses of the sacred and secular.* These diverse elements are compounded in a variety of ways by A. M. Ramsey, John A. T. Robinson, and sometimes Harvey Cox.

All three patterns agree in several basic respects in their revolt against biblical theology:

- Reality, as they see it, is one-layered; rejected is a divine supernatural-moral realm antecedent to and independent of the world of nature.

- Only within the immanent natural process do they accommodate the dimension of transcendence.

- Cognitive knowledge of the super-sensory is excluded.

- Many theological antitheses are rejected, including the traditional contrasts of Creator-creation, eternity-time, infinite-finite, supernatural-natural, good-evil, Church-world, belief-unbelief, salvation-judgment.

Yet for all their common disagreements with biblical theology, the new trends nonetheless also differ significantly from one another:

- The latest attempts to synthesize the ebb and flow of the sacred and the secular proceed in contrary directions. Harvey Cox works Teilhard de Chardin in a secular direction and Bishop Robinson works secular theology in Teilhard's panentheistic direction; meanwhile A. M. Ramsey's correlation (*The Sacred and the Secular*) is more mediating.

- Cox locates the "transcendent" (God's special activity) at revolutionary frontiers of social change and regards centrality for I-Thou personal relations as a threat to the fundamental importance of justice, which is no respector of persons. But Robinson considers the personal as the decisive category for interpreting reality. Here, again, antithetical views have predictably emerged from an earlier dilution of justice to love.

Noteworthy is the fact that current expositions increasingly shroud the personal dimension in ambiguity. Neo-orthodoxy had elevated the I-Thou encounter to decisive centrality, correlating this emphasis with the supernatural revelation of a personal God wholly other than man and nature. Existentialism diluted and restated this relationship in terms of transcendent personal encounter. But recent mediating writers weaken it still further by discarding the reality of a personal God and the emphasis on revelational confrontation. Teilhard, Whitehead, and Robinson, rejecting transcendent personal individual revelation, speak of divine-human relations in mystical and experiential terms only, and see the whole of reality as one field in which the All and the personal constitute a single cosmic movement toward interpersonalization in love.

The theological consequences of this surrender of biblical terrain are grave. In at least four respects the new views signal a strategic loss of Christian perspective:

a. The loss of God as *other* (and revival of a view of God as merely *more* than we are)—hence the forfeiture of an independent Creator of the universe who is antecedent to it and sovereign over it.

b. The loss of God's special once-for-all manifestation in revelation and incarnation. The new Christology dicards the doctrine of the two distinct natures in Jesus of Nazareth.

c. The loss of an absolute distinction between good and evil. If, as secular theologians assert, "God is where the action is," must we not look for a revelation of God in Hitler as well as in Jesus? And does any reason then remain for preferring peace to social revolution? What authentically evangelical interpretation can possibly be placed on Bishop Robinson's emphases that "God is in everything and everything in God—literally everything . . . evil as well as good" (*Exploration into God* 1967, p. 92), and that "no aspect of history, however resistant to personal categories, is not ultimately to be seen in terms of spirit, freedom and love" (p. 102)???? Does this not undermine a lively sense of moral conscience in the presence of evil—and quite understandably breed a "new morality"? In the name of a Christian view of God are we to expect the six million Jews who died in Hitler's Germany to discern God's spirit and love in Nazi bestiality? Could such speculation ever have evoked the indignation that shaped the Barmen Confession over against Nazi tyranny?

    d The loss of a final judgment and separation of the righteous from the wicked.

In short, the emergence of the frontier tendencies signals the collapse of the neo-orthodox attack on modernism and the reappearance of a pre-Barthian theological mood. The influence of Schleiermacher is once again registering its force. Defection to pre-Barthian modernism is attested by several features of the current trend:

• Its vague concept of divine personality, not as wholly *other* personal Creator and Redeemer of man and the world, but as a loosely defined quality structuring the whole of reality.

• Its evasion of a metaphysical objectification of the God-idea and confinement of the content of religious affirmations to statements about God-in-relation to us. Here one finds a revival of emphases in Kant and Schleiermacher. God becomes a postulate demanded by man's moral nature, but the reality of God is asserted without the existence of God as an objectively metaphysical being. The mood is anticipated in Kant's *Opus Postumum:* "The concept of God is a concept of a subject outside me *who imposes obligations* on me . . . This Imperious Being is not outside man in the sense of a substance different from man. . . . The All, the universe of things, contains God and the world. . . ."

• Its shift of emphasis away from divine initiative to human exploration in the theological arena. This trend so adjusts Christianity to one segment of the contemporary mind by removing the reality of revelation and by conforming theology to speculation that it makes revealed religion superfluous. It rejects the religion of the Bible as a form of mental bondage to the culture of the past, while enslaving itself to modern prejudices as a true mirror of the Divine.

The new theories, in short, sacrifice what biblical theism preserves: an authentic view of a supernatural, personal God and of his relations to man and the world— the living, sovereign Creator and Preserver of men and things and moral Judge of the universe, who became incarnate in Jesus Christ in order to offer redemption to a fallen race.

7 *The case for theism is now "up for grabs"; issues are pressing to the fore that reach back through the long history of philosophy and theology and demand a comprehensive depth-investigation of theological concerns.* Disciplined students are becoming impatient with shortshrift, emaciated approaches promoted out of all proportion by denominational publishing houses, and advanced in ecumenical discussions that are shaped to preserve a certain "theological mix" in dialogue but that routinely underrepresent the existing support for historic Christian theism. The proliferation of subjectivistic theories about God has lost its excitement and is becoming wearying; scheme after scheme now has only a half-day popularity or a one-campus visibility.

In any generation, the truly influential theologians are not the clever itinerants who pick and choose which issue to attack and which to avoid but those who spell out their views comprehensively and systematically in a classroom context, and in relation to the history of ideas (eg., Barth, Brunner, Bultmann, Whitehead, Tillich, Teilhard; among evangelicals, Machen, Berkouwer, Clark, Dooyeweerd, Van Til, Carnell).

The death-of-God theology is increasingly seen, not as merely a radical deviation, nor as simply a malignant surface growth, but as a conjectural development rooted in the basic concessions of recent theological speculations and rising from them as a matter of logical inescapability. The unifying negation in the entire tradition connecting Ritschl-Barth-Bultmann-Altizer and the linguistic theologians was supplied by Kant: Man can have no cognitive knowledge of the supernatural. The predictable result is metaphysical agnosticism. Whoever overturns that premise (and neither Isaiah nor Paul would have changed his mind about the truth of God had he read Kant's *Crittique of Pure Reason*) strikes a knockout blow against the basic bias in contemporary theology.

There is now a growing demand for a comprehensive investigation of theological concerns in which the prejudices of our present age are compared and contrasted with those of earlier ages, and assessed anew in the context of the biblical exposition of God.

8. The sacred religious motifs to which Judeo-Christian revelation gave a decisive meaning are now used in so many senses by theologians and clergymen that institutional Christianity has become almost a modern Tower of Bable. The term "God" is so diversely employed that *The Encyclopedia of Philosophy* (1967) declares it "very difficult—perhaps impossible—to give a definition . . . . that will cover all usages" (III, 244).

Gerhard Ebeling says we are dying of "language poisoning"; I prefer to say, of Word-distortion.

Consider the lessons so clearly taught by the drift of twentieth-century religious thought:

• The disjunction of the self-revealing God from the word of prophets and apostles as the Word of God leads to the loss of the self-revealing God. Barth's bold effort to revive a theology of the Word of God faltered when he refused to identify the scriptural word with God's Word.

• The dialectical dogma that divine revelation is never *objectively* given (in human concepts and words and in historical events) leads to the subversion of divine revelation into human self-understanding. Bultmann not only subverted dialectical divine disclosure into existential self-understanding but lost the incarnate Word as well.

The next move was inevitable—either the *wordless God* (the "silent" God, the "hidden" God) of the *"Word" without God* (secular Christianity).

Already the "death-of-God" theology as an option has exhausted itself and is ready for burial except by the faddists. Its proponents are divided internally: Vahanian's emphasis that God is existentially dead for modern man was misappropriated by some who argue for God's ontic death; Altizer's position is an embarrassment to other death-of-God theologians because it lacks significant epistemological underpinning. According to Van Buren, the empirical scientific method "excludes" miracle and the supernatural; yet he inconsistently spares the unique values associated with Jesus from the same guillotine. The truth is that the scientific method is an impotent arbiter of these concerns. Scientists who must live daily with the scientific method are as "modern" as Altizer, Hamilton, and Van Buren; yet many recognize the limits of their method and confess that it cannot settle the issue of the reality of the supernatural.

But that is not yet the terminal stage of a sick theology. Contemporary theology cannot stop with God-is-dead bulletins, for that headline has already exhausted all possible reader interest. What more can one say about God, once he has said that God is dead? People don't care to linger long around a corpse. Book sales are falling off, and publishers are looking for new trends on which to capitalize.

9. *"The resurrection of theism" after the death of God can be a live option if the evangelical vanguard becomes theologically engaged at the frontiers of modern doubt.*

The time is ripe to recanvass evangelical rational theism with its emphasis on the revelation and manifestation of the Logos as the critical center of theological inquiry. A new prospect for systematic theology is at hand, and a growing demand exists for a comprehensive world-view that does full justice to the real world of truth and life and experience in which man must make his decisions.

In the Western world today only three major options survive. Sooner or later one of these will carry off the spiritual fortunes of the twentieth-century world. Each of these views, significantly, holds that man can know the ultimately real world. But each differs from the others in important ways about ultimate reality.

One view is Communism, which dismisses the supernatural as a myth.

The other views, to which neo-Protestant agnosticism has forfeited the great modern debate over the faith of the Bible, are Roman Catholicism and evangelical Christianity. The really live option, in my opinion, is evangelical rational theism, a theology centered in the incarnation and inscripturation of the Word (a theology not of the distorted Word but of the disclosed Word). This, I feel, offers the one real possibility of filling the theological vacuum today.

Evangelical Christianity emphasizes:

- The universal as well as once-for-all dimension of divine disclosure.
- Authentic ontological knowledge of God.
- The intellible and verbal character of God's revelation.
- The universality of religious truth.

10. The problem of God is the critical problem of the next decade (1968-1978) and is the fundamental issue for all mankind. For Americans the problem of God is more decisive for human life, liberty, and happiness than the issues of the American Revolution two centuries ago. For Protestants, the problem of God is more decisive than the issues of the Protestant Reformation four and a half centuries ago. For Christians, the problem of God is as decisive as the confrontation by Christ's disciples of the polytheistic Greco-Roman culture of their day, and of their own preparatory Hebrew heritage. For modern man come of age, the problem of God is no less decisive than was that ancient conflict between man's trust in the gods of pagan superstition and trust in the revelation of the sov-

APPENDIX IV

ereign Creator-Redeemer God. The problem of God now stands before us as the critical problem of the next decade, and it is the fundamental issue for all mankind.

From *Christianity Today* (March 1, 1968), used by permission. Dr. Carl F. H. Henry is the initiator of this book. The present author is grateful to him for his encouragement, for otherwise this book would never have been written at all.

GLOSSARY

Anatta — 'no soul' (doctrine); none-ego; "not-self".

Avidya — Ignorance; delusion; a false belief in the dichotomy of the self and the external world.

Baso — (see under Ma-tsu)

Bhikshu (or Bhikhu) — Medicant monk; member of the Order.

Bodhi — Wisdom; enlightenment; a direct intuition of the essential truth without recourse to logical inference or reasoning.

Bodhidharma (Daruma, in Japanese, A.D. 480-528) — Twenty-eight Patriarch in India, came to China about A.D. 520. during the reign of Emperor Wu (A.D. 502-547) of the Liang Dynasty, and became the founder and the first Zen Patriarch in China. A legend said that he sat cross-legged in meditation in a cave for nine years without speaking to visitors.

Buddha Nature — the true Self or Self Nature. The Buddha nature knows neither increase nor decrease. Zen signifies the mystical experience in which subjectivity and objectivity merge. True self is not conditioned by distinction between "I" and "you," "this" and "that." It transcends the duality, and is therefore above birth and death, as they imagine.

Ch'an (Zen, in Japanese) — is an abbreviation of the orignal phrase Ch'an-Na, which is the Chinese phonetic rendering of the Sanskrit word Dhyana or the Pali Jhana. It means to hold one's thought collected, not to let thought wander away from its legitimate path, so as to discipline the mind and to make it its own master through an insight into its true nature.

Chih-Yueh-Lu — See under Finger Pointing at the Moon.

Daruma — See under Bodhidharma.

Dharma (or Dhamma) — The Law; norm; truth; the saving doctrine or way of life; or the Teaching of the Buddha on the fundamental law of life and the universe.

Dhyana—the Sanskrit word of Ch'an in Chinese or Zen in Japanese.

Doshin — See under Tao-hsin.

Dukkha—Suffering, pain, misery, sorrow; the first of the Four Noble Truths.

Eka — See under Hui-Ko.

Eno — See under Hui-Neng.

Finger Pointing at the Moon (Chih-Yueh-Lu) — one of the famous Zen classics, containing many stories of the sayings of Zen masters, warning that one should not forget his final goal by emphasizing on teachings or words which are simply "the pointing fingers" to the "moon" (the goal).

Gatha — Stanza, usually contains of four verses. The typical one was given by Hui-Neng. (See under the Southern School).

Gunin — See under Hung-Jen.

Hsin — Mind or Heart. The ordinary mind involves a duality of seer and seen; but the Buddha mind transcends the distinction beween "I" and "you," "this" and "that." The fundamental of Zen is to see the real nature of one's own mind.

Hsin-Tsung — Mind doctrine or the teaching of Mind. One of the interpretations of the meaning of Zen as the way of the full realization of the Mind or the complete unfolding of the "Inner Mind."

Huang-Po (Obaku, in Japanese, A.D.d.850) —also known as Master Hsi-Yun and Master T'uan-hi. This is his post-humous name taken from the place he used to live — Mount Huang Po. He is the author of The Doctrine of Universal Mind'' (translated into English by John Blofeld). He transmitted the 'Wordless Doctrine' to I-Hsuan of Lin-chi who became the founder of the great Lin-chi Sect, so he is regarded as the founder of this school which flourishes in Japan.

Hua-tou — Literally means 'the end of a speech' or the critical word of a question. At first, this word was used for Koan (See under Koan.)

Hui-Ko (Eka or Yeka, in Japanese, A.D. 487-593) — the second Zen Patriarch.

Hui-Neng (Eno or Yeno, in Japanese, A. D. 638-713) — the sixth or the last Zen Patriarch, founder of the Southern School of Sudden Enlightenment. (See under Southern School.)

Hung-Jen (Gunin, in Japanese, A.D. 605-675) — the fifth Zen Patriarch.

I-Hsuan — Known as Lin-Chi (q.v.).

Jinshu — See under Shen-Shiu

Karma — Deed, action; retribution of action; principle of causality in moral experience. According to the Law of Karma, one's destiny is determined by the result of his own deeds. This law applies from past to present as well as from present to future. Zen aims to be free from all forms of bondage and the law of Karma. Our straining to possess, to become, to improve, to dominate and even to purify creates attachment and therefore, bondage. As Huang Po pointed out: "If you fail to comprehend how to be devoid of mind, your attachment to objects will all be those of devil-karma. Even if you do things with a view to the Pure Land, these too produce a karma."

Koan (Kung-an, in Chinese; at first the word 'Hua-tou' was much used. See Hua-tou) — Koans are the principal means used by Zen masters to assist the disciple to clean his mind of the fetter of thought, to get rid of different types of conceptionalism and mental fixation. The worst enemy of Zen experience, we are told, is the intellect which consists and insists on discriminating the subject from object. Koan is used as a means to cut short such discriminating intellect, and to put one in a dilemma out of which one must contrive to escape, not through logic, but through a "mind of higher order." There are many impossible demands, such as: (1) "Talk without tongue." (2) "Play your stringless lute." (3) "Clap with single hand." (4) A long time ago, a man kept a goose in a bottle. It grew larger and larger, until it could not get out of the bottle any more; but he did not want to break the bottle, nor did he wish to hurt the goose; how would you get it out?," etc. The number of Koans is traditionally estimated at 1,700; but, as they alleged, perhaps just one may be sufficient to open one's mind to the ultimate truth of Zen.

Kung-an — See under Koan.

Lin-Chi (Binzai, in Japanese, A.D. d. 867) — Founder of Lin-chi Sect which flourishes in Japan, noted for his hawling and beating rough methods which he learned from his own master Huang Po. It is said that once he saw his master Huang Po and asked "What is the principle of Buddhism"? Before he could finish his question, his master gave him several blows!

Mahakasyapa (or Kasyapa) — One of Buddha's disciples; the first Patriarch in India, according to Zen tradition.

Mahayana — Greater Vehicle of salvation; one of the two major divisions of Buddhism.

Ma-Tsu (Baso, in Japanese, A.D. d. 788)—Also called Tao-i, a disciple of Huai-jang, a disciple of Hui-neng. He was the originator of the Koan exercise.

Māyā — Illusion.

Mayoi — State of doubt or uncertainty as contrasted with Satori.

Nirvana (or Nibbāna) — Literally means cooling off; blowing out as the extinguishing of a candle flame; going out of three-fires, i.e., (1) Lust, (2) Hatred, (3) Ignorance. It is the raison d'etre of Buddhism, or the true law of Buddhism. It is an end of ever-recurring of birth and death; an extinction of the everywhere and always miserable consciousness; or a state of eternal extinction as a result of release from Karma and Samsara.

Northern School — It is called 'Gradual School,' holding a view of continuous movement; also known as the 'dust wiping' school,

represented by Shen-hsiu (A.D. 605-706) in his gatha:
"The body is like unto the Bodhi-tree,
And the mind to a mirror bright.
Carefully we cleanse them hour by hour.
Lest dust shall fall upon them."
This school no longer survives.

Obaku — See under Huang Po.

Paramita — Spiritual perfection; ideal virtue.

Prajna — Transcendent wisdom or insight; Buddha's illumination, or Void — void of the limitations of body and mind. The word is composed of two parts: Pra, "going forth" and jna, "to know."

Pure Land — One of the schools of Buddhism, emphasizing devotion to Amitabha as Saviour.

Rinzai — See under Lin-chi.

Samadhi — Absorbed contemplation; concentrated state of mind, trance.

Samsāra — The wheel of birth and death; the realm of transmigratory existence or the region outside Nirvana. The essence of Zen consists in suppressing the activity of Ego, in emerging from cocoon of self-centered thought. If one deliberately seeks to become Buddha, then his Buddha is just his Samsara!

Satori — Enlightenment or Illumination; the state of consciousness of the Buddha-mind which cannot be expressed by language.

Seng-Tsan (Sosan, in Japanese, A.D. d. 606)—The third Zen Patriarch, author of Hsin-hsin-ming (a celebrated poem on the "Believing Mind"). Its theme is that the perfect way is realization of the unity of all things; liking and disliking are diseases of the mind. The dichotomy of subject and object comes from self-delusion. When "ten thousands things" are viewed in unity and harmony, according to his teaching, we are back to 'origin,' and then our mind will have rest.

Shen-Shiu (Jinshu, Japanese, A.D. 606-706)—Regarded as the sixth Patriarch, according to the Northern school. (See under Northern School.)

Sosan — See under Seng-tsan.

Southern School — Known as the "Abrupt or instantaneous school," represented by Hui-neng with his famous gatha which is antagonistic to Shen-shiu:
 Originally there was no Bodhi-tree,
 Nor was there any mirror.
 Since originally there was nothing that has real existence,
 How then could the dust settle there on?
This school advocates that the movement from "ignorance" to "enlightenment" is abrupt and not gradual; discrete and not continuous, altogether beyond calculation. There is a "leap."

Sunyata — Emptiness; Void; the realm of transitory and relative existence. In the Prajnaparamita and other Mahayana Sutra, the ultimate nature of all things is emptiness. The unattainability of all things is Reality itself which is the most exquisite form of Tathagata. Form is void, void is form. Since all is void, originally there was nothing (Pen - lai - Wu - i - wuh). Zen is to free from all forms of bondage. The only abiding principle in life is the Buddha nature; while separate things or forms have no permanence of reality. Self nature is not seen by the eye or as known by the mind. It is "that," which has no part. It is void of any conception related to the parts. In the word of Huang-Po: the void is both one and many.

Sutra (Pali, Sutta) — Sermon; discourse; scripture.

Tan-chin — Platform Sutra, the basic teachings of Hui-neng, the sixth and the last Zen Patriarch.

Tao-Hsin (Doshin, in Japanese, A.D. 580-651) — The fourth Zen Patriarch.

Tao-i — Ma-tsu (see under Ma-tsu)

Tathagata (Ju-Lai, in Chinese) — The Perfect One. A significant appelation of the Buddha, honoring him as one who has full realization of the truth; the Truth-finder. It is made up of: (1) Tatha (meaning "in that manner") and (2) Gata ("gone") It means one who has gone in that manner, or has trodden the path which he taught. Another interpretation: "He who has come from the suchness," that is back from the Tathata after reaching enlightenment.

Tathata — Literally means: "that-way-ness," or "suchness"

Tzu-hsin — Self nature (See under Buddha nature.)

Ummon — (See under Yun-Men).

Wu-nien — This is one of the three principles of Hui-neng's teachings of Zen, i.e., "(1) Wu-nien (no-thought) as the essential; (2) Wu-hsian (no-phenomenon) as the substance: and Wu-chu (no abiding) as the basis." Wu-nien does not mean not to think anything at all; nor does it mean that complete expulsion of thought; but it is to see and to know things with the mind free from attachment.

Yun-men (Ummon, in Japanese, A.D. d. 949) — Founder of Yun-men Sect. One of his legs was caught and broken when his harsh master Wu-chou (senior disciple of Lin-chi) pushed him out of his door, because he hesitated to answer his master's question. It is said that he was thus enlightened by the intense pain!

BIBLIOGRAPHY

Alexander, Hartley B., **God and Man's Destiny**, N.Y.: Oxford Univ. Press, 1936.

Allport, Gordon W., **Becoming**, N.H.: Yale Univ. Press, 1955.
The Individual and His Religion, The Macmillan Co., 1951.
Personality, Henry Holt and Co., 1937.

Altizer, Thomas J. J., **Oriental Mysticism and Biblical Eschatology**, Philadelphia, Westminister, 1961.
Mica Elide & Dialectic of the Sacred, Philadelphia, Westminster, 1963.
The Gospel of Christian Atheism, Philadelphia, Wesminster, 1966.

Anderson, Gerald H., (ed.), **The Theology of the Christian Mission**, N.Y., McGraw-Hill, 1961.

Andrews, Elias, **Modern Humanism and Christian Theism**, Grand Rapids: Zondervan, 1939.

Arnold, Sir Edwin, **The Light of Asia**, London, 1879, 1891.

Barrett, William (ed.), **Zen Buddhism-Selected Writings of D. T. Suzuki**, Garden City, N.Y.: Doubleday, 1956.

Bavinck, **Herman, Gereformeerde Dogmatiek**, Kampe, 1906-1911.
Our Reasonable Faith, Grand Rapids: Eerdmans, 1956.
The Philosophy of Revelation, Grand Rapids: Eerdmans, 1953.

Bavinck, J. H., **Impact of Christianity on the Non-Christian World**, Grand Rapids: Eerdmans, 1949.

Becker, Ernest, **Zen: A Rational Critique**, N.Y., Norton, 1961.

Benoit, H,. **The Supreme Doctrine**, N.Y.: Pantheon, 1955.

Berdyaev, Nicholas, **The Fate of Man in the Modern World**, Milwaukee: Morehouse, 1935.
The Divine and the Human, London: Geoffrey, 1949.

Berkhof, L., **Introductory Volume to Systematic Theology**, Grand Rapids: Eerdmans, 1956.

Berkouwer, G. C., **The Triumph of Grace in Theology of K. Barth**, Grand Rapids: Eerdmans, 1956.

Bevan, Edwyn, **Symbolism and Belief**, Boston, Beccan, 1957.

Blakney, Raymond B., **Meister Eckhart-A modern Translation**, N.Y.: Harper, 1941.

Blanton, Smiley; and Peale, Norman Vincent, **Faith is the Answer,** N.Y., Abingdon-Cokesbury, 1940.
Blofeld, John (tr.), **The Zen Teaching of Huang Po,** N.Y.: Grove Press, 1959.
Blyth, R. H., **Buddhism Sermons on Christian Texts,** Tokyo, 1952.
Zen in English Literature and Oriental Classics, Rutland, Vt.: Charles Tuttle, 1957.
Bobbio, Norferto, **The Philosophy of Decadentism-A study in Existentialism,** Oxford: Blackwell, 1948.
Boisen, Anton T., **Religion in Crisis and Custom,** N.Y., Harper, 1955.
The Exploration of the Inner World, N.Y., Harper, 1936.
Bonhoeffer, Dietrick, **Letters and Papers in Prison,** Fontona Books, 1960.
The Cost of Discipleship, London, S.C.M. Press, 1954.
Brinton, Crane, **The Shaping of the Modern Mind,** N.Y.: Menton Books, 1953.
Brunner, Emil, **Revelation and Reason,** Phil.: Westminister Press, 1943.
The Divine-Human Encounter, Phil.: Westminster Press, 1943.
Buber, Martin, **I and Thou,** N.Y.: Scribner's, 1957.
Eclipse of God, N.Y.: Harper, 1957.
Bucke, Richard R., **Cosmic Consciousness - A Study in the Evolution of the Human Mind,** N.Y.: Dutton, 1923.
Bultmann, R. K., **Existence and Faith,** N.Y.: Meridian, 1960.
The presence of Eternity: History and Eschatology, N.Y., Harper, 1962.
Burtt, E. A., **The Teachings of the Compassionate Buddha** ,N.Y.: New American Library, 1955.
Cailliet, Emile, **The Christian Approach to Culture,** N.Y.: Abingdon, 1953.
Calhoun, Robert R., **What is Man?** N.Y.: Association Press, 1939.
Calvin, John, **Institutes of the Christian Religion,** 2 vols., Grand Rapids: Eerdmans, 1957.
Camus, Albert, **The Rebel,** N. Y., Knopf, 1958.
Carrington, W. L., M.D., **Psychology, Religion, and Human Need,** Channel Press, 1957.
Chan, Wing-Tsit, **Religious Trends in Modern China,** Columbia University Press, 1953.
Chang, Chen-Chi, **The Practice of Zen,** N.Y., Harper, 1959.
Chang, Lit-sen and others, **The Challenge of the Cults,** Grand Rapids: Zondervan, 1961.
Chu Chan, **The Huang Po Doctrine of Universal Mind,** London: 1947.
Clark, Gordon H., **Thales to Dewey — A History of Philosophy,** Boston, Houghton Mifflin, 1957.

A Christian View of Man and Things, Mich.: Zondervan, 1952.
Religion, Reason and Revelation, Philadelphia, Presbyterian and Reformed Publishing Co., 1961.
Clark, Walter Houston, Psychology of Religion, The Macmillan Co., 1958.
Coleman, James C., Abnormal Psychology and Modern Life, Scott, Foresman and Company, 1950.
Cochrane, Arthur C., The Existentialists and God, Phil Westminster.
Collins, James, The Existentialists — A Critical Study, Chicago: H. Henry Regnery, 1952.
Copleston, F. C., Contemporary Philosophy, London, Burns, 1956.
Craig, Samuel G. Christianity — Rightly So Called, Phil.: Presbyterian and Reformed Pub. Co., 1953.
Davies, D. R. Down, Peacock's Feathers, N. Y. MacMillan, 1961.
Davis, A. W., Existentialism and Theology, N. Y., Philosophical Library, 1957.
Dawson, Christopher, Enquiries into Religion and Culture, N. Y.: Sheed and Ward, 1936.
Religion and Culture, N.Y.: Meridian, 1958.
Religion and Rise of Western Culture, N. Y., Doubleday, 1958.
Desan, W. D., The Tragic Finale, Cambridge: Harvard Univ. Press, 1954.
De. Waelhens, A., La Philosophie De Martin Heidegger, Louvain: Publications Universities, 1955.
Dewey, John, Problems of Man, N.Y.: Phil. Library, 1946.
De Wolf, L. H., The Religious Revolt Against Reason, N. Y., Harper, 1949.
Diem, Herman, Kierkegaard's Dialectic of Existence (Tr) Endinberg, Oliver, 1959.
Dixon, William M., The Human Situation, London, Arnold, 1917.
Dollard, John & Others, Personality and Psychotherapy, McGraw-Hill Book Co., 1950.
Doniger, Simon, Healing: Human and Divine, N. Y., Association Press, 1957.
Religion and Human Behavior, N. Y., Association Press, 1954.
Sex and Religion Today, N. Y., Association Press, 1953.
The Minister's Consultation Clinic, Channel Press, Inc., 1955.
Dowey, Edward A., The Knowledge of God in Calvin's Theology, N. Y., Columbia, 1952.
Driesch, Hans, Man and the Universe, (Eng. Tr.), London, Allen and Unwin, 1929.
Dumoulin, H., and Sasaki, R. F., The Development of Chinese Zen after the 6th Patriarch, N. Y., First Zen Institute, 1953.
A History of Zen Buddhism, (Tr.) N.Y., Pantheon, 1963.
Dutt, K. Guru, Existentialism and Indian Thought, N. Y.: Phil. Library, 1960.

Edwards, David L., (ed), **The Honest To God Debate**, London, S.C.M. Press, 1963.
Edward, Jonathan, **Freedom of the Will**, N. H., Yale, 1959.
Eliade, Mercia, **The Sacred and the Profane**, N. Y., Harcourt, 1959.
Eliot, T. S., **Christianity and Culture**, N. Y., Harcourt, 1960.
Falk, Orson, (Selected), **The Works of Nietzsche**, N. Y., Tudor, 1931.
Figgis, J. N., **The Will to Freedom — The Gospel of Nietzsche and The Gospel of Christ**, N.Y., Scribner, 1917.
Flewelling, R. T., **The Survival of Western Culture**, N.Y., Harper, 1943.
Frank, Lawrence K., **Nature and Human Nature**, Rutgers Univ. Press, 1951.
Frankl, Viktor E., **The Doctor and the Soul**, N. Y., Alfred A. Knoph, 1955.
From Death-Camp to Existentialism, Boston, Beacon Press 1961.
Freeman, David H., **Tillich**, Philadelphia, Presbyterian and Reformed, 1963.
Freud, Sigmund, **The Future of an Illusion**, N.Y., Doubleday, 1957.
Fromm, Erich, **Psychoanalysis and Religion**, N. H., Yale Univ. Press, 1950.
Escape From Freedom, N.Y., Rinehart, 1941.
The Fear of Freedom, London Routledge 1942.
Man For Himself, N.Y., Rinehart, 1947.
The Heart of Man, its genius for good and evil, N.Y., Harper 1964.
Fromm, E., Suzuki, D. T., and DeMartine, R., **Zen Buddhism and Psychoanalysis**, N. Y., Harper, 1960.
Fujisawa, Chioako, **Zen and Shinto**, N. Y., Philosophical Iibrary, 1959.
Fung, Paul F. and George D., (Tr.) **The Sutra of the Sixth Patriarch on the Pristine Orthodox Dharma**, San Francisco, Buddha's Universal Church, 1965.
Fung, Yu-lan, **A History of Chinese Philosophy**, (Tr. by D. Bodde), N.J., Princeton, 1953.
Galdston, Lago, M.D., **Ministry and Medicine in Human Relations**, International Universities Press, 1955.
Gilson, Etienne, **God and Philosophy**, N.H., Yale University Press, 1941.
Graham, Billy, **Peace with God**, N.Y., Pocket Books Permabook, 1960.
Grene, Marjorie, **Introduction to Existentialism**, Chicago: Chicago Univ. Press, 1949.
Griffis, W. E., **The Religions of Japan**, N.Y., Scribner's 1895.
Hall, Calvin S. & Lindzdy, Gardner, **Theories of Personality**, N.Y., John Wiley & Sons, 1957.
Hamilton, Kenneth, **God Is Dead—The Anatomy of a Slogan**, Grand Rapids, Eerdmans, 1966.

Revolt Against Heaven, Grand Rapids, Eerdmans, 1966.
Hamilton, William, The New Essence of Christianity, N.Y., Association Press, 1961.
Hamilton, William, and Altizer, Thomas J. J., Radical Theology and The Death of God, Indianapolis, Merrell, 1966.
Harrison, E. J., The Fighting Spirit of Japan, London: Unwin, 1913.
Harper, Ralph, Nostalgia: An Existential Exploration of Longing and Fulfillment in the Modern Age, Cleveland, Ohio, Western Reserve Press, 1966.
Harper, Ralph, Existentialism, Cambridge, Harvard Univ. Press, 1948.
Hass, William, The Destiny of Mind, East and West — Its Basic Difference, Edinburgh, James Thin.
Heideger, Martin, An Introduction to Metaphysics, (Tr. by R. Manheim), N.Y., Yale University Press, 1959.
Essays in Metaphysics: Identity & Difference, N.Y., Phil. Library, 1960.
Being and Time (Tr. by Marquarrie & Robinson), N.Y., Harper, 1962.
Existence and Being, Chicago M. Regnery, 1949.
Kant and the Problem of Metaphysics, Indiana Univ. Press, 1962.
Heinemann, F. H., Existentialism and Modern Predicament, N.Y., Harper, 1954.
Henry, Carl, F. H., (ed.), Revelation and the Bible, Grand Rapids, Baker Book House, 1958.
Remaking of the Modern Mind, Grand Rapids, Eerdmans, 1946.
Frontiers of Modern Theology, Chicago, Moody, 1966.
Herberg, Will, Four Existentialist Theologians, Gordon City, N.Y., Doublday, 1958.
Herrigee, Eugen, The Method of Zen, (Tr. by R. F. C. Hull), N.Y.: Pantheon, 1960.
Hindus, M. G., Humanity Uprooted, N.Y., Blue Ribbon, 1929.
Hocking, W. E., Living Religion and a World Faith, London, MacMillan, 1940.
Rethinking Missions, N.Y., Harper, 1932.
Hodge, Charles, Systematic Theology, Vols, I. II, Grand Rapids, Eerdmans, 1946.
Horney, Karen, The Neurotic Personality of Our Time, N.Y., W. W. Norton & Co., 1937.
Hudson, Cyril, E., Recent Psychology and the Christian Religion, N.Y., George H. Society, 1948.
Hughes, Margaret M. & others, The People in Your Life, N.Y., Alfred A. Knopf, 1952.
Hui Hai, The Path to Sudden Attainment, (Tr. by John Blofeld), London Buddhist Society, 1948.
Humphreys, C., Zen Buddhism, London: Allen and Unwin, 1957.
Zen Comes West, London: Allen and Unwin, 1960.

Jackson, Edgar N., **Understanding Grief**, N.Y., Abingdon Press, 1952.
James, William, **The Varieties of Religious Experience**, N.Y., The Modern Library, 1902.
Jaspers, Karl, (Tr. E. B. Ashton, **Existentialism and Humanism**, N.Y., Moore, 1952.
General Psychopathology (Tr. by Hoenig & Hamilton) Chicago Univ. Press, 1963.
Man in the Modern Age, London, Routledge, 1951.
The Future of Mankind, Univ. of Chicago Press, 1961.
Reason and Existence, N.Y., Noonday Press, 1957.
Reason and Anti-Reason in our Time, London: S.M.C., 1952.
and Bultmann, Rudolf, **Myth and Christianity**, N.Y., Noonday, 1958.
Jenkins, Daniel, **Beyond Religion**, London, 1962.
Jewett, P. K., **Emil Brunner's Concept of Revelation**, London, James Clarke, 1954.
Johnson, Paul E., **Personality and Religion**, N.Y., Abingdon Press, 1952.
Jung, Carl G., **Modern Man in Search of Soul**, (Tr. by Dell and Bayness), N.Y., Harcourt Broce, 1933.
Psyscology and Religion, N.H., Yale, 1950.
The Development of Personality, (Tr. by Hull), N.Y., Pantheon, 1954.
The Integration of Personality, (Tr. by Dell), London, Routledge, 1952.
The Undiscovered self, Boston, Brown, 1957.
Kaufmann, Walter, **Existentialism from Dostoevsky to Sartre**, N.Y., The World Pub.Co., 1961.
Kerouac, Jack, **The Dharma Bums**, N.Y., Viking Press. 1958.
Keyserling, Count Herman (Tr. by Reece), **The Travel Diary of a Philosopher**, 2 Vols., N.Y., Harcourt Brace, 1926.
Kierkegaard, Soren, **A Kierkegaard Anthology** (Ed by Robert Bretall), N.J., Princeton 1937.
King, W. P. and Others, **Humanism, Another Battle Line**, Nashville, Cokesburg, 1931.
Kraemer, H., **The Christian Message in the Non-Christian World**, N.Y., Harper, 1938.
World Culture and World Religions, Phil., Westminster, 1960
Kuyper, Abraham, **Calvinism**, London, Sovereign Grace Union, 1932.
The Work of the Holy Spirit, N.Y., Funk and Wagnalls, 1900.
Lao Tzu, **Tao Te Ching**, (Tr. by R. B. Blakney), N.Y., New American Library, 1955.
Lewis, C. S., **The Abolition of Man**, N.Y., MacMillan, 1947.
The Problem of Pain, Fontana Books, 1957.
Lecomte Du Nouy, P. **Human Destiny**, N.Y., New American Library, 1955.

Lieu, Wu-Chi, A Short History of Confucian Philosophy, Baltimore Penguin Books, 1955.
Liebman, Joshua, Peace of Mind, N.Y., Simon and Schuster, 1949.
Lindsell, Harold, A Christian Philosophy of Missions, Wheaton, Kampen, 1942.
Linn, Louis, M.D., & Schwarz, Leo W., Psychiatry and Religions Experience, N.Y., Randon House, 1958.
Linssen, Robert, Living Zen, (Tr. by D. Abrahams Curiel), N.Y.: Grove Press, 1958.
Machen, J. G., The Christian Faith in the Modern World, Grand Rapids, Eerdmans, 1947.
MacQuarri, John An Existentialist Theology—A Comparison of Heidegger and Bultmann, London, S.C.M., 1955.
McNeill, John T., History of the Cure of Souls, N.Y., Harper, 1951.
Mairet, Phillip, Christian Essays in Psychiatry, N.Y., Philosophical Library, 1956.
Martin, Florence, When They are Nine To Eleven, N.Y., Philadelphia Board of Christian Education of Presbyterian Church, 1950.
Humanism Integral, Paris, Aubier, 1936.
Martin, Walter, R., The Christian & the Cults, Grand Rapids, Zondervan, c. 1956.
The Kingdom of the Cults, Grand Rapids, Zondervan, 1965.
Marcel, Gabriel, L'Homme Problematique, Paris, Oubier, 1955.
The Philosophy of Existence, N.Y., Philosophical Library, 1949.
Marills, Rene, Jean Paul Sartre: Philosopher Without Faith, (Tr. by W. Baskin), N.Y., Philosophical Library, 1961.
Maritain, Jacques, (Tr. M. R. Adamson), True Humanism, London, Geoffrey, 1954.
Man's Approach to God, PA, Archabey Press, c. 1960.
Religion of Culture, Paris, Desclée de Bronwer, 1930.
Mascall, E, L., The Secularization of Christianity, London, Longman, 1965.
May, Rollo & Others, Existence, N.Y., Basic Books, 1958.
May, Rollo, Psychotherapy and Religion, N. Y., Harper, 1957.
The Art of Counseling, N.Y., Abingdon-Cokesbury, 1949.
Messier, L. J. A., The Challenge of Humanism, N.Y., Oxford Univ. Press, 1953.
Michalson, Carl (ed.) Christianity and Existentialists, N.Y., Scribner, 1956.
The Witness of Kierkegaard, N.Y., Association Press, 1960.
Montgomery, John W., The 'Is God Dead' Controversy, Grand Rapids, Zondervan, 1966.
Morris, Leon, The Abolition of Religion—A Study in 'Religionless Christianity', Chicago, I. V., Press, 1964.
Murphy, Gardner, Human Potentialities, N.Y., Basic Books, 1958.

Mudge, Lewis S., **Is God Alive?**, Philadelphia, United Church Press, 1963.
Murray, J. A. C., **An Introduction to a Christian Psychotherapy**, Edinburg: T. & T. Clark, 1947.
Niebuhr, Richard, **Christ and Culture**, N.Y., Harper, 1958.
Niebuhr, Reinhold, **The Nature and Destiny of Man**, N.Y., Scribner, 1941.
Nietzsche, Friedrich, **The Works of Friedrich Nietzsche**, N.Y., Tubor, 1931.
Notovick, Nicolas A. **La Vie Inconnue de Jesus Christ**, Paris, 1894.
Oates, Wayne E., **Religious Factors in Mental Illness**, N.Y., Association Press, 1955.
The Bible in Pastoral Care, Phila. The Westminister Press 1946.
The Christian Pastor, Philadelphia, The Westminster Press, 1946.
The Religious Dimensions of Personality, N.Y., Association Press, 1957.
Ogata, Sohaku, **Zen For the West**, N.Y., Dial Press, 1959.
Ogletree, Thomas W., **The Death-of-God Controversy**, N.Y., Shingdon, 1966.
Orr, James, **God's Image in Man**, London, Hodder and Stoughton, 1905.
The Christian View of God and the World, N.Y., Scribners, 1893.
Otto, M. C., **Kingdom of God and the Son of Man - A Study in the History of Man**, London, Lutherworth.
Otto, Rudolph, **The Idea of the Holy**, N.Y., Oxford Galaxy Book, 1958.
Outler, Albert, **Psychotherapy and the Christian Message**, N.Y., Harper, 1954.
Parker, William R. & Others, **Prayer Can Change Your Life**, N.J., Prentice-Hall, 1957.
Parker, T. H. L., **The Doctrine of The Knowledge of God**, Edinburgh, Oliver and Boyd, 1952.
Pascal, Blaise, **Pensee and the Provincial Letters**, N. Y., Modern Library, 1941.
Paterson, R. T., **Irrationalism and Rationalism in Religion**, Durham, Duke Univ. Press, 1954.
Philips, J. B., **God Our Contemporary**, N.Y., MacMillan, 1960.
Pike, James A., **Beyond Anxiety**, N.Y., Scribner, 1953.
Pratt, James Bissett, **The Pilgrimage of Buddhism**, N.Y., MacMillan, 1928.
RadhaKrishnan, S., **Indian Philosophy**, 2 Vols, London, Allen and Unwin, 1927.
East and West in Religion, London, Allen and Unwin, 1933.
Eastern Religions and Western Thought, Oxford University Press, 1940.
East and West,-The End of Separation, N.Y., Harper, 1956.

BIBLIOGRAPHY

Reichelt, Karl L., **Meditation and Piety in the Far East**, N.Y., Harper, 1954.
Rienhard, K. F., **The Existentialist Revolt**, N.Y., Frederick Ungar, 1960.
Richardson, Alan, (ed.), **Four Anchors from the Stern**, London, 1963.
Riley, I. W., **From myth to Reason**, N.Y., Appleton, 1926.
Roberts, David E. **Psychotherapy and a Christian View of Man**, N.Y., Scribner, 1951.
Existentialism and Religious Belief, N.Y., Oxford, 1949.
Robinson, John A. T., **Honest to God**, Philadelphia, Westminster, 1963.
Ross, Nancy W., **The World of Zen**, N.Y., Random House, 1960.
Ruggiero, Guido De, **Existentialism-Disintegration of Man's Soul**, N.Y., Social Science Pub., 1948.
Rushdoony, R. J., **By What Standard?** Philadelphia, Presby & Reformed, 1959.
Intellectual Schizophrenia, Philadelphia, Presby & Reformed 1961.
Freud, Philadelphia Presby & Reformed, 1964.
Sartre, Jean Paul, **Extentialism**, (Tr. by Bernard Frenchtmon), N.Y., Phil. Library, 1947.
Nausea (Tr. by L. Alexander), Conn. New Directions, 1938.
The Psychology of Imagination, N.Y., Citadel, 1961.
No Exit, and Three Other Plays, N.Y., Vintage, 1961.
Existentialism & Human Emotions, N.Y., Philosophical Library, C. 1957.
Existential Psychoanalysis (Tr. by H. E. Barnes), N.Y., Philosophical Library, C. 1953.
The Emotions: Outline of a Theory (Tr. by Bernard), N.Y., Philosophical Library, C. 1948.
Existentialism and Humanism, (Tr. Philip Mainet), London, Methuen, 1948.
Being and Nothingness, (Tr. by H. E. Bernes), N.Y., Philosophical Library, 1956.
Le Diable et le Bon Dieu, Paris, Gallimard, 1951.
The Transcendence of the Ego, an existential Theory of consciousness, N.Y., Noonday Press, 1962.
Sauer, Erich, **The Dawn of World Redemption**, Grand Rapids, Eerdmans, 1953.
From Eternity to Eternity, Grand Rapids, Eerdmans, 1959.
Schaff, Philip, **History of the Christian Church**, Vols. II, IV, Grand Rapids, Eerdmans, 1949, 1950.
Schaier, Hans, **Religion and the Care of Souls in Jung's Psychology**, N.Y., Bollingen Foundation, 1950.
Senzaki, N., and McCandless, R., **Buddhism and Zen**, N.Y., Phil. Library, 1953.

Senzaki, Nyogen, and Reps, Paul, **The Gateless Gate**, (Tr. of Mumon-Kan), Los Angeles, 1934.
Schweitzer, Albert, (Tr. C. T. Campain), **The Philosophy of Civilization**, N.Y., MacMillan, 1950.
   The Decay and Restoration of Civilization, London, 1923.
Scott, N. A. Jr., **The Tragic Vision and the Christian Faith**, N.Y., Association Press, 1957.
Shaku, Soyen, **Sermon of a Buddhist Abbot**, Chicago, Open Court, 1906.
Sheen, Fulton, **Peace of God**, N.Y., Doubleday, 1954.
Singer, C. Gregg, **Toynbee**, Philadelphia, Presbyterian & Reformed, 1964.
Singh, Surgit, **Christology and Personality**, Philadelphia, Westminster Press, 1961.
Sorokin, P. A., **Social and Cultural Dynamics**, N.Y., 1937.
   Man and Society in Calamity, N.Y., Dutton, 1946.
   The Reconstruction of Humanity, Boston, Beacon, 1948.
   Social Philosophy of an Age of Crisis, Boston, Beacon, 1951.
   The American Sex Revolution, Mass., Porter Sargent Publisher, 1956.
Spencer, Sidney, **Mysticism in World Religion**, Baltimore, Rengion Books, 1963.
Spengler, Oswald, **The Decline of the West**, N.Y., Knopf, 1939.
Spiegelberg, Frederic, **Living Religion of the World**, Prentice-Hall.
Spier, J. M., **An Introduction to Christian Philosophy**, Phil., Presbyterian and Reformed, 1953.
   Christianity and Existentialism, Presbyterian and Reformed, 1953.
Stace, W. T., **Religion and the Modern Mind**, Philadelphia, Lippincott, 1960.
Stinnette, Charles R., Jr., **Anxiety and Faith**, Conn., Seaburry, 1955.
Suzuki, D. T., **An Introduction to Zen Buddhism**, N.Y., Phil. Library, 1949.
   Essays in Zen Buddhism, 3 Vols., London, Rider, 1949, 1950, 1951.
   Zen Buddhism, Selected Writings, (Ed. by Wm. Barrett) N. Y. Doubleday, 1956.
   Mysticism: Christian and Buddhist, N. Y., Harper, 1957.
   The Zen Doctrine of No-Mind, London, Rider, 1949.
Swann, Jeffrey, **Toehold on Zen**, Cleveland, World Pub. Co., **1963**.
Temple, William, **Men's Creatrix**, N.Y., Macmillan, 1917.
   Nature, Man and God, N. Y., Macmillan, 1939.
Teilhard De Chardin, P., **The Phenomenon of Man**, (Tr. by Bernard Wall) N.Y., Harper, 1952.
   The Future of Man (Tr. by N. Denny) N.Y., Harper, 1964.
Thornwell, James H., **Discourses on Truth**, N.Y., Robert Carter, 1856.

Thielicke, Helmut, **Between God and Satan**, Grand Rapids, Eerdmans, C. 1958.
  Between Heaven and Zarth, N. Y., Harper, 1965.
  Nihilism, Its Origin and Nature, with a Christian Answer, London, Routledge, 1962.
Tillich, Paul, **The Courage to Be**, N. H., Yale Univ. Press, 1952.
  Dynamics of Faith, N. Y., Harper, 1959.
  Systematic Theology, Chicago Univ. Press, 1957
  The Protestant Era, N. Y., Phoenix Books,
  Theology of Culture, N. Y., Oxford, 1959.
  The New Being, N. Y., Scribner, 1955.
  Morality and Beyond, N. Y., Harper, 1963.
  The Eternal Now, N. Y., Scribner, 1963.
  Ultimate Concern, N. Y., Harper, 1965.
  The Religious Situation, N. Y., Meridian Books, 1956.
  The Shaking of the Foundation, London, Pelican, 1962.
Toynbee, Arnold J., **Civilization on Trial**, N.Y., Oxford, 1948.
Trueblood, D. E., **The Predicament of Modern Man**, N.Y., Harper, 1944.
  Alternative to Futility, N. Y., Harper 1948.
  Signs of Hope in a Century of Despair, N.Y., Harper, 1950.
Underhill, Evelyn, **Concerning the Inner Life**, N.Y., Dutton C. 1926
  Mysticism, A Study in the Nature & Development of Man's Spiritual Consciousness, London, Methuen, 1962.
Van Buren, Paul, **The Secular Meaning of the Gospel**, N.Y., Macmillan, 1963.
  Christ in Our Place, Edinburgh, Olive & Boyd, 1957.
Van Dusan, H. P., (ed.), **The Christian Answer**, N.Y., Scribner, 1946.
Van Hanian, Gabriel, **The Death of God; the Culture of our Post-Christian Era**, N.Y., Braziller.
  Wait Without Idols, N.Y., Braziller, 1964.
  No Other God, N. Y., Braziller, 1966.
Van Riessen, H., **Nietzsche**, Philadelphia, Presbyterian and Reformed, 1960.
Van Til, Cornelius, **The Defense of the Faith**, Philadelphia, Presbyterian and Reformed, 1955.
  Is God Dead?, Philadelphia, Presbyterian and Reformed, 1966.
Walsh, Chad, **Early Christian of the 21th Century**, N.Y., Harper, 1949.
Warfield, B. B., **Plan of Salvation**, Grand Rapids, Eerdmans, 1942.
  Calvin and Augustine, Philadelphia, Presbyterian and Reformed, 1956.
Watts, A. W., **The Spirit of Zen**, N.Y., Grove Press, 1958.
  The Supreme Identity, N.Y., Pantheon, 1957.
  The Way of Liberation in Zen Buddhism, San Francisco, American Academy of Asian Studies, 1955.
  The Way of Zen, N.Y., Pantheon, 1957.
  The Wisdom of Insecurity, N.Y., Pantheon, 1951.

This Is It, N.Y., Pantheon, 1960.
Zen, Stanford, California, James Ladd Delkin, 1948.
Zen Buddhism, London, Buddhist Society, 1947.
Beyond Theology, The Art of Godmanship, N.Y., Pantheon Books, 1964.
Whitehead, A. N., **Science and the Modern World**, N.Y., Mentor Books, 1952.
Symbolism: Its Meaning and Effect, N.Y., Putnam's 1959.
White, Ernest, **Christian Life and the Unconscious**, London, Hodder and Stoughton, 1955.
Williams, J. Rodman, **Contemporary Existentialism & Christian Faith**, N.J., Prentice-Hall, 1965.
Wilson, John T., **Current Trends in Psychology and the Behavioral Sciences**, University of Pittsburg, 1954.
Wise, Carroll A., **Psychiatry and the Bible**, N.Y., Harper, 1956.
Religion in Illness and Health, N.Y., Harper, 1942.
Wong, Mou-lan, **The Sutra of Wei Land (Hui-Neng)**, London, 1944.
Wood, Ernest, **Zen Dictionary**, N.Y., Philosophical Library, 1962.
Wood, Nathan R., **The Secret of the Universe**, (Gordon College Ed.) Boston, Warmick Press, 1936.
Young, Warren C., **A Christian Approach to Philosophy**, Wheaton, Kampen, 1954.
Young, Warren R., and Hixson Joseph R., **L S D on Campus**, Dell Publishing Co., 1966.
Zuidema, S. U., **Kierkegaard and Sartre (Modern Thinkers Series)**, Presbyterian and Reformed, 1960.

OTHER WORKS BY THE AUTHOR

(Besides a score of books on laws in his pre-Christian days)

The New Bible Commentary (Co-translator)
 Hong Kong, Christian Witness Press, (Publishing Center of China Inland Mission), 1958

The Way—An Investigation Concerning the Divine Truth
 Washington, D.C., I.S.I., 1960

Religious Thought of Famous Men of the World
 Hong Kong, Christian Witness Press, 1961

A Christian Criticism of Humanism,
 Hong Kong, Alliance Press, (Publishing Center of Christian and Missionary Alliance), 1963

A Christian Criticism of Humanism (Supplementary Vol.)
 Hong Kong, Alliance Press, 1968

A Christian Criticism of Humanism, (Enlarged edition)
 Hong Kong, Alliance Press, 1968

Christology,
 Hong Kong, Bellman House, 1964

A General Interpretation of Christian Truth
 Hong Kong, Bellman House, 1964

Faith on Trial,
 Hong Kong, Bellman House, 1964

The Way of Salvation
 Hong Kong, Bellman House, 1968

The Way of Life,
 Hong Kong, Bellman House, 1968

A Cloud of Witnesses, (Co-Author)
 Hong Kong, Bellman House, 1963

A Short Biography: An Asian Christian You Should Know (Lit-sen Chang—Ambassador to National Leaders) By Prof. Y. L. Liu, etc.
 Hong Kong, Christian Witness Press, 1967

The Basis and Evidences of Christian Faith (For Printing)

The Defense of Christian Truth: Letters to the Leaders of China (For Printing)

Golden Chips, Devotional Work (For Printing)

The Essence of Christian Faith (In Preparation)

On Religion — Its Origin, Nature, & Finality (In Preparation)

Comprehensive Apologetics (Vol. I, Fundamental)
    Lectures in the Far East, 1968

Comprehensive Apologetics (Vol. II, Philosophical)
    Lectures in the Far East, 1968

Comprehensive Apologetics (Vol. III, Religious)
    Lectures in the Far East, 1968

Comprehensive Apologetics (Vol. IV, Cultural)
    Lectures in the Far East, 1968

A Missionary Tour Around the World: A New Frontier of World Missions (For Printing)

The Challenge of the Cults — A Christianity Today Symposium (Co-author on "Zen-Buddhism"), Grand Rapids, Michigan, Zondervan, 1961

A Bold Look At the Church in a Broken World (Symposium, Co-author, on "Asia's Cultural Challenge"), Texas, Word Books, 1967

Strategy of Missions in the Orient: Christian Impact on Pagan World Hong Kong, 1968